ADMINISTRATION and DEVELOPMENT in MALAYSIA

*Institution Building and
Reform in a Plural Society*

ADMINISTRATION *and* DEVELOPMENT *in* MALAYSIA

Institution Building and
Reform in a Plural Society

MILTON J. ESMAN

Cornell University Press | Ithaca and London

First published 1972 by Cornell University Press.
Published in the United Kingdom by Cornell University Press Ltd.,
2–4 Brook Street, London W1Y 1AA.

International Standard Book Number 0-8014-0685-4
Library of Congress Catalog Card Number 71-173991
PRINTED IN THE UNITED STATES OF AMERICA
BY VAIL-BALLOU PRESS, INC.

Librarians: Library of Congress cataloging information
appears on the last page of the book.

Preface

As these lines are written, a modified form of parliamentary government is being reinstituted in Malaysia after a lapse of nearly two years. On May 13, 1969, the delicate understandings and institutions which had maintained a tolerable equilibrium in this plural society broke down under the strain of a hard-fought election campaign. The same group of politicians and civil servants who had governed the country since Independence in 1957 picked up the pieces and carried on. Despite the reservations of their supporters and the misgivings of their opponents, Malaysia's political future is in the hands of this elite, for there is no feasible alternative to their rule, given the lines of cleavage in this society. Contrary to prevailing doctrines in comparative politics and political sociology which emphasize the self-serving qualities of bureaucrats and the desirability of substituting political for administrative processes, Malaysia's senior officials have been the indispensable steel frame which has held this precarious state together even when political processes failed. These administrators were not adequately prepared for their roles either as development administrators or as conflict managers, but they made do with the capabilities and the resources they had.

Many of the political systems of new states—and of older ones as well—are composed of diverse and often hostile ethnic, religious, racial, and linguistic solidarity groups. In states where the major cleavages and political issues are drawn along these primordial lines, processes and instruments of conflict regulation are few and fragile. One reasonably successful pattern has existed in Malaysia. This book concerns an effort to strengthen one section of Malaysia's governmental elite, its senior administrators, through a strategy of planned and guided change designated as "institution building."

For the opportunity to participate in the experiences which this book describes and analyzes, I am grateful to Tun Abdul Razak, a superb development administrator and institution builder who was Deputy Prime Minister when these events occurred and has since succeeded to the Prime Ministry. Successive Chief Secretaries of Government, Tan Sri Abdul Jamil bin Abdul Rais and Tan Sri Tunku Mohamed bin Tunku Besar Burhanuddin, and Mr. Thong Yaw Hong, Director of the Economic Planning Unit, facilitated and supported this institution-building effort. Financial support for the analysis of this experience and for writing this book was provided by Dean Donald C. Stone of the Graduate School of Public and International Affairs of the University of Pittsburgh and by the Development Advisory Service of the Harvard University Center for International Affairs.

The conceptual model for this study was fashioned in an extended series of stimulating and intellectually fruitful weekend meetings by the members of the Executive Committee of the Inter-University Research Program in Institution Building. To Hans Blaise, Julian Friedman, Eugene Jacobson, Saul Katz, Jiri Nehnevajsa, Fred Riggs, William Siffin, Ralph Smuckler, and Irving Swerdlow I extend my appreciation for their collaboration and my hope that this application of our model is reasonably faithful to the original design.

My greatest debt is to the scores of Malaysian educators, politicians, professional and business men, and particularly senior officials of all services and all races who, over a two-year period, provided the insights and information—the reality of Malaysian social relations, governmental behavior, and administrative practices—on which this study is grounded. Because of the large number of informants, the sensitive character of much of the data, and the conventions of impartiality and anonymity in the civil service, I cannot publicly acknowledge by name my deep obligation to these men. I would be especially remiss, however, were I not to single out for special thanks my dedicated and enthusiastic colleagues in the Development Administration Unit of the Prime Minister's Department. I am grateful to Merle Fainsod, Lester Gordon, James Guyot, and John Montgomery for their painstaking and critical reading of earlier stages of this book and for their very helpful suggestions and to Janet Bell for typing and preparing the manuscript for publication.

The problems treated in this book are associated with recent events and rapidly changing conditions. I have tried to cover comprehensively developments between July 1965 and February 1969 when I was personally involved and to account systematically for events until September 1970 when Tun Razak succeeded Tunku Abdul Rahman as Prime Minister. This is the effective cut-off point beyond which I make no effort to account for events, though there are occasional references to subsequent developments.

M. J. E.

Ithaca, New York

Contents

Contents

x

Tables

Diagrams

ADMINISTRATION and DEVELOPMENT in MALAYSIA

Institution Building and Reform in a Plural Society

1

Development Administration
and Communal Conflict

Development administration is a new and rapidly growing field of academic inquiry and professional practice. Its outer limits are not clearly defined, but its central core is the role of governmental administration in inducing, guiding, and managing the interrelated processes of nation building, economic growth, and societal change.[1] It is an interdisciplinary field, drawing on concepts and analytical methods from sociology and social psychology as well as from political science and economics. In practice it is multiprofessional in its concern with the management as well as the outputs of action programs in such major sectors as education, agriculture, industry, and transport. It has a twin focus: to develop administrative institutions and capabilities which would improve the managing of change processes, and to administer—shape and implement—development programs in all sectors of public policy.

As a field of action, development administration is universal in scope, for the intense pressures of new technologies and ideas are forcing rapid change in all contemporary societies. The most fruitful scholarly work to date has focused on the less

---

[1] A good recent summary of the scope and meaning of development administration is given in Edward S. Weidner's paper "The Scope and Tasks of Development Administration: Recapitulation of Variations on a Theme," in *Meeting the Administrative Needs of Developing Countries*, a report of a project conducted by the American Society for Public Administration under sponsorship of the Agency for International Development, Washington, D.C., July 1967.

industrialized nations, where traditional administration with its emphasis on officeholding, routine services, and control functions has proved unable to cope with the requirements imposed by change-oriented political elites and by increasing public demand for more dynamic governmental performance. Broadly speaking, the field covers administrative capabilities and performance in governmental, quasi-public, and private institutions, but the emphasis to date has been on the public sector, because most of the scholars working with these concepts have been interested in government and in public administration. Especially in the less developed countries, economic growth, systems change, and social justice are not regarded as spontaneous developments, but as the outcome of governmental policy and action. This study draws on recent experience in Malaysia, one of the more affluent of the newly independent, less industrialized countries. It is primarily concerned with public administration, though it does not ignore administrative capabilities and behavior outside government.

Development administration at any level of government in any sector of activity has four interrelated elements: (1) The *substantive* element is concerned with the goals and outputs of public action, with shaping policy choices, allocating resources, and planning and guiding programs of action. The administrator participates in shaping policy and thus in impressing his preferences on present and future events. He is concerned with the ends of public policy as well as with the means of achieving them. (2) The *managerial* element guides actions toward established substantive goals with the objective of maximizing program effectiveness and the efficient use of means. This requires competent use of management technologies and information systems and a managerial definition of the administrative role. It also sanctions the mixture of instruments—bureaucracy in its various forms, market incentives and mechanisms, associational and voluntary groups, local authorities—to achieve public objectives. (3) *Social change* uses governmental initiative to induce attitudinal and behavioral changes among clientele groups consistent with publicly determined objectives, for example, inducing farmers to double crop, persuading women to use contraceptives, or providing incentives for manufacturers to produce for export. Such activities draw administrators into institution-building activities and into close and continuous interaction with clients. Because they involve a high degree of uncertainty, experimentation, bargaining, and dialogue are required to determine what changing mixtures of incentives, services, and regulation are likely to be effective. (4) The *political* element represents the needs of the polity to constituent groups, responds to demands for the differential distribution of the costs and benefits of public services, and mediates and regulates conflict among individuals and groups affected by public programs of action. These four elements of administrative action can be summarized as policy, management, change agent, and political roles.

These elements are analytically distinct but operationally inseparable. Many administrative positions involve their incumbent more in one element than another, but the prime function of general administrators is to keep all of them in view in making choices and in guiding action. Much public decision making is done by bureaucrats, and nearly all decisions are influenced by them, but they are not a monolithic group in any society nor are they the only decision makers. Politicians, businessmen, educators, and other "influentials" participate in public decision making, depending on the issue. The main public responsibility is borne by senior politicians, but only the most innocent maintain the fiction that administrators merely carry out decisions made by others.

In most developing countries the increased and expanded roles of government have imposed new demands on administration. The image of the colonial administrator as the high-status mandarin keeping order and performing routine services by deploying instruments of authority toward a passive and compliant public, from whom he maintains an appropriate social distance, now appears archaic and dysfunctional. New role definitions and new intellectual and operational capabilities are required if administrators are to be effective political

3

decision makers and program managers in the context of nation building and induced socioeconomic change. While the need for this transformation has been widely recognized, the old behavior patterns have a remarkable sustaining quality, and performance tends to lag behind normative requirements. This problem takes different forms in different countries.

The Situation in Malaysia

In Malaysia, as in other former British colonies, the civil service retains its continuity and legitimacy and is not under serious attack as an institution, but is under strong external pressure to increase its performance capabilities and play a more developmental role.[2] Any program to modernize Malaysia's public administration must take account of the four dimensions of development administration already discussed, especially the political. Malaysia's main political problem is of a particularly dangerous kind, conflict among ethnic groups, particularly Malays and Chinese. Ethnic tension within a single polity can be vicious and destructive because it engages more primordial loyalties than other forms of political conflict.[3] Communal issues in Malaysia are so salient, interwoven into every issue of public policy and public management, that they must be explicitly calculated in every policy decision. Thus a planned program for modernizing Malaysia's administration must consider its ability to contribute to conflict management. Administrative improvement must be directed not merely to strengthening its instrumental managerial capacity, the tradi-

[2] The leading comparative treatment of this theme appears in Ralph Braibanti and associates, *Asian Bureaucratic Systems Emergent from the British Imperial Tradition* (Durham, N.C.: Duke University Press, 1967).

[3] Recent general and theoretical treatments of this subject include R. A. Schermerhorn, *Comparative Ethnic Relations: A Framework for Theory and Research* (New York: Random House, 1970); Philip Mason, *Patterns of Dominance* (London: Oxford University Press, 1970); and Tamotsu Shibutani and Kyan Kwan, *Ethnic Stratification* (New York: Macmillan, 1965). The Schermerhorn volume contains a good bibliography.

tional objective of technical assistance in public administration, nor to building its substantive policy-making and planning capabilities, nor even to guiding social change, important as these certainly are, but specifically to enhancing its political capacity to participate in the management and regulation of communal conflict.

Every society requires instruments for conflict management. Among them are participative processes and institutions, which mediate and regulate interpersonal and intergroup disputes among their constituents. Political parties, local governments, and voluntary and associational groups are participative institutions, and they resolve conflict by enforcing accepted norms or by bargaining. The more intense the disputes and the less institutionalized the participative structures and processes, the less competent they are to mediate. Where there is limited intergroup trust and little consensus on what constitutes proper procedures and legitimate norms, participative institutions are ineffective in managing conflict. Conflicts can also be regulated by authoritative institutions like courts, bureaucracies, or political elites, so long as they are considered legitimate, and can maintain their cohesion and mobilize sufficient power to enforce their judgments.

In Malaysia participative institutions are relatively weak, especially among ethnic Malays, and most are organized along communal lines. The existing participative institutions channel and escalate communal claims more than they mediate conflict. Since they are ineffective for the management of communal conflict, the main burden falls on a small group of political leaders, particularly in the central government, and on the bureaucracy. While the senior politicians are in touch with their communally organized constituents, they have enjoyed sufficient autonomy from these conflicting forces to manage and to resolve most of the conflicts that arise. But as groups mobilize and make greater demands on the system and as communal tensions increase in complexity and intensity, the politicians will need more effective support from the higher civil service, which has been available but not technically or psychologically equipped for

5

conflict management roles. As the pressure on the politicians increases, the very survival of the polity may depend on the capacity of the higher civil service both to provide more effective public services and to assist in regulating communal conflict.

The governing elite in Malaysia is composed of two sections which maintain a symbiotic pattern of relationships: the Alliance Party politicians who head the political section and the senior administrators who operate the bureaucracy. Despite tensions between them, their relationships are mutually supportive. Their style of rule is paternalistic, and together they symbolize authoritative government and deploy the authoritative instruments of this administrative state. Chapter 2 elaborates on the properties of an administrative state and its relevance to Malaysia.

The burden of the argument is that a society whose main problem is the management of communal conflict and whose secondary problem is the guidance of far-reaching social and economic change is likely to be better served if its authoritative institutions are stronger than its participative institutions and if the former are able to discipline the latter. This proposition is especially valid if, as in Malaysia, the existing participative institutions are more likely to make demands on public authority for allocations than to promote self-help or resolve disputes among their members, and if their membership and demands polarize along antagonistic communal lines.[4]

---

[4] This position is contrary to the stream of writing which deplores the "premature" growth of bureaucracy and assigns priority to strengthening participative organizations in order to control bureaucracy. The latter doctrine ignores the importance of guidance in modernizing societies and especially of conflict management, which are the imperative needs of such a country as Malaysia. For this reason such advice has been so little heeded in developing countries, even those that espouse revolution, whose single parties soon develop highly centralized patterns of control. This doctrine is valid only for societies with high consensus on the legitimacy of the regime and long experience in the arts of political compromise. This would not include Malaysia. Among the stream of writings emphasizing the importance of controlling bureaucracy on behalf of democratic de-

6

Aside from the use of coercive instruments, the authoritative institutions can maintain themselves by cultivating their legitimacy and their effectiveness. The legitimacy of the bureaucratic wing of the Malaysian establishment springs from its tradition and its ability to draw men of the highest educational attainment. One test of its effectiveness is its ability to plan and manage action programs. The need to expand this capability prompted the technical assistance reported in this book. The legitimacy of the political wing of the Malaysian establishment has been sustained—at least until the communal riots of May 1969 —by periodic popular elections and by maintaining open channels to its principal constituencies. Their effectiveness depends on their will and ability to act decisively in the maintenance of order, the management of conflict, the satisfaction of public demands, and the fulfillment of development programs, for which the politicians must rely heavily on the bureaucracy. In return for protecting the civil service, the politicians expect substantial assistance in managing all aspects of public affairs, in developmental and conflict management as well as the routine functions of government.

Paradoxically, however, no regime in a modern or modernizing polity can survive unless it can maintain communication with its constituents. Communication enables it to explain the requirements of the polity, to respond to group demands, and to test public responses to administrative programs. Effective communication is impossible unless the publics are organized, not

---

velopment are those by Fred Riggs and Joseph LaPalombara, "Bureaucrats and Political Development: A Parodoxical View," and "Bureaucracy and Political Development: Notes, Queries and Dilemmas," in Joseph LaPalombara, ed., *Bureaucracy and Political Development* (Princeton: Princeton University Press, 1963). An extreme statement of the participationist position prompted by Title IX of the U.S. Foreign Assistance Act of 1965 which mandates an emphasis on "maximum participation" by the people of AID-recipient countries is David Hapgood, ed., *The Role of Popular Participation in Development* (Cambridge, Mass.: MIT Press, 1969). An example of writings which emphasize the priority of order and effective government is Samuel P. Huntington, *Political Order in Changing Societies* (New Haven: Yale University Press, 1968).

7

only to make demands, but also to process some of their demands by providing services to their members. Therefore, effective interaction among administrative agencies and their constituents requires the development of participative capabilities and institutions. In societies where associational skills and propensities are weak, the initiation of such organizations must often be a function of political leadership or of bureaucracy. Yet where societies are conflict-prone, especially along communal lines, the development of these capabilities should be secondary in time and emphasis to the capacity of authoritative institutions to govern and control them. The experiment reported in this book emphasizes the priority of strengthening the operational capabilities of the Malaysian administration, recognizing that more attention must also be devoted to building participative capabilities and processes if administration itself is to become more effective.

The Malaysian bureaucratic cadres retain a high degree of legitimacy inherited from colonial times. They have maintained their integrity, discipline, and organizational coherence. They remain competent in the discharge of routine service and control activities. Their attitudes, role definitions, and operational capabilities, however, are not adequate to the requirements of development administration in any of its four dimensions, but the structure is there to build on. Key members of the central political elites have perceived the need for strengthening the country's administrative capabilities because they have found the civil service to be deficient in "delivering the goods," in shaping and implementing the development programs on which the Alliance politicians consider that their own survival depends. This need impelled the government of Malaysia to request assistance from the Ford Foundation in 1965.

The Malaysian Development Administration Project

The request from the Malaysian government to the Ford Foundation originated with the Deputy Prime Minister and was strongly promoted by the leadership of one of his principal staff arms, the Economic Planning Unit. This request resulted in a brief two-man reconnaissance and a set of recommendations to initiate a program of administrative reform.[5]

Prospects for a sustained program in administrative development through foreign technical assistance appeared to be favorable. The senior political leadership was highly supportive, particularly the Deputy Prime Minister, Tun Abdul Razak, one of Asia's most dynamic development politicians and Malaysia's superadministrator.[6] Like many Malay aristocrats, Razak began his career as an administrator, advancing rapidly to the position of state secretary of Pahang, his native state, before moving into nationalist politics ("I was a civil servant long enough to learn all of their tricks, but not long enough to be taken in"). Since 1956 he has been struggling to modernize the civil service through continuous exhortation to officers to give up their old colonial ways and to become dynamic development administrators. He has been responsible for major innovations in the administrative system, including the introduction of development planning and the internationally renowned "operations room–red book" system of project planning, scheduling, and monitoring, which is analyzed in detail in later chapters. Frustrated by the sluggishness of the civil service in implementing development activities, he has intervened frequently (and contrary to the conventions of the service) in the posting of officers and in modifying its governing rules and procedures. He is vitally interested in administration, in administrative performance, and administrative innovation. His enthusiastic acceptance of the Montgomery-Esman report meant that the Development Administration Unit set up in the Prime Minister's Department as the center for administrative innovation would be within the ambit of his concern and protection.

Another favorable factor was the continuing stability and viability of the administrative system. It had survived the shock of

[5] John D. Montgomery and Milton J. Esman, *Development Administration in Malaysia* (Kuala Lumpur: Government Printer, 1966). The content of this report is analyzed in Chapter 5 of this volume.

[6] A very sympathetic description of his earlier efforts and his operational style by an American scholar is in Gayl Ness, *Bureaucracy and Rural Development in Malaya* (Berkeley: University of California Press, 1967).

9

rapid Malayanization virtually intact; it had not been debauched by nationalist politicians; it had retained its integrity, discipline, public respect, and effective capacity to carry out routine services throughout the country down to the village level. While its officers were not clamoring for reform, certainly not for reform introduced under unfamiliar and unpredictable American auspices, many, especially the younger officers, recognized that change was inevitable. Ten years of exhortation by Tun Razak had softened them up. While their attitude sets, role definitions, and operational capabilities were not conducive to development administration, few were enthusiastic, and some were frankly hostile, many more were willing to listen and to learn.

Strategy of Adminstrative Reform

It was decided that the program in administrative reform would be closely associated with a parallel and mutually reinforcing effort to strengthen Malaysia's economic planning capabilities. Technical assistance for both activities was assumed by the Development Advisory Service of Harvard University under the Ford Foundation's sponsorship and financing.[7] The strategy would be guided by lessons from previous efforts at induced administrative reform and from judgments of what might be effective and feasible in Malaysia:

1. The reformer's task is not only technical but highly political. Thus change agents must cultivate and maintain a favorable climate for reform in their environment. They must invest their energies in building support among those within the government and outside who can influence the results of their efforts.

2. A campaign of induced administrative reform which attempts to produce changes in administrative behavior must deploy a mixture of mutually reinforcing instruments. These are *technological* (changes in systems, methods, and cognitive

[7] The author was asked to help launch this program as senior advisor to the Prime Minister's Department. He was thus a participant-observer in this reform program from September 1966 to August 1968.

knowledge), *cultural* (changes in values, beliefs, sentiments, and attitudes), and *political* (changes in the distribution of power and the system of rewards). Priority should be assigned to technological approaches because they are more tangible, more acceptable to clients, and more likely to facilitate behavioral changes.

3. The introduction of new systems and methods in an organization must be regarded as a process of guided group learning and adaptation, not as the "installation" of prepackaged technologies. Hierarchical authority is a necessary but not sufficient condition for the introduction and institutionalization of administrative reforms.

4. Reformers must exercise influence simultaneously at multiple points within the administrative network and in its immediate environment so that momentum may be established at many sectors and changes may be mutually reinforcing.

5. Reformers' targets should be selected in order to achieve maximum strategic impact within the limits of political feasibility. In Malaysia, the central government-wide systems—personnel, finance, supply, organization—would receive initial priority. They would afford maximum leverage for influence. Improvement in these systems would loosen up the entire administrative structure and thus increase the government's total capacity to absorb more complex activities. Within the civil service, the elite administrative grade officers, the Malaysian Home and Foreign Service (MHFS) would be the prime targets because they are the legitimate leadership cadres and their influence permeates the entire government. Sufficient resources would have to be reserved, of course, to meet targets of opportunity, and satisfy urgent requests for services from politically important sources.

6. Inducing administrative reform is basically an institution-building activity.[8] Institution building has three main programming implications: (*a*) Major reforms occur in and through

[8] The leading work in institution-building theory has been done by and under the auspices of the Interuniversity Research Program in Institution Building. See Section IV of the bibliography for references to this literature.

formal organizations. Therefore new organizations must be built or older ones remodeled with the capacity to protect and promote innovations in their environment. (*b*) Building indigenous capabilities—individuals and organizations—which have the capacity to sustain innovations and to continue innovating takes precedence over achieving short-term operational results. This implies a high priority to staff development and to investing in the organization. The emphasis of foreign advisers should therefore be on developing capabilities and commitments among local staff and building their influence within the system rather than on the organization's immediate outputs, except as the latter are required to protect the new organization's standing in its environment pending the development of local expertise. (*c*) Every program of action involves the innovative organization in transactions and in "linkage" relationships with other organizations whose behavior it is attempting to influence along innovative lines. Each such linkage must be managed so that compatible relationships are established and maintained while the innovations are being transferred, adapted, and institutionalized in the linked organization.

How these general propositions were applied experimentally through specific programs of action and how these change strategies fared when they encountered the realities of Malaysia's administrative environment are reviewed and evaluated in this study. From the early history of these experiments judgments can be drawn about the utility of these approaches to administrative reform when applied to a relatively stable and prestigious administrative system like Malaysia's.

On Feasibility and Desirability

Conclusive judgments about the feasibility of the change strategies which were attempted will depend upon the evaluation of results which are only partially available at the time of writing. The early tests of these change strategies, measured by the ability of change agents to launch reforms which represent major deviations from previous practice and to achieve significant clientele involvement, suggest a favorable preliminary judgment of the program and methods of reform. *Feasibility,* broadly meaning that enhanced administrative capability can contribute to major national goals, is the implicit assumption underlying this experiment. Social scientists are skeptical about the capacity of public bureaucratic institutions to become effective instruments of development. In some polities, the conservative and compulsive commitment to routine, precedent, and status, in others the debilitating consequences of spoils politics, in others the self-serving abuse of office combined with disregard for responsive public service, reinforce the prevailing fear and contempt among many scholars for bureaucratic institutions. It has proved easier to reject bureaucratic institutions than to find convincing substitutes for achieving governmental effectiveness. If one is interested in the developmental outputs of governmental action and even if one allots large roles to political, market, and voluntary institutions, development cannot proceed very far without strong and sustained contributions by public administrative agencies. The evident gap between required and actual performance indicates a high priority for strengthening administrative effectiveness, rather than the anxious concern expressed by so many contemporary scholars for "controlling" public bureaucracy in developing countries.[9]

Feasibility can be distinguished from *desirability* by only a fine line. Like other institutions—private enterprise, the judiciary, churches, political parties, legislatures—the social impact of bureaucracy can range from the benign to the exploitative. Since administration is a plural phenomenon, it may, in the same country at the same time, be dynamic and client-serving in one sector, stagnant and even abusive in another. There is no a priori reason to worry about the "control" of bureaucracy any more than about the control of other institutions that wield power. Bureaucracy may sometimes be more benign, more responsible, and more effective than alternative or competing institutions. In Malaysia there is little likelihood that civil ser-

[9] See Riggs and LaPalombara. A position closely akin to mine is in Ralph Braibanti's "Introduction" to *Asian Bureaucratic Systems.*

13

vants will usurp anything and far greater danger that they will fail to discharge both the instrumental and the political roles for which they have the potential and for which their polity has no substitute capacity. If Malaysia's administrators can be equipped to contribute to the management of its most critical problems, economic development and communal conflict, and if in the process it may at times be necessary for bureaucracy to restrain political and participative institutions in the interest of internal peace and orderly development, then it is a rational and humane political strategy to strengthen the operating capabilities of the civil service. In Malaysia both participative and authoritative institutions and capabilities must be strengthened, but the latter take priority.

The environment of Malaysia, as of many societies, particularly those subject to communal conflict, is more Hobbesian than Jeffersonian. Such a society cannot risk weak authoritative structures because there is insufficient intergroup trust to permit political and participative institutions to manage the inevitable conflicts. Thus public bureaucracy is strengthened not alone as a force for order, but, in the style of development administration, to help define goals, shape policies, and carry out action programs that will serve national goals, including the groping and experimenting for viable patterns of communal coexistence and accommodation. While one may question the feasibility of the efforts reported in this study, those who are concerned with orderly development in the Malaysian situation cannot doubt their desirability.

It is impossible to treat administrative reform in Malaysia outside the societal context in which it functions. The environment of Malaysian administration is thus analyzed in Chapter 2. Chapters 3 and 4 describe and analyze the Malaysian administrative system and personnel in the late 1960s and thus provide a baseline for the reforms. Chapters 5, 6, and 7 review and evaluate the early experience with reform following the strategies just outlined.

Chapter 8 speculates on the management of communal conflict, a problem that now afflicts many nations. A number of approaches are suggested as worthy of testing. Much of the hard thinking, the program management, the social experimentation, and the institution building related to communal conflict will fall upon Malaysia's hard-presssed administrators now and in the future. More will be required than pragmatic responses to crises. The present political and administrative leadership is as moderate and as civilized on these issues as their peers anywhere in the world, and far more so than most of their constituents, but they urgently need longer-term strategies for the management of communal conflict, particularly after the tragic outbreaks of May 1969. These strategies must be supported by experimentation, structured bargaining, and other forms of accommodative communication, and supplemented where necessary by the coercive power of government in those heartbreaking episodes when efforts at understanding break down in the face of intractable conflict.

Finally, Chapter 9 summarizes what has been learned from this inquiry.

2

The Malaysian Context

"Ecology" has been an important orientation of recent writing in comparative administration.[1] According to ecological concepts, administration cannot be viewed, as by scientific management or the more recent decision-theory writers, as a self-contained system relentlessly pursuing the goals of instrumental efficiency or cost effectiveness. Instead it is a subsystem of the larger society with which it maintains a continuous pattern of transactions. The prevailing societal values, distribution of political power, communication flows, economic and technical arrangements, and political styles condition the behavior of public administration, for it must depend on them for its authority and resources and for approval of its outputs. Thus in a society which attaches little value to efficiency, administration will probably not behave efficiently, but it will subserve more salient values. This does not mean that administration must be a pale reflection of the prevailing culture or balance of political forces in the larger society. Some groups of administrators may work for change; some may respond to demands originating in society, regarding organized groups as constituents; others may attempt to deliver prepackaged services, regarding their consumers as clients; others may prefer simply to hold office and maintain the *status quo*. Most of them are likely to participate

[1] See John Gaus, *Reflections on Public Administration* (University, Alabama: University of Alabama Press, 1947); and Fred Riggs, *The Ecology of Public Administration* (New Delhi: Asia Publishing House, 1961).

16

in the competition for resources, status, influence, and even political power.

Throughout this book, I shall refer to elements of Malaysian society which condition the behavior of its public administration and which administration, in turn, regulates or serves. A few of the main contextual or ecological elements are outlined below.

Communal Pluralism

Communal pluralism is the essential reality of Malaysian society and government. Ethnic Malays constitute slightly less than a majority of the new nation and the Chinese are a very significant 37 percent. Though relations between these two blocs is the most salient political issue, the ethnic problem is even more complex. In peninsular Malaya—now called West Malaysia—there is an "Indian" minority of 10 percent, predominantly Tamil, but including an important group of bearded and turbaned Sikhs. There is also a small but strategically placed group of Eurasians. In East Malaysia, the Borneo states of Sarawak and Sabah, where Chinese outnumber Malay Muslims, the largest of the many indigenous ethnic groups are the Ibans and Kadazans respectively, sharing little with Chinese or Malays except their membership in a newly formed political entity (see Table 1).

COMMUNAL IDENTITIES

Statistical pluralism is not as important as how people behave and identify themselves, how interests are perceived, and how issues are defined. Malaysia came into being in 1963, and its predecessor, Malaya, achieved independence from Britain in 1957 without a hard struggle.[2] To most of its citizens Malaysia

[2] A concise history of these political events is presented by R. S. Milne, *The Government and Politics of Malaysia* (Boston: Houghton Mifflin Co., 1967); also Willard F. Hanna, *The Formation of Malaysia* (New York: American Universities Field Staff, 1964), and K. J. Ratnam, *Communalism and the Political Process in Malaya* (Kuala Lumpur: University of Malaya Press, 1965).

The Malaysian Context

Table 1. Malaysian population statistics:
Estimated population by state and race, 31 December 1967

State	All races	Malays	Chinese	Indians and Pakistanis	Others *
Johore	1,316,772	654,936	532,083	98,434	31,319
Kedah	936,825	635,287	189,007	88,888	23,643
Kelantan	684,554	626,640	38,033	8,171	11,710
Malacca	416,795	210,639	164,213	33,745	8,198
Negri Sembilan	517,451	219,598	206,989	78,120	12,744
Pahang	431,747	246,069	148,398	31,823	5,457
Penang	761,194	219,937	433,925	90,871	16,461
Perak	1,656,985	666,285	721,944	242,510	26,246
Perlis	118,987	91,606	21,395	2,167	3,819
Selangor	1,431,707	426,889	678,311	278,476	48,031
Trengganu	382,282	353,135	23,125	4,739	1,283
West Malaysia	8,655,299	4,351,021	3,157,423	957,944	188,911
Sabah	590,660	145,000 †	145,000 †	–	300,660
Sarawak	902,841	163,022	296,977	–	442,842
East Malaysia	1,493,501	308,022	441,977	–	743,502
All Malaysia	10,148,800	4,659,043	3,599,400	957,944	932,413

Source: Malaysian Government Statistics Bulletin, 6 November 1968.
* Others include Eurasians, Kadazans, Melanaus, Ibans, and Land Dyaks, but not aborigines, who are listed with Malays.
† Crude estimate by author.

is still an abstraction, a very new nation. Its symbols have little emotional meaning to large sections of the population, and to some its legitimacy is questioned, largely on communal grounds. There is little social or instrumental communication among the communities, and much of this communication is fraught with tension.[3]

Most Malaysians identify themselves and others by communal categories, which take precedence over class, regional, and occu-

[3] Compare with J. S. Furnival's theory of plural society in his *Colonial Policy and Practice: A Comparative Study of Burma and Netherlands Indies* (New York: New York University Press, 1956).

18

pational rubrics. Thus Chinese and Malay farmers growing the same crop in the same district will have no communication and few common institutions except those imposed on them by public authority. To simplify, I shall speak primarily of Malays and Chinese, the largest, most important, and most antagonistic communal groupings, though they are not monolithic. There is much actual and even greater potential class conflict within them, and these sources of conflict will not be neglected. But the intracommunal cleavages and issues are frequently mitigated, especially among the Malays, by the perception of threats to the community and its common interests originating in other communal groups.[4]

Members of each major community use simplistic but highly significant gestalts to identify themselves and others. Malays identify themselves esssentially by race, religion, and language, the latter two being the more important. All "Malays" in Malaysia are Muslims, and to abandon Islam calls for such severe sanctions that it very seldom occurs. Malays communicate among themselves in the Malay language. Because Malaya has been a crossroads country, Muslims of diverse racial origins, Arabs, Pakistanis, Achinese, have beeen assimilated into the Malay community. "Race" is part of a Malay's self-identification and, though glorified by Malay nationalists, it is a highly accommodative concept. So long as a man professes Islam, speaks the Malay language, follows Malay customs, and considers himself a member of the Malay community, he is accepted as a Malay.

Malays consider themselves the *bumiputera* (sons of the soil), the native, indigenous people of the peninsula. Although they know that many of their number migrated from Indonesia within the past half-century, they do not appreciate being reminded of this by non-Malays because the *bumiputera* doctrine legitimizes their fundamental aspiration for political con

[4] These attitudes among village Malays have been described by Marvin L. Rogers, "Political Involvement in a Rural Malay Community" (Ph.D. diss., University of California, Berkeley, 1968), and Peter J. Wilson, *A Malay Village and Malaysia: Social Values and Rural Development* (New Haven: Human Relations Area Files, 1967).

trol of the country. They regard non-Malays as sojourners, who were invited into their country by the British colonial masters to develop its resources. They came to make money and return home, and their basic loyalties and emotional attachments were (and in the judgment of many Malays still are) to China or India. The *bumiputera* doctrine, which Malay nationalists and even their moderate representative in the current government proclaim, with its implication that non-Malays are in Malaysia by sufferance, is a source of continuous irritation to non-Malays, a reminder of second-class status.

Malays regard themselves as scrupulous in their dealings with outsiders as well as one another, faithful in all obligations to their families, friends, religion, and rulers, and concerned more with the quality of human relations and with the unhurried enjoyment of simple, decent living than with material acquisition. Modern education and information media and the fear that their race is losing its struggle for survival against Chinese competition are causing the younger and better educated Malays to redefine the latter theme and emphasize the need for dynamism, development, mastery of modern technologies, and changes in their group's image of a desirable way of life. Difference in this view is a mark of generational change among Malays which has important political significance.

Malays have a less flattering image of Chinese: hard-working, ambitious, insatiably acquisitive, clever but unscrupulous in transactions outside their family, coarse and insensitive in interpersonal relations, ritually and physically unclean, unreliable in their values except their enduring obligation to ancestors and thus to Chinese culture and to China, regardless of the regime temporarily in power.

Chinese regard themselves as hard-working, progressive, concerned with improving their lot through their own efforts in a competitive and often hostile environment, and faithful to their family and social obligations. To the Chinese, a "typical" Malay is lazy and superstitious, without motivation to improve himself through education or hard work, preferring to subsist on handouts or patronage from relatives or the government than to earn his way through diligent work. The Chinese believe it was largely Chinese immigrant labor and entrepreneurship which built modern Malaysia. Thus what they have they earned themselves through hard and honest effort and therefore enjoy as a right. Some of their ancestors have been in Malaya for centuries and the rest came from China not much more recently than did many of the Malays from Indonesia. Though they desire to retain their communal identity and their Chinese culture, they claim to be loyal Malaysians, entitled to full equality in all respects, not to sufferance or second-class citizenship. As the more economically productive citizens, they pay the bulk of taxes, another reason for full and equal participation in public decision making and in the benefits of government. Their fathers may have accepted any terms that assured their physical safety, economic opportunity, and cultural expression, but the emergent Chinese generation, except for the minority of China-oriented chauvinists, regards anything less than full equality as unjust and unacceptable.

INTERCOMMUNAL RELATIONS

There is little effective communication among the communities. The conflicting stereotypes which I have drawn are not caricatures. They actually reflect the way members of the communities look at themselves and at one another and thus orient their behavior. Except for a small group of intellectuals and government officials in the cities, the communities live apart and practice different life styles. There is little intermarriage; Islam forbids intermarriage, unless the non-Muslim party converts, and few Chinese men find Islam an appealing faith. The cultural pride of Chinese as participants through their ancestors in a rich and enduring civilization confronts them with the unpleasant choice of sacrificing something which they value highly to accommodate to the Malay-Muslim society which they regard as an inferior culture. Nothing exists to draw either party toward the other. Chinese love pork, which is forbidden to the Malays; Chinese enjoy noise and garrulous excitement, which is offensive to Malays who prefer more quiet and ordered styles of social intercourse. Chinese are direct and blunt in their style; Malays are more deferential, sensitive, and reserved.

Roles are sharply differentiated in Malaysia along communal lines. The Malays are overwhelmingly rural dwellers in subsistence farming, fishing, and small-holder rubber. There is a significant drift of young Malays to the cities, escaping rural poverty and attracted to urban opportunity, but these migrants find themselves primarily in unskilled, low-paying occupations and are often unemployed. Malays control government at the federal and state levels. Thus they are prominent in the civil service, especially in the administrative and clerical services. They dominate the military and are well represented among schoolteachers, but in commerce, industry, mining, finance, construction, plantation agriculture, and the liberal professions they are barely represented.

In education non-Malays, particularly Chinese, are dominant. The reasons are complex, traceable to differences in the value systems of the communities, to the British neglect of Malay education, and to the superior educational opportunities available to urban dwellers who are mostly non-Malays. At the University of Malaya the enrollment in 1966–1967 was 70 percent non-Malay, and the faculties of engineering, science, and medicine were 98, 93, and 84 percent non-Malay respectively.[5] The Technical College in Kuala Lumpur was 90 percent non-Malay. These figures are ominously disquieting to the Malay political, professional, and intellectual leaders, for they imply that Chinese economic dominance is reinforced by a growing dominance in the modern technologies, which are a complementary source of social power. Malays ask whether their control of government will be sufficient to counteract the growing Chinese power in education and in the modern economy and whether, in addition to their efforts to foster Malay entrepreneurship and educational opportunity, direct government intervention is required to correct these imbalances, even at the risk of reduced efficiency and lower rates of economic growth.

Such proposals are resented and resisted by the Chinese, who

[5] University of Malaya, Eighteenth Annual Report, 1966–1967.

argue that free and open economic and educational competition is the only policy which is fair to all. They also argue that it is against the interests of Malays themselves to be given positions, licenses, scholarships, and other subsidies on a preferential basis, since it accustoms them to handouts and undermines their incentive to compete. Along with many Malays, they charge that the benefits of Malay privilege redound all too often to a small group of highly placed people who enjoy preferential access to government rather than to rank-and-file Malays who benefit very little from privileges which are justified in their name.

This catalogue of differences could be expanded to include other aspects of the norms and styles of the two communities to demonstrate the complexity of shaping common objects of identity for these two peoples coexisting in the same territory and under the same political structure. Geographic separatism is impossible. Nor is it likely that one community will expel or absorb the other for each is too large, relatively, to permit elimination or absorption of either as a feasible, not to mention morally tolerable, objective—even though it is not outside the realm of discourse among extremists, particularly militant Malays. Thus the pattern must move from peaceful coexistence to mutual and incremental accommodation, problem by problem, that will provide sufficient coherence to maintain the polity and prevent disorder and bloodshed. Any expectation of integration or the development of an integrative identity in the foreseeable future is pure rhetoric or fancy. The management of a precarious coexistence and the exploration for further patterns of accommodation are the main tasks of political leadership, a frequent theme in this study.

ORGANIZATION OF POLITICS

Since the identity structure of most Malaysians is communal, it is not surprising that politics, responding to this essential reality, should be organized on that basis. After abortive efforts in the early 1950s to organize political life noncommunally, it became evident that successful political mobilization would have to be communally based. The result was the Alliance

Party, a coalition of three communal groupings, the United Malay National Organization (UMNO), the senior partner, the Malayan Chinese Association (MCA), the junior partner, and the Malayan Indian Congress (MIC), the minipartner. The Alliance provided a pragmatic dominant party system, which made no claim to be monolithic, but candidly recognized the existence of diverse and conflicting communal interests and the need for an instrument to manage and mediate them.

In the original theory of the Alliance each community was to be represented by its "natural" leadership. In the case of the Malays this meant the English-educated members of the traditional aristocracy, for the Chinese, the leading capitalists. The leadership was to represent and reconcile the diverse interests in each community and deliver their electoral and moral support to the Alliance. Issues would be negotiated and compromised, and the benefits and burdens of government would be equitably apportioned among the communities according to the mature judgment of their natural leaders. These leaders, in turn, would be responsible for explaining and justifying Alliance decisions to their respective constituencies and for securing their compliance. Thus communal issues, divisive and explosive as they are in Malaysia, would be removed from the theater of agitational controversy and negotiated quietly by the wisest and coolest heads in each community.

The Alliance was based on a series of explicit and implied understandings about the mutual responsibilities of the parties and the relationships of the communities to each other. The Malays were to be politically dominant, and the style of the polity would be Malay. By the delineation of constituency boundaries, which favored the rural areas, Malays would be assured of safe majorities in the federal Parliament. The Alliance formula would also insure Malay hegemony in state governments even where non-Malays are the majority of the population. Thus the chief ministers of the states and the members of the federal cabinet would be predominantly Malay. The chief of state would be a Malay sultan, chosen by the traditional rulers from among their number for a five-year term, a neat device also for assuring support from the traditional rulers and their entourages for the new federation with its strong central government. The official religion was to be Islam and the national language Malay. Various Malay privileges were to continue.[6] These include quotas and preference in public employment, especially in the administrative and diplomatic services, reservation of certain lands for exclusive ownership and use by Malays, preference in certain forms of licensing and public contracts, and special scholarships and training privileges.[7] The rationale for these privileges was the need to protect the Malays and to offer them special economic opportunities until they are able, at an undetermined future date, to compete on equal terms. Non-Malays, in return, received full and equal citizenship if born in Malaya and more liberal naturalization rights than existed during the colonial regime. They were also accorded full political participation and rights to officeholding, religious freedom, liberal use of communal languages, and opportunity for economic activity with the understanding that no existing economic stake would be abridged by government action. The Chinese partners would finance the Alliance, and Chinese notables would be eligible for their share of honors and other decorations.[8]

This political bargain realized great benefits for all parties, in many cases more than the original participants had expected to achieve. The Malays gained political independence, control of government, and a polity which was to be Malay in style and in its system of symbols. In return the Chinese gained more than overseas Chinese in Southeast Asia had dreamed of—equal citizenship, political participation and officeholding, unimpaired economic opportunity, and tolerance for their language, religion, and cultural institutions. In the decade and a half

[6] Article 153 of the Federal Constitution empowers the King to protect the "special position" of the Malays and specifies these areas of privilege.

[7] The policy of quotas and preference in public employment is discussed in detail in Chapter 3.

[8] For a good, brief, factual outline of these provisions, see Milne, pp. 38–41.

since this great bargain was struck the leadership of the major structures of the Alliance has been remarkably stable, notwithstanding costly defections on both sides. The moderate leaders of both groups, convinced that their political survival and the peace and prosperity of the country were at stake, faithfully abided by the letter and the spirit of these agreements, despite heavy pressure from their own ranks.

As well as awarding benefits, any such compromise imposes costs and dissatisfactions. The benefits are soon taken for granted, but the limitations and unfulfilled aspirations become fresh political issues. New issues emerge that were not anticipated, were glossed over by the original negotiators, or arose on the margins of agreement. Predictably this has happened in Malaysia. The success of an arrangement like the Alliance depends on continuing good will and a spirit of accommodation and mutual loyalty by the leaders as they grapple with new problems. This good will and trust have been abundantly available. Success also depends on continued acceptance by each constituency of the legitimacy, wisdom, and fairness of their leadership, which in turn influences the capacity of the leadership to deliver the support of a majority of their community to the Alliance at election time and in deliberations on specific issues. With increasing political awareness and mobilization, plural and conflicting elements have emerged in each community which the UMNO and particularly the MCA have been hard pressed to manage and to contain within the Alliance structure. These forces deserve attention because they illustrate the dynamic character of communal pressures which the Malaysian political system must continue to cope with.

Among the Malays the most significant pressures are populistic. A substantial body of Malay opinion places a higher value on the fulfillment of Malay nationalism than on communal cooperation or economic development. As its name implies, the Pan-Malayan-Islamic Party (PMIP) is committed to Pan-Malayanism, which indicates a pro-Indonesia policy and perhaps even political association with their Indonesian racial brothers. Their emphasis on the traditional religious element in Malay life attracts support from religious conservatives and has forced the Alliance government to counter by elaborate sponsorship of mosque building and Koran-reading contests and by otherwise emphasizing religious observance in its political program. Essentially the PMIP does not accept the legitimacy of Chinese participation in Malaysian life at its present level. They espouse the cause of the poor and forgotten Malay farmer and fisherman who had been "neglected" by the Alliance government because the dominant Malay establishment in the UNMO has been "bought off" by the Chinese. While the Chinese capitalists and UMNO politicians grow rich, the honest Malay peasant, whom they exploit, continues to suffer. Because of its identification with religious obscurantism, the PMIP has not drawn much support from Malay-speaking intellectuals, who proclaim many of the same economic and cultural themes in even more strident terms. The potential for PMIP recruitment of embittered Malay intellectuals does exist, and despite limited finances and unexciting leadership the PMIP actively competes with the UMNO for the rural Malay vote.

Another anti-UMNO position, with a small mass following but important support among educated Malays, including many younger civil servants, is less obviously communal in its appeal. It accuses the Malay establishment of neglecting the peasants (Chinese as well as Malay) by failing to attack the root cause of rural poverty, the middleman, whom they attack not because he happens to be Chinese, but because of his exploiting role as a monopolist and monopsonist.[9] They also accuse the UMNO of sponsoring *"bumiputera* capitalism," the artificial creation by government favor of a small privileged group of Malay pseudo-

[9] Only "institutional" changes—meaning the replacement of middlemen by cooperatives or government facilities and the enforcement of tenancy laws—will provide the Malay farmer with the necessary incentives to use modern technologies effectively. The most articulate and influential spokesman for this position is Professor Unku Aziz, Vice-Chancellor of the University of Malaya. A recent statement of his position is in his paper, "Agricultural Development and Economic Development in Malaysia," Chapter 5 of *The Structure and Development of Asian Economies* (Tokyo: Japan Economic Research Center, December 1968).

capitalists,[10] and neglecting broadly based institutional reforms that would help large numbers of rural Malays to achieve a better way of life. While concerned with improving the economic and social lot of the poor Malays, this group rejects the government's current emphasis on religion and mosque building (opium for the people), avoids specifically communal appeals, and participates in noncommunal political parties. This group is populistic, and its target is as much the Malay establishment as the Chinese capitalists and middlemen. Many of the younger educated activists in the UNMO share these views, especially on the causes and cures of rural Malay poverty.

Though pressed by these attacks, the UMNO has maintained an active and vigorous mass organization among the Malays. By assimilating and rewarding local elites, by judicious use of patronage and handouts to communities and individuals, and by continued identification with the cause of Malay progress and protection, they have been sufficiently responsive to the needs of their constituents, despite frequent strains, to deliver electoral majorities. They have also used their power to protect and honor their basic commitment to their Chinese partners, even when this hurts them among Malays whose support they must retain.

The problems of the MCA have been more difficult. The Chinese community is occupationally and educationally more differentiated than the Malay.[11] It is more diffusely organized

[10] These pseudo-capitalists seldom perform legitimate entrepreneurial or management roles. Apparently a small group of Malays are permitted to buy the shares of pioneer firms—usually foreign-owned and managed—which are reserved for Malays at issue price. The *bumiputera* capitalists sometimes join the boards of these firms mostly in honorific roles. Frequently, they sell the shares at easy profit to Chinese as they gain in value. A brief description of the National Investment Company is in Sumitro Djojohadikusumo, "Malaysia and Singapore," in *Trade and Aid in South-east Asia* (Melbourne: F. W. Cheshire, 1968), Volume I, pp. 221–232.

[11] A recent and very insightful analysis of politics among Malayan Chinese is by Wang Gung-wu, "Chinese Politics in Malaya," unpublished manuscript, 1970.

by guilds and subethnic regional and language groupings, and its capitalist leadership cannot claim the same customary and emotional support and deference that Malay aristocrats and other high-status persons can still command from their commoners. When the Alliance was formed, only a small proportion of the Chinese community were able to vote or were politically interested. Many of the latter had been drained off in the Insurgency which was failing and the majority of the Chinese were eager to rehabilitate their community politically. This required spokesmen who were acceptable to the British and who could negotiate with Malay aristocrats. The wealthy, English-speaking Chinese who came forward to found the MCA were acceptable for that role. The Chinese community appeared to support them, and British officials and Malay aristocrats saw them as its natural leaders.

Less than a decade after its establishment, the MCA was in deep trouble. Despite repeated assurances by the UMNO leadership that they would treat with no other Chinese political group, the MCA was manifestly unable to command a broad consensus among Malaysian Chinese. One reason is that many Chinese do not feel morally bound by the compromise that founded the Alliance. Some say that they were never consulted while their self-appointed leaders negotiated away their political and cultural rights. Others claim that terms which satisfied their fathers, who were so grateful as overseas Chinese to be given any political rights or economic protection, do not suffice for their sons who were born in Malaya and demand full equality in all respects. Others insist that even within the terms of the great compromise the MCA has done little to assert and protect legitimate Chinese interests. They accuse the MCA capitalist leaders of sacrificing Chinese educational and language interests and of bartering away the economic opportunities of poor and middle-class Chinese in order to protect their own economic position and political power as puppets of the UMNO.

The nature of legitimate political discourse in contemporary Malaysia, allows free expression of Malay chauvinism, as is done by the PMIP and other Malay nationalists. Chinese chauvinism exists but may not be expressed. Right-wing Malays threaten the Chinese that if they become too troublesome they face the prospect of an "Indonesian solution," a union with Indonesia in which the Malays would swamp the outnumbered Chinese. Many Chinese, especially those educated in Chinese-language schools still look to their native cultural and political models for inspiration and are embittered that their language has so little economic value. So far as these alienated Chinese have a political vehicle, it finds ideological expression through the Labor Party. Though its doctrine is Marxian and it would establish a noncommunal peoples' republic in Malaysia, its appeal is as much in Chinese chauvinism as in Marxian socialism. Its leaders are subject to continuous police surveillance and frequent detention, since it is regarded as the overt expression of the underground Malayan Communist Party. Yet it has a substantial following among alienated Chinese youth who find the Malay-style polity offensive to their Chinese identity, the capitalist economy dominated by foreigners and Chinese entrepreneurs unjust and exploitative, and the regime of Malay privileges discriminatory and damaging to their educational and employment prospects. The MCA cannot, obviously, deliver this group of voters.

More significant are the non-Communists who espouse noncommunal politics. Most of the growing educated Chinese middle class takes this political line. Malaysia, yes, "we identify with this nation, we should be neither Chinese nor Tamils nor Malays, but Malaysians all, equal and fraternal." They proclaim the slogan of their hero, Lee Kuan Yew, Prime Minister of Singapore: "a Malaysian Malaysia." The political significance of this slogan is the end of *bumiputeraism* and Malay privileges. Though they preach noncommunalism as a principle, this group are judged by most Malays as hypocrites, for the end of Malay privileges now would signal the dominance of Chinese even in areas now protected for Malays. The non-Malay, basically Chinese parties which advocate the doctrine of noncommunal democratic socialism oppose Malay privilege, but advocate special opportunities for Malays to overcome their educational and economic lag, yet not at the expense of the other races. Like the Labor Party they emphatically reject the stereotype held by many Malays that all Chinese are rich or have rich relatives and are interested only in money, not in politics. They would redefine basic issues on class rather than communal lines, stressing the common interests of the "have-nots," poor Malays and poor Chinese, against the rich and privileged Malay aristocrats and Chinese capitalists who control the Alliance. They accept Malay as the national language but argue that Chinese, Tamil, and English should also have official status as in Singapore, their political model. They object as much to the MCA's style of manipulated, paternalistic, boss politics as to their policy positions.

The MCA leadership is also under pressure from businessmen and other community leaders who have no other political vehicle and work through the MCA itself. This pressure demands that Chinese interests be protected and promoted more vigorously to prevent Malay privileges from being further extended, to open more land for Chinese cultivation, to protect the use of the Chinese language, to demand more job opportunities for Chinese educated youth, to fight for more Chinese candidates on the Alliance slate. They charge that the MCA leaders are too compliant to the UMNO and that when they fight it is primarily to protect a few capitalists rather than more broadly based Chinese interests.

THE SYMBOLS SYSTEM

Communal divisions appear not only on specific issues regarding the economic, social, and cultural benefits and costs of participating in the polity. The problem arises also in the symbols system. The chief of state is a Malay sultan, and so are the heads of all the states, even of Malacca, Penang, Sabah, and Sarawak, whose governors are appointed in the absence of traditional rulers. The national language is Malay; the official religion is Islam, which is actively propagated by the government but without impairing the free practice of other religions. The national flag contains the Islamic star and crescent. Malays

31

can thus identify emotionally with the expressive symbols of the polity. Non-Malays, who are half the population, cannot. So jealous are the Malays of their control of the polity and its style that not a single element in the official symbols system is drawn from the traditions of the non-Malay people. Their attachment to the polity and their willingness to invest support in the system must rest entirely on instrumental judgments and on calculations of how their interests are affected.

A Malay may oppose particular acts of government but continue to regard the regime as legitimate because it is replete with symbols to which he is emotionally attached. There are no similar emotional reserves to hold non-Malays when their particular interests are threatened by the actions of the government. The fact that the federal and state governments confer titles and honors quite generously on non-Malays, especially MCA politicians, wealthy businessmen, and senior civil servants does not compensate for the emotional emptiness of the official symbols system to the mass of non-Malays.

THE LANGUAGE ISSUE

Until May 1969 the Alliance held together despite defections which weakened both major partners, especially the MCA. They met and dealt with new issues and despite hard bargaining were faithful to their original arrangements. A recent example of this cooperation occurred in the early months of 1967 and involved the emotionally charged language issue. The Constitution of 1957 proclaimed Malay as the national language, but permitted the official use of English for ten years, at which time Parliament would take further action. Elementary education was given in four languages and secondary education in English and Malay only, with Chinese and Tamil taught as elective subjects. Malays regarded the ten-year provision as a period of grace to permit non-Malays to learn the language fluently enough to use in official transactions. Since their language is at the heart of their identity structure, Malays attach great emotional and economic significance to this issue. They consider the language provision an essential part of the great compromise, expecting it to insure a Malay-style polity and give Malays a competitive advantage in employment and in government-related transactions. The majority of non-Malays "accepted" Malay as the national language, expecting that a symbolic acceptance or tokenism would satisfy Malay aspirations, but that English would continue to be used officially for a very long time.

Many Chinese were unhappy that Chinese had been denied the status of an official language, and their organizations and spokesmen have continually pressured the MCA on this subject, without avail. Meanwhile the more militant Malays insisted that the UMNO and the Alliance immediately vindicate their pledge that Malay become the sole official language. They were irked by the disinterest in the national language shown by many non-Malay government officials, politicians, lawyers, and educators and were convinced that the Chinese were failing to honor a solemn commitment and that the time for firm legal sanctions had come. They felt it necessary to attack the status of English as an official language because the enemies of the Malay language were using English for their purposes.

Though the Alliance's technique is to mute communally sensitive issues, this was not possible with the language problem in 1967. It was essential, however, that the Alliance leadership present a solid front to its diverse constituencies. They finally concluded that after September 1, 1967, Malay would become the sole official language, but that "liberal use" of English should be permitted in Parliament, the courts, government agencies, and in higher education where necessary to insure the orderly and efficient conduct of business. The MCA leadership reported that the "liberal use" provision was the minimum that would enable them to face their constituency, and even then they anticipated trouble from many who felt that the official-language measure was a brutal form of pressure against non-Malays to reduce their economic effectiveness and competitiveness and represented a form of Malay cultural imperialism. There were rumblings of protest in many MCA branches, and several of the more intransigent protesters were expelled.

But the disquiet of the non-Malays was reduced to insignificance by the Malay nationalists' violent protests, which mobilized broad sympathy in Malay society. A National Language Front was formed which assailed the UMNO leadership, including the Prime Minister, "Father of his country," who had hitherto been virtually immune to public criticism. He was condemned for betraying the Malay language and "selling out" to the Chinese. Rumblings were heard from UMNO branches all over the country, in which Malay-language schoolteachers with strong economic as well as emotional commitments to the language, are prominently represented. The government-sponsored Muslim college near Kuala Lumpur was closed when its students rioted. Protest meetings were held by Malay students in Cairo. Demonstrations broke out in the government-operated National Language and Culture Center which harbors an important group of militant Malay intellectuals, and they were joined by members of the Malay Language Society of the University of Malaya in sponsoring a march on the Prime Minister's residence, an unheard-of form of protest and defiance among Malays. Tensions were high among more militant Malays, and the UMNO leadership began to unleash its biggest guns in the Cabinet, the state governments, and even among the rulers (who are normally above politics) when the dramatic tensions slowly began to recede. The elites of both parties in the Alliance had made a quiet deal which represented the minimum their constituencies were likely to find acceptable. There was no further room for concession or maneuver. Both parties held firm against the demands of their extremists, even when these involved substantial rank-and-file support, and by holding firm they prevailed.

TWO-CURRENCIES RIOTS

In other instances the Alliance was less successful. It is a rule of Malaysian public life that any issue, however innocuous on the surface, may erupt in perverse communal form. Thus communal calculations must be in the forefront of every responsible politician's and administrator's concern. When in Novem-

34

ber 1967 the United Kingdom devalued the pound sterling without consulting Malaysia, most of whose ample foreign exchange reserves were held in sterling, this shock should not have had internal communal consequences. There was no economic crisis or prospect of one. After consulting the banking and financial authorities in Singapore and Brunei, which previously shared with Malaysia the Straits dollar, the Malaysian government decided not to devalue. Incredibly, however, they decided to devalue only the old Straits notes and coins which had not yet been turned in for new Malaysian currency, even though the holders of these notes had recently been assured that they need not hurry to convert.[12] Thus there would be two currencies in circulation, most of it not devalued. Bank deposits, would of course, not be affected. But a small portion of the currency mostly held in modest hoards by peasants and working people, lost 15 percent of its value for reasons that were incomprehensible to them and appeared to be an arbitarary betrayal of trust by the government.

The Communists moved quickly to capitalize on this political folly. In Penang the Labor Party proclaimed a hartal, a suspension of all economic activity, combining a general strike and a closing down of businesses. Labor Party activists, supported by secret society hoodlums who run elaborate protection rackets in all the important cities in Malaysia, induced numerous merchants and street vendors to close shop, some through intimidation, some in sympathy with the theme of the hartal. Soon gangs of Malay youths appeared to protect Malay vendors who refused to suspend business. Violence ensued. In a few hours Penang was an armed camp, polarized along communal lines, and soon the violence spread to large areas of the adjoining mainland of Northwest Malaya. Eighteen days of curfew and massive police and military intervention were required before the island and its neighboring areas were pacified. The government announced that 23 persons had been killed and 326

[12] The technical reason is that the old Straits notes and coins were officially tied to the pound sterling while the new Malaysian currency and bank deposits were not.

35

wounded, but many observers estimated much higher casualty figures. Among the Malays such organizations as an Army of the Holy War sprang up (their members received religious pardons), while the Labor Party and the secret societies bore the brunt of action for the Chinese (large numbers of whom were detained for extended periods by the police).

This is how a problem in monetary management unpredictably triggered vicious and bloody communal riots in a conflict-prone society. Characteristically, the Alliance government rejected requests by leading intellectuals and opposition politicians for a commission of inquiry into the causes of the riots on the grounds that the causes were well enough known (they were provoked by the Communists and communal extremists) and the more basic causes of communal strife were likely to be exacerbated rather than diminished by a public inquiry.

ACCOMMODATION AND THE ZERO-SUM GAME

Former Prime Minister Tunku Abdul Rahman embodied the politics of accommodation.[13] He believes that living the good life is not only a virtue in itself but that "wining, gambling, and womanizing," horseracing, sports, and beauty contests, however offensive to intellectuals, help to keep politics in their proper pragmatic perspective. His principal political objective has been the pursuit of a harmonious multiracial society. A Malay aristocrat, head of the UMNO since 1951, he established wide confidence among Chinese as a Malay who understands the problems of other communities. Yet every gesture toward the Chinese strained his Malay support, as the national language struggle illustrates, and many younger UMNO activists accused him of yielding too much to the Chinese. It is not certain that any other Malay politician can play this balancing and reconciling game so effectively. Indeed, the drive

---

[13] Since this passage was written, Tunku Abdul Rahman, after sixteen years as Prime Minister, stepped down on August 31, 1970, and was succeeded by his deputy, Tun Abdul Razak. There is no adequate political biography of this remarkable man, but for a sympathtic, popular treatment see Harry Miller, *Prince to Premier* (London: G. G. Harrap, 1959).

for development, mobilized behind the Tunku's successor, Tun Abdul Razak, has certain anti-Chinese overtones. Reducing the role of middlemen in the rural economy, expanding public enterprise in industry, increasing special educational opportunities for Malays, all intended to enhance the welfare and opportunity of Malays as economic underdogs, are perceived as threatening and unjust by many Chinese.

In some respects this seems to be a zero-sum game. If there are a hundred student openings in the medical faculty of the University of Malaya, if these facilities cannot be increased, and if the present system of selection based on competitive academic performance fills eight-five of the seats with non-Malays and leaves only fifteen for Malays who comprise nearly half the population, how can a political issue be avoided? Any quota system which would insure more seats for Malays, who find the present distribution intolerable, will be perceived by Chinese as denying them equal opportunity based on merit.[14] Chinese politicians, particularly the MCA leaders who have acquiesced in various forms of Malay privilege from taxi licenses to scholarships and the awarding of small construction contracts as an exercise in macro-politics, helping the have-nots to equalize the existing disparities between the races, have lost support among many Chinese, not on the principle that Malays deserve a better break but because every such privilege denies a competitive opportunity to a deserving Chinese. It is not the clash in value terms—equity versus ability—as much as the consequences, loss of fair opportunity to deserving Chinese as individuals, *not the macropolitics but the microconsequences* that have alienated so many Chinese from the MCA leadership and even from the political system itself. When young, English-educated Chinese refuse to stand in the cinemas as the national

[14] The communal consequences of various patterns of resource allocation are reviewed as an issue of policy in Chapter 8. In its white paper, *Toward National Harmony* (Kuala Lumpur: Government Printer, 1971), the government indiciated its intention to begin to fill student openings on a quota basis in the faculty of medicine and other faculties where the number of Malays is disproportionately small.

anthem is played, this is protest, alienation from a regime that seems to them to distribute benefits and costs unjustly. Yet these same measures appear to Malays to be minimal compensation to overcome intolerable and growing gaps in the economic and educational positions of the two races

These tensions are enhanced by changes in the value systems of younger members of both racial groups. If members of each racial group pursue different goals, and these goals are not incompatible, prospects for peaceful coexistence are good. This situation was observed by several scholars prior to national independence. For the most part Malays did not pursue material or acquisitive values and did not resent the wealth which the Chinese acquired. Their definition of a good life did not include material wealth.[15] Malays were interested in official status, in political power, and in the protection of their traditional institutions and practices, while the majority of the Chinese, regarding themselves as sojourners in Malaysia, were content to leave government and politics to others. During the colonial period, a tolerant administration protected most of the economic opportunities of the Chinese and the modest governmental and cultural aspirations of the Malays and discouraged the entry of each community into the preferred field of the other. This differentiation in values did not prevent all conflict, but it helped keep it in check.

Since Independence this compatible pattern of aspirations has broken down. Young Malays influenced by modern education, information media, and political pressures desire economic power, wealth, income, and entry into the modern economy, which brings them directly into conflict with non-Malays. They are frustrated by their inability to compete in these areas, which they attribute in part to a monopolistic conspiracy among non-Malays. Virtually every Malay believes the Chinese use naked economic power to suppress competition by aspiring Malay businessmen. Thus they turn to government to intervene to in-

[15] See, inter alia, Kennelm O. Burridge, "Report on Field Work in Batu Pahat, Johore," mimeo. (Kuala Lumpur: University of Malaya, February 1956).

crease their opportunities by subsidies, quotas, and public enterprise, and some advocate the elimination of Chinese from some economic activities by government monopoly or government-sponsored cooperatives. These activities are perceived by non-Malays as discriminatory and as deprivations of their rights and opportunities.

The young Chinese, born in Malaysia, unlike their fathers, are no longer satisfied to be politically inert. They reject the comfortable Malay image of the Chinese as interested exclusively in making money, therefore unconcerned with government and undisturbed by the implications of Malay privileges in government and politics. The appeal of the "Malaysian Malaysia" slogan to young, educated, middle-class Chinese is fundamentally a demand for equal treatment and equal status in government employment and political activity. It was so recognized and therefore rejected by Malays. Now the members of both communities increasingly aspire to similar goals and make competing demands on the political system. The original Alliance agreement that provided for a rough differentiation of roles is increasingly unacceptable to the younger generation of both races, yet the outlines of a revised distribution of roles which could be mutually acceptable has not emerged. Younger Malays, while demanding greater economic power, are not prepared to yield on Malay privileges or political hegemony; young Chinese who demand greater political and cultural opportunity and reduction of Malay privileges are unwilling to yield the economic position which they feel they and their fathers have achieved through fair competition. The potential for conflicts thus increases and the tasks of conflict management are magnified.

GROWTH ECONOMICS AND THE DISTRIBUTION PROBLEM

Management of such conflict is facilitated if the quantum of benefits or satisfactions available for distribution increase as fast or faster than the demands on the system. This applies as well to noneconomic as to economic goods. Growth economics offers the political system a continually expanding pie, which

39

permits it to break out of the zero-sum game. The need for a larger pie is one reason that the government of Malaysia has embarked on a planned development program and has taken a serious view both of the planning process and of substantive development programs. But even the rationality of growth-oriented activities is frequently constrained by communal considerations.

An illuminating example is land policy. The most efficient growth policy the government could follow would be to put the vast acreage of unused land owned by state governments into production, thus increasing the productivity both of the land and of unemployed and underemployed labor. West Malaysia alone has nine million acres of currently unused arable land, about the same acreage as is now in cultivation. Government is engaged in large and expensive land-development programs for resettling Malays, but does not have the financial or managerial resources to open up land at the required rate.[16] The private sector, meaning Chinese, have the money, management, and skills to develop unused land and would be willing to do so because the returns would be adequate, but the Malay-controlled state governments have been reluctant to alienate state land, which they consider the patrimony of the Malays, for long leases to Chinese capitalists. Economic growth per se does not excite them unless substantial benefits accrue to Malays. Chinese investors who have alternative uses for their capital rapidly

[16] The most effective land development program of the Alliance government is incorporated in the program of the Federal Land Development Authority (FLDA). For a good political analysis, see James F. Guyot, "Creeping Urbanism and Political Development in Malaysia," mimeo. (Bloomington, Indiana: Comparative Administration Group Occasional Paper, February 1968). For an economic analysis, see Robert Ho, "Land Settlement Projects in Malaya: An Assessment of the Role of the FLDA," *Journal of Tropical Geography*, 20 (June 1965) pp. 1–15. According to the First Malaysia Plan (pp. 117–118), by the end of the plan period, the FLDA will have settled 34,450 families. Professor Unku Aziz estimates that this is a small fraction of the Malay peasants who have become landless during this period, not to mention additions to the agricultural labor force.

lose interest if they are required to share a substantial portion of their profits, control, or employment with Malays. The Malay politicians put a higher value on control of resources and benefits to Malays than on over-all economic growth. Chinese have recently been awarded some tracts through private arrangements with royalty, officials, and politicians in some states and by agreement to settle a minimum number of Malays on their projects and provide them with various processing services, but land for estates is alienated only grudgingly and slowly to Chinese. This is one example of how measures to accelerate economic growth and incidentally make economic resources gradually available for distribution through fiscal measures for the benefit of Malays often founder on communal grounds, especially on issues of control and distribution.[17] Malays are no longer willing to subsist on the crumbs of economic growth while the Chinese increase the economic gap between the races by exploiting "their" natural resources.

DENOUEMENT: THE CRISIS OF MAY 1969

In May 1969, after governing Malaysia for more than fifteen years, the Alliance was badly damaged, perhaps beyond recovery. In the quinquennial Parliamentary elections on May 10, which they confidently expected to win, the Alliance's share of votes in West Malaysia fell from 58.5 percent in 1964 to 49.1 percent; of 104 seats they dropped from 89 to 67. Although still a Parliamentary majority, this was far less than the two-thirds that the Alliance had hoped for and which would be needed in order to amend the Constitution. The UMNO's vote fell from 66 percent to 56 percent in predominantly Malay constituencies

[17] The naive view that economic growth alone can deal with the problems of development was rudely shaken by the events of early 1969 in Pakistan. Despite high and sustained rates of over-all economic growth, the inequities in the distribution of benefits and control of resources by region and class and the notorious corruption in high places undermined the legitimacy of the regime and contributed to the downfall of the Ayub government. Men are moved by other values than over-all economic growth, including justice in the distribution of benefits, however meager.

41

while the populistic, anti-Chinese PMIP increased its vote proportionately. The MCA and the MIC votes in non-Malay constituencies fell from 49 percent in 1964 to an abysmal 39 percent, the winners being the moderate, nominally noncommunal, non-Malay parties which achieved an effective working alliance in this election. Two-thirds of the Alliance's losses were in non-Malay constituencies. The Alliance lost the states of Kelantan (which the PMIP retained) and Penang (which was won by the new Gerakan Party); in Perak the combined opposition gained a small majority of seats and in Selangor there was a dead heat.

The results appeared to reflect a protest in both communities against the establishment politicians for complacency and for not prosecuting vigorously enough the incompatible interests of their community. No one expected that any group other than the Alliance could or would govern for the next five years.

UMNO leaders were shocked at the outcome. They blamed the Chinese for abandoning the Alliance and attributed their loss of Malay votes to their moderate stance on racial issues. The MCA, repudiated by its constituents, declined to participate in the new Cabinet, although it would vote with the UMNO in Parliament. To many Malays the results portended a dangerous threat to their political hegemony, and their apprehensions were not diminished by the boisterous public celebrations of the opposition parties, with ugly racial overtones, especially in Kuala Lumpur. Through a series of complex events,[18] serious communal rioting broke out in Kuala Lumpur on the night of May 13, 1969, which the police were unable to quell. Arson, rioting, and murder continued for two weeks. Official figures list 196 dead, including 169 non-Malays, and 439 injured. These figures seem conservative to many on-the-spot observers. More than nine thousand were arrested and countless thousands lost their homes. Some observers reported

[18] For an account which reflects a Malay viewpoint, see Tunku Abdul Rahman, *May 13 Before and After* (Kuala Lumpur: Utusan Melayu Press, September 1969). An opposite view is expressed by John Slimming, *Malaysia, Death of a Democracy* (London: John Murray, 1969).

that the Malay Regiment, which was called in to maintain order after the police had been unable to control the riots, interfered flagrantly on the side of the Malays. The effects of this crisis were to erode intergroup trust to the vanishing point and to heighten communal hostilities among all strata of Malaysians, including the forces of public order. Most seriously perhaps, it undermined confidence among Chinese in the impartiality of government and its ability or willingness to protect their lives and property. These suspicions seemed to be confirmed by the fact that Malaysia had become in effect a one-race government.

The government suspended Parliament and postponed elections in Sabah and Sarawak, which had been scheduled for later in the month. Although the Prime Minister and Cabinet retained their formal status, effective power was transferred to a nine-man National Operations Council (NOC), chaired by Tun Razak and composed of senior Alliance politicians, civil servants, and military officers. The heads of the MCA and the MIC were the only non-Malay members. In each state, an Operations Council was organized consisting of the chief minister, the local police director, and military commander. A similar pattern was established in each district with the district-officer in charge. Competitive politics were set aside and the NOC declared that "there can be no question of a return to Parliamentary democracy so long as racial harmony does not exist among the communities. So long as communal sensitivities are tender they can, through irresponsible political propaganda be easily exploited to precipitate another, indeed more serious racial clash." [19] The government's information output was not entirely consistent. The Prime Minister—deeply shaken by this setback to his lifetime effort to create a harmonious multiracial society—blamed the outbreaks entirely on secret society members, Communists, and racialists, all Chinese. The NOC was more balanced in its appraisal, acknowledging that some responsibility rested with Malay hoodlums.

[19] National Operations Council, *The May 13 Tragedy* (Kuala Lumpur: Government Printer, 9 October 1969), p. 77.

43

Although it has ruled by decree, the NOC's policies have been moderate. It has rebuffed the efforts of militants in the UMNO, including some of its most prominent younger politicians and their student supporters, to unseat the Prime Minister and to move more vigorously against the economic power of the Chinese. Aside from a flurry of threats to the citizenship status of many non-Malays and the cancellation of work permits of noncitizens, there have been no direct threats to the security or economic interests of non-Malays, and the government has attempted to reassure the Chinese. While emphasizing the importance of drastically reducing racial economic disparities, the government has also announced as its objective the elimination of poverty among all races. It has moved vigorously to increase employment opportunities, especially for young Malays in urban areas who are considered a serious source of disaffection. Other distributional measures are contemplated, even at the cost of economic growth. New efforts to expand credit for Malay farmers and to establish public industrial enterprises with Malay management and staff, especially in rural areas, are in prospect.

The government intends to "entrench" certain provisions of the Constitution and remove them from future political debate. These relate to the prerogatives of the Malay rulers, the official status of the Malay language, the responsibility of the King to safeguard the special position of the Malays and their privileges in land, civil service, scholarships, and licenses, and the right of the Council of Malay Rulers to veto any constitutional provision which would impair any Malay rights:

The entrenched provisions in the Constitution are the result of agreement between all the communities in this country. They are the product of consultation and compromise. They represent binding agreements between the various races in this country and are the underpinnings on which the constitutional structure, such as fundamental liberties, the machinery of government and a score of other detailed provisions are built. If these entrenched provisions are in any way eroded or weakened, the entire constitutional structure is endangered and with it the existence of the

44

nation itself. It was the failure to understand and the irresponsible and cavalier treatment of these entrenched provisions that constituted one of the primary causes of the disturbances on May 13, 1969.[20]

The Malay leadership intends that these provisions become nonnegotiable and out of bounds in future political debate. They appear to believe that when discussion of these issues, in public or even in Parliament, is proscribed the most important provocation for communal conflict will be eliminated.

Departing from its earlier practice of avoiding public discussions on communal issues, the government set up a new agency, a Department of National Unity, to devise public policies and programs for improving intercommunal relations. It also activated a National Consultative Council made up of sixty-six representatives of political, legal, economic, and other organizations to search for improved patterns of intercommunal accommodation. At the time of writing these institutions have just begun to function.

It is difficult to conceive of a stable and legitimate political structure in Malaysia which is not a functional substitute for the impaired Alliance. Multicommunal political groupings based on ideological or class alignments, which many observers have frequently proposed, are an unlikely prospect for years to come. A one-race government cannot establish and maintain legitimacy. The problem for the UMNO leadership is to find associates who are more representative of the Chinese than the MCA and will accept the entrenched provisions outlined above. The problem for the moderate Chinese parties is to find terms of cooperation which are acceptable to both the UMNO and their constituencies. It will not be easy to reconcile the *bumiputera* doctrine, sacred to the Malays, and "a Malaysian Malaysia," which is the aspiration of the younger generation of non-Malays. To compound the difficulty, the emergent and more articulate generation of younger politicians, both Malay and non-Malay, are less inclined to compromise on these basic issues than were

[20] *Ibid.,* p. 85.

their elders who founded the Alliance and are now passing from the scene.[21]

Dual Socioeconomy

Income levels and living standards in Malaya are high in comparison with most preindustrial countries. Per-capita income was $323 U.S. in 1967, the highest in Asia except for Japan, Singapore, and Hong Kong. The growth trend averaging above 5 percent per year from 1960 to 1967 has been satisfactory, though more than half has been dissipated by a net annual population increase exceeding 3 percent (see Table 2).

Unemployment has been increasing in the cities and in the rural areas. The Minister of Finance in his 1969 budget speech put the over-all unemployment figure at 6.8 percent of the labor force, about 20 percent in the 15- to 24-year age group, and 11.2 percent in the major urban areas. The figure is likely to increase in the next few years as the British withdraw their military bases and as land development and new manufacturing struggle to keep pace with the growing labor force. The secondary school system will soon produce three times more general graduates—equipped only to be clerks and contemptuous of

[21] Faithful to his commitment, Tun Razak convened Parliament on February 20, 1971. The results of elections in Sarawak, including the alignment of the Chinese-based Sarawak United Peoples Party (SUPP) with the Alliance assured the latter the two-thirds majority required to amend the Federal Constitution. The first act of the new Parliament was to amend the Constitution to "entrench" the provisions involving citizenship, Malay privileges, national language, and the prerogatives of the Rulers and to proscribe public or even Parliamentary discussion of these issues. The National Operations Council retired to the background to scrutinize security issues. The government is controlled by UMNO in which the relative position of its communally more militant wing has been strengthened by the retirement of former Prime Minister Tunku Abdul Rahman. It is likely that any overt expression of the Malaysian Malaysia theme may in the future be construed as subversive. The MCA and MIC are participating in the government. A serious effort has been undertaken to expand the base of the MCA so that the Chinese wing of the Alliance may be more representative of its constituency.

46

Table 2. Gross national product and population

Item	1960	1961	1962	1963	1964	1965	1966	1967 *
Gross National Product (GNP) ($)	6,648	6,681	7,047	7,512	7,959	8,775	9,345	9,714
Midyear population ('000)	8,108	8,368	8,644	8,915	9,155	9,421	9,725	10,017
Per-capita GNP ($)	819	798	816	843	867	933	960	969
GNP annual growth rate	–	0.5	5.5	6.6	5.9	10.2	6.5	3.9
Per-capita annual growth rate	–	(−2.5)	2.2	3.3	2.8	7.6	3.4	0.9

Source: Government of Malaysia, Department of Statistics, Kuala Lumpur.

* All financial figures in thousands of Malaysian dollars at current prices (M$3 = US$1).

manual occupations—than the society will be able to absorb. Thus unemployment, in addition to great economic waste, may become a deeply destabilizing political problem, both in rural and urban areas. While underemployment, much of it ill-disguised, and other forms of low-productivity employment characterize a large proportion of both the rural and urban labor force, there is no visible evidence of the desperate, grinding poverty, disease, and malnutrition found in India, Java, Egypt, China, and other preindustrial societies where dense population presses on land resources.

The per-capita income figures conceal vast differences in income distribution. While there are no authoritative figures, they can be inferred from observation, income tax records, and other sources. The best available estimates indicate that rural incomes per capita are less than half of urban incomes, one obvious indicator of the well-known phenomenon of socioeconomic dualism in transitional societies. It is likely that income distribution both within and among the communities has become less equitable as the economy has grown.

T. H. Silcock estimates that average per-capita Chinese income is about two and a half times that of the average Malay, more than 80 percent of whom are rural dwellers.[22] There is other statistical evidence. In 1966 the crude death rate among Malays was 8.6 per 1,000 compared to a Chinese rate of 6.4. Infant mortality was 61 per 1,000 live births for Malays, 32 for Chinese. Toddler mortality was 7.9 per 1,000 among Malays, 3.2 among Chinese. It is widely recognized that rural schools are inferior to urban schools because of the quality of teachers and the support of parents and that Malay medium schools are inferior to English medium schools. Ambitious parents of all races try to enroll their children in English medium schools, which are usually located in urban areas. This is a cruel dilemma for Malays, torn between supporting the national language and providing their children with the most useful education. This is why Malay nationalists insist that the English-language schools must be eliminated if the national language policy is ever to succeed.

The modern urban economy, including plantation agriculture and tin mining, is dynamic and growing; it employs modern, sophisticated technologies, and its large, complex organization realizes the benefits of scale, specialization, and cooperation. The rural economy is essentially impoverished and stagnant, using primitive technologies and highly fragmented organizations. The two sectors are poorly integrated since they share relatively few transactions. The backward rural sector receives little service from the modern commercial sector, but government roads, schools, health clinics, and information media are beginning to provide the infrastructure for greater future integration.

[22] T. H. Silcock, "Approximate Racial Division of National Income," in T. H. Silcock and E. K. Fisk, *The Political Economy of Independent Malaya* (Canberra: Australian National University Press, 1963), pp. 276–281.

The urban economy is non-Malay. The rural economy is dominantly Malay, though 50 percent of Chinese live outside large cities. The urban areas contain a large proletariat, mostly Chinese, reinforced by a growing stream of Malay migrants who find their way into unskilled, low-paid occupations or unemployment. Members of the Chinese proletariat are not rich, and contrary to a widespread Malay myth, very few of them have rich relatives from whom they can ask and receive support. Many of them earn the equivalent of $30.00 U.S. a month when they are working. They are poor and often embittered, and from their ranks the secret society criminals and the Communists recruit their members.

Aside from the white foreigners, who continue to occupy upper-income and upper-status roles, and the small group of Malay civil servants, politicians, and professional men, the upper and middle classes are filled predominantly by Chinese. Their numbers are growing and so is their wealth, status, and competence. To witness this phenomenon, one need only observe the members of the Royal Selangor Golf Club, drive through the new housing developments around Kuala Lumpur, look at the shops in any Malaysian city or town, examine the ethnic composition of the faculty and students of the University of Malaya, or visit the offices of any large modern enterprise, whether European or Chinese-owned. If, on the other hand, one travels through the rural areas anywhere in Malaysia and observes the standard of living and styles of life, the contrast is overwhelming. Bicycles, motor scooters, and transistor radios indicate that some rural folk now live above the subsistence level, but very few, mainly small landlords, schoolteachers, and government clerks, have moved into the middle class. Malay peasants are deeply in debt, and their expenditure patterns, low productivity, and the exactions of middlemen keep them in debt. Tenancy is widespread; a survey in the Muda Valley rice bowl of Kedah indicated that 55 percent of the land was held in tenancy to Malay landlords, many of whom are active in the UMNO. Many peasants lose their land annually through frag-

49

mentation in the Islamic tradition and through foreclosures. Few alternative economic opportunities have developed in the rural areas. There is little evidence that per-capita consumption levels have increased since Independence. On the other hand, improved educational and health facilities, roads, and piped water resulting from public expenditures have contributed to increased opportunity and public consumption for rural Malays.

These marked differences in control of wealth and the availability and use of income are symptoms of deep-seated differences. The children of overseas Chinese are socialized into a culture that puts a high premium on economic and other achievement values, on competitive styles, on calculating and manipulative skills. The world is hard and does not owe a man a living. He is taught that he must work, compete, achieve, or fail, and the gods help only those who help themselves. Pleasures are available, but they are secondary to work. These values apply as much to the worker and the clerk as to the boss. This is a functional equivalent of the familiar Protestant ethic with a vengeance. The overseas Chinese are tough competitors.

The rural Malay child is socialized into a culture that accents other values. The fulfillment of religious and family obligations and rituals takes precedence over work and the prudent use of money. The fear of shame drives many peasants to borrow heavily to finance religiously and socially sanctioned festivals celebrating birth, circumcision, marriage, and death. The present is more real than the future, so it is better to consume than to save. The enjoyment of leisure and dignified friendship is more important than wealth and the disciplined work, study, and conflict necessary to achieve it. Interpersonal sensitivity is highly cultivated; calculating, organizing, and manipulative skills are not.[23]

The rural Malay pattern of life is not a prescription for successful participation in a modern, technological, competitive

[23] For one study of rural Malay behavior on the East Coast see Hock Tjoa Soei, *Institutional Background to Modern Economic and Social Development in Malaya* (Kuala Lumpur: Liu and Liu, 1963).

society.[24] Unless Malays can break out of this pattern, they develop a trained incapacity to function effectively in modern roles, especially in competition with Chinese. Their growing awareness of backwardness, however, is contributing to greater frustration among Malay youth. Exacerbated by unemployment, this frustration may be expressed in deeply destabilizing rage as they revolt against the symptoms of backwardness, but lack the technological equipment, the social discipline, or the institutional opportunities to compete in modern roles.

Through regular educational programs and special enterprises like the MARA Institute of Technology—which provides residential training for five thousand young Malays—the government is attempting to help these youths function competitively in a modern economy. A number of talented Malays have broken away from the traditional culture pattern and are participating in modern roles, primarily in government and government-related activities. Their children, in turn, will be socialized into a modern set of values and skills, but these measures to date have not reduced the economic or educational gaps separating the communities. Indeed the gaps are widening in favor of the Chinese.

Like most developing countries, Malaysia has been attempting to shift its economic structure away from the colonial pattern of dependence on a few primary products. Most of the essential features of a colonial economy still prevail, however. Virtually no manufactured goods are exported. Four primary products, rubber, tin, oil palm, and timber contributed about 70 percent of export earnings in 1967, and about half of the gross domestic product is exported (see Table 3). Pressure to diversify has been less pronounced than in other countries because the traditional products, rubber and tin, have remained

[24] In his controversial book, *The Malay Dilemma* (Singapore: Asia Pacific Press, 1970), Dr. Mahatir bin Mohamad argues that Malay privileges must be expanded and extended for an indefinite period because Malays, due to their ethos, value system, and biological handicaps resulting from excessive inbreeding, are unable to compete economically with Chinese.

profitable over long periods of time. As the world's largest and most efficient producer of natural rubber (50 percent of the total) Malaysia has felt the pressure of competition from synthetics, but the efficient Rubber Research Institute has developed improved genetic technologies which have reduced costs,

Table 3. West Malaysia: Gross domestic product by sector of origin, 1961–1967

	1961	1965	Average annual rate of growth 1961–1965	1966	1967	Average annual rate of growth 1965–1967
Agriculture forestry and fishing	1,706	1,943	3.3	2,066	2,155	5.3
Rubber planting	909	1,012	2.7	1,070	1,109	4.7
Other agriculture	528	530	0.0	557	561	2.9
Livestock	87	172	18.6	176	180	2.3
Forestry	73	93	6.2	106	117	12.2
Fishing	109	136	5.7	157	188	17.6
Mining and quarrying	477	532	2.8	547	562	2.8
Manufacturing	444	702	12.1	790	860	10.7
Construction	206	318	11.5	330	340	3.4
Electricity, water and sanitary services	82	129	12.0	144	160	11.4
Transport, storage, and communications	201	247	5.3	255	268	4.2
Wholesale and retail trade	902	1,052	3.9	1,082	1,120	3.2
Banking, insurance, and real estate	69	108	11.9	118	129	9.3
Ownership of dwellings	255	295	3.7	297	310	2.5
Public administration and defense	351	462	7.1	484	505	4.5
Services	685	912	7.4	962	1,010	5.2
Gross domestic product at factor cost	5,378	6,700	5.6	7,075	7,419	5.2

Source: Mid-Term Review of the First Malaysia Plan, 1966–1970, Table 1–7, p. 14.

All figures in millions of Malaysian dollars at constant 1964 prices.

improved quality, and thus kept natural rubber competitive in an expanding world market. The benefits of the new production and marketing techniques have accrued mostly to the foreign and Chinese-owned estates which have been able to assimilate them and handle subsidized replanting programs. The small holders, especially the Malays, who produce 50 percent of the rubber, have benefited less and suffer acutely when the rubber price declines as it did dramatically in 1967 and 1968.[25] Rubber acreage is not being expanded, and large tracts are being re-planted to oil palm, a vegetable oil with an apparently expanding world market. Logs and timber have recently joined the list of major exports, now growing at the amazing rate of 17 percent a year, most of it shipped unprocessed from Sabah to Japan, which benefits from the value added at every subsequent pro-cessing stage. With the vigorous demand for tin, Malaysia has retained its share of the world market and now contemplates off-shore mining as the older deposits on the West Coast of Malaya are gradually depleted. With luck, Malaysia may bring in oil on its impoverished East Coast; drilling operations are already under way.

As a percentage of gross domestic product, manufacturing grew very slowly to 11 percent in 1966 from a very low base at the time of Independence. It is heavily concentrated in the highly urbanized Kuala Lumpur and Penang-Butterworth areas with smaller outcroppings in Ipoh and Johore Baru. The own-ership and management are foreign or Chinese, and the labor force is Chinese. Few Malays participate in or benefit directly from these industries. Most is import-substituting and survives by quotas and tariff protection averaging a moderate 25 per-cent ad valorem, but gradually increasing. In industry, as in the other sectors, diversification objectives are hampered by very limited governmental research, information, developmental, and other services and by acute shortages of esssential technical, economic, and managerial skills. Except for the oil sheikdoms,

---

[25] According to the First Malaysia Plan (p. 99) an estimated 80 percent of estate acreage but only 50 percent of small-holder acreage were in high-yielding rubber in 1965.

few countries have reached Malaysia's per-capital income level with so limited a stock of trained professional and technical manpower. There is no policy on industrial priorities and tariffs, with the result that indiscriminate low-volume, high-cost, import-substituting industries stimulated by tax subsidies and import quotas are developing instead of competitive, specialized lines with export possibilities.

There are no significant agricultural research facilities outside rubber, though a new Agricultural Research and Development Institute was started in 1969. Nor are existing government agencies equipped to communicate research results to the farmers and to help influence and modernize their economic behavior. Increased productivity and diversification among Malay farmers are limited by lack of tested practices suitable to Malaysia, by the weakness of present delivery systems for new technologies, by the conservatism and the traditional value systems of the peasants, by landlordism and inadequate credit and marketing facilities which decrease peasant initiative and which Malays tend to blame on Chinese middlemen. From 1961–1965, while the economy enjoyed an annual over-all growth rate of 5.6, no growth was registered in peasant agriculture ("other agriculture" in Table 3) where most Malay farmers are employed. The growth rate in this sector from 1965–1967 was probably less than the population increase. These figures underline the stagnation of Malay rural life and indicate that the peasants are not sharing equitably—if indeed they are sharing at all—in Malaysia's economic growth.

Aside from the maintenance of peaceful communal coexistence, the Alliance government is committed to two main and often conflicting objectives: development, an important ingredient of which is economic growth, and equalizing the opportunities and rewards among the races, helping the have-not Malays. However, none of the traditional institutions of Malay society are to be impaired in this process. The authority, privileges, and status of the traditional rulers, who are far from exemplars of modern achieving man, are to be fully respected. The conservative and ritualistic form of Islam in Malaysia is to be protected and encouraged. The economic role and stake of the Chinese will not be abridged, nor indeed will the rights of Malay landlords. The established administration will not be harassed or controlled by participatory institutions. The Malay, particularly the peasant, is to be made more efficient and more productive *within* the existing social system. The "silent revolution" which the Alliance government proclaims will be orderly and controlled from above. There will be no social revolution and no change in the power structure. Nothing will be taken from him who now has. With government help, the poor Malays must earn more for themselves within the present system. Since little is available for redistribution, the size of the economic pie must grow so that rank-and-file Malays may have a larger share of the increments, but more growth must come from their own efforts and the mastering of modern technologies since no way has been found to capture for them a larger portion of the Chinese-induced growth which would prevent the existing economic gap from growing. The Minister of Finance has declared repeatedly that the current tax burden which claims 18 percent of the gross national product is "optimal" and should not be increased.

If economic growth and efficient resource use were the only goals, Chinese through free competition would successfully dominate virtually all the resources and opportunities at the disposal of Malaysian society. Under present conditions they can use resources more efficiently, not as a community but as individuals and firms. They would also claim an even greater proportion of university places and civil service positions, but this would be intolerable to the Malays who feel they never had a fair chance. And the Malays control government. If a choice must be made, Malays to a man are more interested in reducing through institutional changes the present socioeconomic dualism, which so closely matches communal lines, than in overall economic growth, though they would like to reconcile these two desirable goals. Their bias in individual decisions is increasingly running in the direction of preferring communal equity to growth because not enough Chinese-managed growth

55

can be captured through taxes to finance equalization measures and prevent further widening of the communal gap. Chapter 8 deals more fully with the management of this critical problem.

Openness and Permeability of the System

Malaysian society is so open to external influences and maintains such an active network of external transactions, information flows, and personal contacts that they constitute an important total influence in its public affairs. Malaysia is the polar opposite of a hermit kingdom, in fact and in aspiration. Notwithstanding the passing of political colonialism, Malaysia's elites have not turned their backs on foreign contacts nor expressed any desire to be self-contained. This openness to external influences is both a predisposition of the elites and a response to the hard facts of geography, economic structure, and ethnic pluralism.

There are many dimensions to this openness; the first relates to security. With its long coastline and narrow heartland, Malaysia is not an easy country to defend, and its eastern half is separated by hundreds of miles of air and water from the west. There is still a dangerous Communist insurrection in Sarawak involving an estimated two thousand hard-core alienated Chinese, with an undetermined number of sympathizers. A decade after the official ending of the costly twelve-year insurrection on the peninsula, harassing bands of Communists are still active on the northern border with Thailand. Malaysia is a small but rich country in a world of poor and ambitious giants—Indonesia, China, and India. Smaller, more equal powers, like the Philippines and even Singapore, present other forms of uncertainty, which require prudent security measures. Malaysia's leaders feel that the country is unable to meet its defense needs without assistance. In the past they have relied heavily on the British, and to a lesser extent other Commonwealth partners, particularly Australia and New Zealand. British protection was seen implicitly as a *quid pro quo* for Malaysia's tolerance of a substantial British investment and trade position in that country and for the investment of Malaysia's substantial reserves in the sterling area.

The Malaysian elites of all races trust and admire the British. All their models are British. They remember how the British protected them from guerrilla Communism during the protracted insurrection and defended them at the time of confrontation with Indonesia. The British presence seemed to be a reassurance that independent Singapore would not make her facilities available to unfriendly Chinese power. The Commonwealth defense presence was perceived as a stabilizing influence, reducing Malaysia's need to contribute financially to its own defense, while helping to develop the organizational and fighting capabilities of its inexperienced armed forces. The substantial reduction in British military commitments confronts the Malaysians and the Singaporeans with a much more dangerous world which cannot be averted by turning in on themselves. They are actively cultivating regional cooperation with their neighbors. They are relieved that Australia and New Zealand have pledged to maintain forces in the area. Malaysia has agreed, in principle but warily, to common security planning with Singapore. Though they desire a continuing United States presence in Southeast Asia, they hope to normalize relations with the People's Republic of China. And they are distressed that their defense bill now consumes 25 percent of their budget and may even rise in the next few years.

The second dimension of openness inheres in Malaysia's economic structure. With its population of less than ten million, Malaysia has a relatively small and territorially fragmented internal market, too small to achieve economies of scale for a widely diversified line of manufactured products. Therefore, she must continue to specialize in order to compete in world markets, even though this leaves considerable room for agricultural and industrial diversification. Indeed she has specialized successfully, but in primary products only, and exports about half of what she produces. She is thus involved in an active network of international commercial and financial transactions. Her modern sector is outward-oriented, and her consumers are accus-

57

tomed to and prefer products from the established industrialized countries. This openness is abetted by a virtually free foreign exchange regime due to a comfortable reserve position—eight months of imports in 1968—and a desire to maintain the confidence of existing foreign investors and to attract new investment and foreign aid.

One element of instability in the open economic structure is the large and very conspicuous residue of European ownership and control in the modern economy. Europeans still live very well in Malaysia, and they are highly visible. While there has been some new investment from Japanese, American, and other European firms, the British investment which dominates the plantations, tin mines, large commercial houses, and some modern industry has been stagnant, financed primarily from reinvested earnings, and there is evidence of gradual disinvestment. An estimated 15 to 20 percent of foreign exchange earnings are devoted to profit and salary remittances, capital repatriation, and luxury and semiluxury imports for the benefit of resident foreigners (who enjoy much higher living standards, under less competitive conditions, than would be possible in England). The large foreign enclave in Malaysian society has thus far been protected because the government elites respect private enterprise and hope to attract more private investment. The Malay leaders also recognize that there are not yet enough qualified Malays to operate modern enterprises, and they prefer the continuation of foreign ownership and control to the expansion of Chinese power. Chinese capitalists, who feel quite competent to run any kind of modern enterprise, calculate that the presence of high-status foreign businessmen maintains a favorable climate for enterprise. This protects all businessmen against tendencies to encroach on the private sector or to expand the area of public enterprise. Thus both parties favor and assure a continuation of the *status quo* for foreign enterprise as the most feasible short-run alternative.

The government has been pursuing a policy of Malaysianization of managerial and where possible professional and technical personnel. The process has been completed in government and government enterprises, and current focus is on the private sector. The target is to achieve Malaysianization gradually so that by 1985 only a few top technical and managerial posts will be held by foreigners. Schedules have been fixed by negotiation for existing firms and are required for new firms prior to receiving "pioneer" licenses, which entail valuable tax concessions. Malaysianization, however, is not satisfactory unless ethnic Malays, not merely Chinese and Indians, are taken into such posts, for Malays are not prepared to see Chinese become the sole heirs and beneficiaries of western enterprise in their country. The present acute shortage of qualified Malays at the technical, professional, and managerial levels is the most significant factor which has induced the government to stretch out the period of Malaysianization and incidentally retain an important element of openness in the society.

Information flows into Malaya are quite free, and only those identified with Chinese Communism or with Israel are restricted.[26] There is a liberal inflow of foreign publications. The mass media, particularly the cinema and television, are dominated by the output of the United States and the United Kingdom. The society's propensity to absorb foreign information is enhanced by the widespread use of foreign languages, particularly English. Thus the growing middle class who own TV sets, and indeed all who are tuned into modern communications media through transistor radios, which are widely diffused even in the rural areas, are influenced by the latest foreign idioms, tastes in clothing, music, sports, consumer goods, gadgets, and news events. Until the disturbances of 1969 there was an enviable climate for foreign scholars and researchers.

External communication is sustained also by personal movements which, despite tight immigration controls, are highly permissive. In 1968 an estimated 2,500 students from West

---

[26] Chinese Communism is regarded as politically subversive; the Malays as Muslims have a strong emotional sympathy with the Arabs while most Chinese admire the more modern style of the Israelis.

Malaysia were enrolled in higher-education institutions in the United Kingdom, 6,000 in Australia, 3,000 in Taiwan, and more than 1,000 in other countries, nearly three times the number enrolled in Malaysia itself. Though there is a small brain drain, mostly of highly educated Chinese to Australia and Canada, most students return to Malaysia. Their models of foreign living and their overseas contacts continue. There are deep and active religious contacts among Malays, with 6,000 annual pilgrimage trips to Mecca and more than 300 studying Islam, primarily at El Azhar University in Cairo. Family contacts in the form of letters, remittances of funds, and personal visits to ethnic sources —Tamils to India, Chinese to Taiwan and Hong Kong (and beyond), Malays to Indonesia—keep the mails, the banks, the consulates, and the transport companies busy all year round. In addition, traffic between Malaysia and Singapore is active, and nearly 30,000 workers cross the causeway each day, an equal number moving in each direction for employment and other normal economic activities.

This openness appears to be a fixed element in the Malaysian system, a reflection of its economic structure, ethnic composition, and geographic realities, as well as the habits of its people and the preferences of its leadership. The rural Malays and the indigenous peoples of Sabah and Sarawak have the least stake in the open society; they are parochial in scope, but not hostile to foreign informational and economic influences. The current pattern is not likely to change radically unless political victory should come to the Malay extremists, whose xenophobia extends to all people, except perhaps Arabs and Indonesians, and who might be prepared to pay a very high price in economic welfare and intellectual development for the strident assertion of Malay identity. If the Chinese Comunists should prevail in Southeast Asia, informational, personal, and economic movements would be rigidly controlled by the state and party apparatus.

An open and permeable society insures invaluable inflows of technological, market, financial, cultural, and political information, which helps to avoid parochialism and extremism and maintain a proper perspective of Malaysia's real size and importance in the world. It increases the capacity of its people and institutions to empathize, learn, and adapt. These are very considerable advantages which wise national policy would seek to maintain. But is it consistent with the long-term national objective of integration? Does the openness of Malaysian society produce a cacophony, too many clashing styles, symbols, and loyalties, too many tugs of psychological and political influence in too many directions? Does its permeability do more to retard the development of a national identity than to divert attention from communal tensions? Can a polity survive under such centrifugal pressures, and can a coherent pattern emerge from so much looking outward and from so many external stimuli operating on so fragmented and loose-knit a society? The uncertainty is plausible enough that many even of the more moderate Malays favor reducing the foreign, especially English, content in the mass media so that more materials incorporating indigenous content, idioms, and styles can be introduced. A national news agency was established in 1968, among whose objectives is the introduction of more local news and feature material.

How is this society to find a distinctive identity? The Prime Minister condemns the Tamil-language press for devoting ten pages to mourning the death of the Chief Minister of Madras, the hero of Tamil nationalism. He rebukes Chinese theater audiences for cheering a sequence showing Mao Tse-tung and Malays for their fascination with events in Indonesia. The pressures for a more closed society come primarily from Malay nationalists with potential support from rural Malays, a group which is likely to become politically more articulate. The other ethnic groups and the current elites have a stake in and a preference for the maintenance of the present open situation. Yet some introversion, some greater concern with Malaysian identity, styles, symbols, and problems will inevitably enter into their nation-building strategy, at some cost to the prevailing openness.

An Administrative State [27]

The administrative state as an ideal type is one in which the state is the dominant institution in society, guiding and controlling more than it responds to societal pressures, and administrative (bureaucratic) institutions, personnel, values, and styles are more important than political and participative organs in determining the behavior of the state and thus the course of public affairs. According to these criteria Malaysia qualifies as an administrative state.

Interest groups function in Malaysia, and are not instruments of government or "transmission belts." Among the Tamils trade-unions are the most important associational groups. The Chinese have an elaborate network of chambers of commerce, guilds, and linguistic-regional associations.[28] Among the Malays, however, there are virtually no organized interest groups except government-sponsored cooperatives, which have failed more often than they have succeeded. A few cross-communal professional societies and welfare organizations exist, but they engage only very small urban elites. Most of the prestigious welfare organizations, nationally and locally, such as Boy Scouts, Red Cross, and the Cancer Society are headed by senior administrators. Many interest-type organizations, including the Muslim religion (but not the other religious denominations), are formally incorporated into the bureaucracy through the state departments of religious affairs, and the same may happen to the farmers' associations now being organized by the Department of Agriculture.

[27] The origin of this term is Dwight Waldo's classic, *The Administrative State* (New York: Ronald Press, 1948). It was also used by Fritz Morstein Marx, *The Administrative State* (Chicago: University of Chicago Press, 1957). The definition is mine.

[28] These represent the Chinese "establishment," paternalistically controlled and associated with the MCA. They are targets of opposition among younger, middle-class Chinese, who, however, have not developed effective organizations of their own.

Membership and participation in organized associational groups is highest among the Chinese and lowest among the Malays, even if the UMNO is regarded as having some of the properties of an associational group. Except for the unions, whose style is predictably disputatious, interest groups find it more effective to petition government than to demand or threaten. Government maintains effective autonomy in relation to these groups. Most of the pressures they exert are particularistic—for jobs, licenses, land titles, contracts, scholarships—benefiting an individual or firm, rather than a group or policy. And while the society is becoming politicized, mobilizing to make demands on government, the balance of pressures originating in government and beamed to the society is still greater than pressures flowing in the opposite direction. This situation could change as the urban Chinese and especially the rural Malays become more politicized and multiply their claims through communal channels, claims which the government may not have the available resources to satisfy and which may be mutually incompatible. Common fears of the consequences are likely to insure the continuation of an administrative state in Malaysia.

Political organizations perform representational, conflict management, interest communication, and especially solidarity functions for members of the various communities, but except for occasional heated issues like national language, communication between national and state legislators selected by national party leaders and their constituents is thin and infrequent. It usually involves the enlistment of politicians for particularistic purposes rather than demands on government for group interest, community service, or policy measures. The channels of petition lead either to a senior administrator or to a senior politician—a state chief minister or a federal cabinet minister. The latter control the political parties through a process of highly centralized decision making which has been occasionally challenged but never seriously threatened. Many senior Malay politicians are former administrators turned politician, who maintain administrative attitudes and styles of work and who associate and communicate closely with serving administrators. Political organizations and personalities provide channels for communicating demands and for pressuring the administration, but the diffidence and limited sense of efficacy among the masses, the tight centralization of political control, the prevailing consensus that the job of government is to govern more than to respond, and the administrative backgrounds and styles of senior politicians, especially among the Malays who control government, all reinforce the power of government and its administrators.

Not much is done by or expected of participative organs. Through centralized party control and strict party discipline, reinforced by respect and deference for authority, Parliament has been weak and manipulated by the senior political leadership. An intricate pattern of local government units, installed after World War II as direct copies of the British model, have failed to work. They have evoked little citizen interest and have been seriously mismanaged and victimized by corruption. To compound these problems, most municipalities and larger towns have fallen into the hands of opposition parties. Several municipal and town councils controlled by non-Malay opposition parties have been superseded by state governments, Malay- and Alliance-controlled, and governed administratively. All local elections were suspended in 1965 and a Royal Commission is preparing recommendations which are expected to increase administrative control over local government. Boards of education, hastily installed in all schools in 1956 have, except in a few upper-income schools and those traditionally operated by Chinese organizations, failed to function. A Royal Commission on Teachers has recommended that the boards be transformed into parent-teachers' associations and control of the schools revert to the Ministry of Education. As previously mentioned, cooperatives, despite government sponsorship and subsidy, have sustained many more failures than successes because of poor management, disinterest among members, inability to enforce repayment, and lack of social discipline. These experiences demonstrate that participant experience, skills, and even aspirations are not prominent, especially among Malays. There is little confidence among the elites that participant values and capabilities can be rapidly cultivated, or any strong conviction that they should be.

Public power in Malaysia tends to gravitate to and be exercised by administrators or senior politicians. There is growing conflict between district administrators and local and state politicians who have never functioned in administrative roles and are newer and less educated participants in the political process. These conflicts are temporarily resolved by the senior politicians who have been administrators and share the conviction that rational administrative institutions must be protected from "excessive" political interference. These conflicts force a painful and reluctant accommodation for junior administrators taught to believe that politicians should not interfere with administrative decisions and local politicians determined to demonstrate their power to influence local allocations of land, licenses, and other government benefits. The outcome will probably allow greater scope for political influence on local decision making than the current generation of administrators consider legitimate. Administration will be more politicized, especially in dealing with particularistic claims for small public services and concessions sponsored by politicians, but not to the point that the administrative style of the polity or the important political role of senior administrators will be seriously impaired.

Strong government in Malaysia is considered both legitimate and necessary to maintain a precious but precarious order, to control unruly passions and antisocial behavior, and to move reluctant or indifferent people through externalized discipline to do what the survival or the advancement of society or their own real interests require. In brief, the state is considered morally superior to man, strong government is part of the natural order, governments are expected to govern, and administration is the core of government. There is little confidence in the efficacy of participative institutions and little expectation that they can or should supplant or control authoritative and centralized organs, political or administrative. Despite chronic complaining about government and administration—much of it clearly justified—there is little attack on the institutions and much deference and respect, especially among Malays, for persons who represent authority, most of whom are administrators. In times of crisis, as in May 1969, the instinctive response is to fall back on administrative institutions and personnel.

3

A Profile of the Malaysian Administrative System, circa 1965

This chapter proposes to draw a descriptive and evaluative baseline, a point of departure for the innovations and reforms outlined later in the book. The administrative system of any modern country has many plural features resulting from the diverse professional orientations of its component groups and their relationships to different clienteles, as well as common features resulting from dependence on the same political authority, a common framework of legal and personnel regulations, and in many cases a common leadership corps. While in Malaysia as in other countries there are important differences between the police, education, public works, and diplomatic services, this chapter will emphasize their common elements.

In Malaysia "the administration" was the most powerful and most prestigious set of structures in the society. Before Independence government was the most important institution and, in the absence of politicians, the administration was the government. Since Independence that power had been shared with politicians, but many of the senior politicians were former administrators. They had no desire to undermine the status or effectiveness of bureaucracy, despite occasional grass-roots conflicts and the need to lubricate political organizations with patronage. In this administrative state the senior civil servants were far more decorated than politicians or businessmen. They were prominently in evidence at all official occasions. Their shifts in postings and appointments to higher positions were newsworthy events. They were a highly privileged and protected segment of Malaysian society. Especially in the administrative and professional grades they were well paid and, with the help of a conservative fiscal policy which preserved price stability, they maintained a comfortable and dignified upper-middle-class standard of living and could accumulate substantial savings. While the private sector paid better for some specialized skills (medicine, accounting, industrial management) government salaries in these grades were generous when measured by qualifications, job requirements, risk, and standards of living in the larger society. Their salaries were supplemented by numerous paternalistic benefits like noncontributory retirement, government-provided housing, full medical and hospital coverage for officers and their families, very generous leave provisions, interest-free car loans, and a once-in-a-lifetime round-the-world trip (first class with wife) after ten years of service. Conditions in the intermediate and lower ranks of the service were, of course, far less munificent, but they provided similar paternalistic services—housing, medical care, noncontributory annuities on a more moderate scale.[1]

Much of the time of the most senior administrators was absorbed in governing the system, in personnel decisions. This could be traced to colonial practice when the expatriate officers who operated the government were very much concerned with their own rights and welfare. There were relatively few demands and little effective pressure from the society for services, and a *laissez-faire* economic policy kept the business of government quite simple. Much of the time of headquarters personnel was devoted to construing the General Orders (the complex personnel regulations) and applying them to the problems of individual staff members. The service was largely self-governing, and its corporate interests and those of its individual members were carefully protected.

[1] Braibanti's data indicate that in 1964 to 1965, the disparity in base monthly salaries between the highest- and lowest-ranking employees in Malaysia was 47.79/1, compared with 63.64/1 in India and 7.24/1 in the United States (p. 656).

This tradition persisted in a completely Malaysianized post-Independence service and in a political government which faced economic and social problems of vast complexity.[2] The reason is that the senior administrators were esssentially untrained in their policy areas and in the processes of program development and program management. They were qualified and indeed tested in "administration," defined in the colonial tradition as routine personnel, financial, housekeeping, legal, and land matters. Thus a majority of those who occupied the "commanding heights" of the system continued to concern themselves with things they felt most competent to do and were consistent with their role definitions. The maintenance of the administration with its complex General Orders and numerous paternalistic services remained one of their major preoccupations. It is estimated that the secretaries of ministries, the most senior civil servants, in their weekly meetings devoted more than half their time to relatively minor personnel matters.

Structure of Civil Service

Structurally the civil service reflected its colonial origins and the configurations of Malaysian society.[3] The system was stratified by "divisions" and fragmented into "services." The "divisional" structure based on academic attainment and job requirements determined the levels of perquisites available

---

[2] From 1961 to 1968 operating expenditures of the federal government doubled and development expenditures quadrupled as government moved decisively from the colonial pattern of maintaining order and providing minimum public services to an emphasis on economic growth and expanded public services. This vast expansion covered not only the size and complexity of established activities (e.g., education, health services, roads, water supply) but entirely new activities (e.g., family planning, land development, agricultural marketing, housing). An analysis of this process of expansion during the 1950s appears in Gayl Ness, *Bureaucracy and Rural Development in Malaysia* (Berkeley: University of California Press, 1967). For an analysis of the pattern of federal expenses, see Federation of Malaysia, *Budget Summary of Federal Government Expenditure, 1969* (Kuala Lumpur: Government Printer, 1969).

[3] The most systematic source is Robert Tilman, *Bureaucratic Transition in Malaya* (Durham, N.C.: Duke University Press, 1964).

69

to officers. The system had become extremely complex as the tasks of government multiplied and individual decisions accommodated new fields of work and salary claims by the staff unions. In principle, Division I covered professional and administrative work for which university graduation was usually prerequisite. Division II positions were essentially office-management posts requiring at least secondary school graduation, and they were usually filled by advancement from junior services. Division III jobs required secondary school graduation and covered a wide range of clerical, subprofessional, and technical occupations. Division IV were blue-collar positions and the relatively unskilled office jobs requiring usually only grammar school education. These occupations were hard to distinguish from the "Industrial and Manual Group," a category which existed only in West Malaysia.

The most authoritative available estimate of government employment was made by the Royal Commission on the Revision of Salaries and Conditions in the Public Services, as shown in Table 4.[4] To these figures should be added an estimated 15,000 employees of statutory corporations (considered nongovernmental) and 60,000 schoolteachers (employed by school boards but totally compensated by public funds). This would produce a rough total of 310,000 civilian public employees in a labor force of about 3.2 million, about 10 percent of the total or 11 percent of employed workers. By international standards this is a high figure, comparable to such countries as the United Kingdom and Denmark, double the rate for Japan, and four times the rate for India.[5] Professional and managerial employees in

[4] Data on government employment have never been accurate or comprehensive and will not be until the DAU completes the development of a computerized staff records system which is now under way. The Royal Commission figures do not specify the year, but we assume they are for 1965 as are the data on labor force and high-level manpower drawn from the manpower survey of 1965. The latter covers only West Malaysia, but the proportions would not be greatly affected by the addition of East Malaysia.

[5] International comparative data on public employment are highly unreliable since there are no standard definitions to govern the ordering of

Table 4. Government employees in West and East Malaysia

	Railways	State services	Federal service	Total
West Malaysia				
Division I	70	530	3,320	3,920
Division II	90	1,170	3,840	5,100
Division III	2,470	12,030	84,190	98,690
Division IV	1,610	7,150	33,990	42,750
Industrial and manual group	8,190	28,680	25,780	62,650
TOTAL	12,432	49,560	151,120	213,112
East Malaysia				
Division I	–	477	472	949
Division II	–	1,067	1,041	2,108
Division III	–	3,197	4,737	7,934
Division IV	–	3,150	10,093	13,243
Industrial and manual group	–	–	–	–
TOTAL	–	7,891	16,343	24,234
ALL MALAYSIA TOTALS	12,432	57,451	167,463	237,346

the public sector represented about 47 percent of the national stock of high-level manpower. This indicates the weight of government in Malaysian society and the continuing expectation that government is obligated to find a suitable place for all educated people.

Vertically the bureaucracy was divided into "services," for most of which there was a published "scheme of service" setting forth specific qualifications for entry, salary schedules, and re-

data. Thus the figures in the text should be regarded only as rough orders of magnitude. Bruce Russett's 1959 figure for Malaya of 5.47 obviously excludes schoolteachers and public-enterprise employees. Comparative figures are from Russett, *World Handbook of Political and Social Indicators* (New Haven: Yale University Press, 1964), p. 70. Braibanti makes a detailed effort to compare public employment in India, Pakistan, Ceylon, Burma, Nepal, and Malaysia (pp. 648–649). The data cited for Malaya in his analysis underrepresent public employment in 1963 by a factor of two-thirds.

71

quirements for promotion. Each "service" was included in one of the four divisions, and the salary ranges within each division were roughly similar, though they overlapped. There were approximately one thousand active schemes of service to govern the approximately 212,000 employees in West Malaysia. The schemes in East and West Malaysia had not yet been harmonized. Each service was closed and protected. Entry was from the bottom after meeting educational (or in some cases experience) qualifications. Advancement was usually by seniority, though promotion by merit was increasingly emphasized in official doctrine. Lateral mobility was extremely rare, each service jealously protecting its scarce promotion posts from outside competition. The governing rationale was the protection of "standards" from political interference. Upward mobility from one division to another based on experience could occur. Thus senior clerks could be admitted to the Executive Officer Service, members of the Malay Administrative Service (MAS) to the Malaysian Home and Foreign Service (MHFS), accounting assistants to inland revenue-officer posts without additional education, but they were admitted regardless of age and experience at the bottom seniority and salary range, at the same pay as recent graduates.[6] The structure was so rigid both vertically and horizontally that it encouraged psychological and jurisdictional parochialism and discouraged self-improvement and innovation by staff members. The services tended to be inbred and to resist external communication and programmatic coordination.

STATUS SYSTEM

There was a definite status system which generally followed divisional lines. It was reinforced by salary differentials and legitimatized by the high social premium placed on educational

[6] During the colonial period and until 1966, the higher administrative service in Malaya and Malaysia was known as the Malayan Civil Service (MCS). In 1966 the government combined the MCS and the recently established diplomatic service into a Malaysian Home and Foreign Service (MHFS). Though the administrative elite is still popularly known as the MCS, the present designation, MHFS, is used throughout this book. The

attainment. In government service education was the key to opportunity. Superordinate positions were held by members of the MHFS, the former Malayan Civil Service, the senior and most prestigious service. The MHFS were the "administrators" in the British tradition. They were generalists, university honors graduates in any discipline. Their intellectual training, character, and ultimately experience presumably qualified them to occupy commanding positions and to move flexibly from one policy field or type of administrative work to another. Administrative officers were expected to help shape policy for ministers, supervise the management of operational programs, coordinate the work of departmental specialists, and handle "administration," defined as personnel, finance, and housekeeping work in ministries. In the districts they were responsible for land transactions, revenue collection, and summary judicial work. There were about seven hundred established MHFS positions in 1965. Though MHFS officers entered at about the same pay levels as other Division I services, their average grade and pay were far higher. Forty percent of MHFS officers occupied superscale posts, compared with 20 percent of doctors, 35 percent of engineers, 16 percent of veterinarians, 14 percent of statisticians, and 21 percent of educators. Of the senior superscale positions (superscale D and above) MHFS officers held 61, all other services combined held 41. The MHFS comprising less than 20 percent of all Division I officers held 60 percent of the most senior jobs.

Immediately below them were the professional officers (such as engineers, medical officers, agronomists, educators), who held honors degrees in an established professional field and the non-professional Division I services (such as immigration, social welfare, inland revenue, cooperatives, police). The nonprofessional services required liberal arts university degrees, though less-qualified nongraduates had been promoted. According to the prevailing doctrine, Division I officers other than the MHFS

Malay Administrative Service (MAS) was a junior service to which Malays were admitted with less than honors degrees from universities or by transfer from state administrative services.

performed strictly professional or technical functions, which excluded policy concerns or management from which they should be protected so that they might freely practice their specialized skills, while MHFS officers took care of all administration. In practice many of these officers administered large, complex action programs with major policy and management concerns (the state agriculture, education, and public works officers and the federal heads of the Veterinary, Radio, Immigration, Customs Departments, etc.). These services in turn preferred and rewarded their own generalists and provided little training or promotional incentives or rewards for specialists, except in medicine. Virtually no provision was made for postgraduate specialized training. There was a relatively low salary ceiling for specialists and an invariable preference for generalists in higher positions in the professional services.[7] The system harkened back to colonial days when government was simple, the services were small, and there was little need for specialization or postgraduate training within the established professions.

The subordinate services below Division I enjoyed relative status roughly according to their pay levels. The sharp gradations in pay and perquisites reflected the limited availability of higher and secondary education in the colonial period and continued acquiescence in sharp patterns of stratification in a society which had not experienced a social revolution.

There was an important ethnic dimension in the Malaysian bureaucracy. The Malays controlled government and through it the administration. The strategic point of control was the MHFS. This Malay privilege was governed by a quota system of four Malays to one non-Malay,[8] which was interpreted to

[7] For an analysis of the opportunities for specialist training and the distribution of senior posts among specialists and nonspecialists, see the DAU and Staff Training Center publication, *Training for Development in West Malaysia* (Kuala Lumpur, October 1968), mimeo.

[8] The 4:1 quota for new entrants into the MHFS was initiated in 1953. It derives its legal force from section 153 of the Constitution which authorizes the King to set such quotas to protect the special position of the Malays.

74

apply only to admissions through the university honors graduate stream. Other Malays could be admitted from the state services and from the Malay Administrative Service, a junior Division II service, accepting Malays with less than honors degrees and previously without a university background. This was the main avenue of Malay recruitment to the administrative service before and immediately after Independence, and most of the current incumbents of senior posts had entered without university training. So concerned were the Malays with maintaining firm control of the MHFS that in 1965, when there were a hundred vacancies due to an insufficient supply of Malay honors graduates, these posts were kept vacant rather than filled with qualified non-Malays, even though the effective ratio at that time was about eight to one. The quota assured Malay control of this elite service, an aspect of hegemony in government to counterbalance Chinese predominance in the economic and educational fields. There can be little doubt that the country paid a price in reduced administrative effectiveness. Administrative careers were denied to many talented non-Malays who were among the outstanding university graduates, while many Malays with marginal academic records, especially in the field of Malay studies, gained entry into the MHFS. This quota was also a symbol of second-class citizenship and thus a generator and target of discontent, especially among intellectual and middle-class non-Malays.

Yet Malay control of the MHFS was only part of the ethnic picture. While it was widely believed that the government informally practiced Malay preference in appointments and especially promotions, the figures in tables 5, 6, and 7 do not substantiate that view so far as appointments are concerned. Many non-Malays believed, however, that achievement criteria would have yielded an even higher percentage of non-Malay appointments. The professional services were predominantly non-Malay, ranging from 90 percent in medicine and health, 84 percent in public works (engineering), 100 percent in statistics, 63 percent in agriculture and in education. In the decade from 1957–1968, the Malay proportion of Division I posts ac-

Table 5. Analysis of professional services (Division I) by ethnic groups as expressed in percentages

Ethnic group	Services									
	Education	Agriculture	Drainage and irrigation	Public works	Telecoms	Medical	Statistics	Forest	Veterinary	Geology
Malays	32.2	32.6	8.6	16.4	17.9	10.1	–	53.7	34.4	4.7
Chinese	40.3	51.7	74.2	63.8	44.3	40.7	64.5	36.6	21.9	66.7
Indians	24.0	15.7	17.2	18.7	31.1	44.6	35.5	9.7	43.8	28.6
Others	3.5	–	–	1.1	6.7	4.6	–	–	–	–

Source: Data extracted from the Government of Malaysia Staff List, 1968.

Table 6. Analysis of nonprofessional services (Division I) by ethnic groups as expressed in percentages

Ethnic group	Services								
	MHFS	Police	Customs	Registration	Prisons	Immigration	Income tax	Labor	Cooperatives
Malays	86.7	43.2	63.4	30.8	71.4	50.0	5.7	15.7	76.8
Chinese	6.4	30.8	32.7	30.8	7.1	41.7	53.5	52.9	7.7
Indians	6.4	21.7	4.9	38.4	7.1	–	23.9	31.4	15.5
Others	0.5	4.3	–	–	13.4	8.3	16.9	–	–

Source: Data extracted from the Government of Malaysia Staff List, 1968.

Table 7. Comparison of population/staffing of federal public service (Division I) according to ethnic groups
(in percentages)

Ethnic group	Ethnic composition of population	Ethnic composition of public service	Differential
Malays	49.8	37.4	−12.4
Chinese	37.2	35.9	− 1.3
Indians	11.3	23.2	+11.9
Others	1.8	3.5	+ 2.7

Source: Data extracted from the Government of Malaysia Staff List, 1968.

tually declined from 46 to 37 percent.[9] Non-Malays held 63 percent of all professional and administrative posts in the federal government, but a somewhat smaller percentage of superscale positions, indicating the possibility of Malay preference in promotions.[10]

A substantial majority of the clerical and the various technical services were also held by non-Malays. Prior to Independence, the urban non-Malays had easier access to English and to educational opportunities. They were also considered by the British to be better suited to technical work and to office and labor discipline than the easygoing Malays, a few of whom from aristocratic backgrounds were directed through the Malay College and other centers into junior administrative posts. For these reasons, non-Malays predominated in the professional as well as the clerical and technical services. Because of the overwhelming numerical superiority of non-Malays in the university faculties of medicine, engineering, science, and even

[9] Tilman, p. 72, indicates that the Malay percentage of Division I posts had declined from 46.5 in 1957 to 41.5 in 1962.

[10] For example, in the Public Works Department Malays held 16 percent of all posts, but 38 percent of superscale positions. In Police the figures were 43 and 52, in Agriculture 33 and 39, indicating the possibility of Malay preference for promotions in these services. But in Education where Malays held 32 percent of Division I posts, they filled only 18 percent of the superscale positions. These figures are derived from an unpublished study using 1968 data.

agriculture and education, it seemed likely that they would predominate in these services for many years, despite the efforts of government to reduce the disparities by generous scholarships to Malays and by informal but universally recognized preferences in key promotions. In the technical and especially the clerical services, it appeared that the gap would be closed sooner as educationally qualified Malays became available. The growing emphasis on Malay as the official language of government also favored Malay applicants.

Malay control of the MHFS and non-Malay predominance in the professional services created strains in the administration. There were inevitable frictions between professionals who controlled the operating departments and wished to maximize their programmatic autonomy and the general administrators who dominated the ministries and the central guidance and control agencies, especially when the professionals considered themselves better educated and more knowledgeable both on substantive problems and on relevant administrative matters. Malay professionals complained as vigorously as their non-Malay counterparts about the MHFS officers in the ministry secretariats. These frictions, which would ordinarily exist, were exacerbated by the ethnic differences and by a government tendency to appoint to the top professional posts Malay officers who neither by seniority nor the consensus of their non-Malay colleagues were best qualified. The alleged ineffectiveness of the Malayan Chinese Association in protecting the merit system in appointments and in these key promotions contributed to their loss of support among Chinese youth, intellectuals, and middle class. Non-Malay officers in all services strongly preferred seniority to merit criteria for promotion since seniority is objective, while judgments of "merit" may be abused.

ADMINISTRATIVE STRUCTURE OF THE CENTRAL GOVERNMENT

Though Malaysia was a federal state, the center was dominant. The main political parties were national, and their financing and control were highly centralized. The judiciary was unitary. Financial resources were overwhelmingly in central hands. Total state revenues, minus federal grants, were about 10 percent of federal revenues. State expenditures including federal grants averaged 12 percent of combined federal recurrent and development expenditures.[11] Aside from the usual functions of defense, foreign relations, and monetary policy, which are found in virtually all federal systems, in Malaysia education, health, police, commerce and industry were federally operated, and federal funds were spent on behalf of virtually anything, including rural development and even religious buildings, though these functions are assigned constitutionally to the states.

The traditional structural unit in the federal government was the department, of which there were more than forty. The main ones preceded Independence: agriculture, education, veterinary, drainage and irrigation, radio Malaysia, inland revenue, public works, immigration, telecommunications, post office, customs and excise. Since Independence new ones like statistics, civil aviation, and television had been created. The departments were functionally specialized, self-contained operating units conducting programs in well-defined spheres. Some, especially the older professional ones, contained a major professional service, and the head of the department was ex officio head of the service. Thus all veterinarians worked in the Veterinary Department, its head was head of that professional service, veterinary positions were normally controlled by that department, and all postings of veterinary officers were determined by its director. The same applied to agriculture, public works, medical and health, accounting, and other "professional" departments, which operated agencies and personnel systems. They were jealous of their jurisdiction, maintained rigid patterns of hierarchical authority, and therefore had difficulty communicating and cooperating among one another. Before Inde-

[11] *Monthly Statistical Bulletin of West Malaysia*, May 1968, pp. 147–153, and Bank Negara Malaysia, *Quarterly Economic Bulletin*, Vol I, No. 1 (March 1968), pp. 42–45.

pendence these departments—all headed by expatriates—dealt directly with the central control agencies, the Treasury, Federal Establishments Office (FEO), and the Chief Secretary.

Now things were different, much more complex and much less to their liking. With Independence came ministers, with ministers came ministries, and with ministries came new decision centers controlled by the MHFS, the administrative generalists. Soon the proud old departments found themselves subordinated hierarchically to the new ministries that were staffed by people who knew very little about their special problems—whether they be telecommunications, forestry, irrigation, or environmental sanitation—but who insisted on getting their funds, reviewing their staffing decisions, and, above all, controlling their access to the central agencies and even to the minister.

Three types of ministries evolved: (1) those like Foreign Affairs and Commerce and Industry which were staffed in all key posts by MHFS officers and were not bedeviled with the problems of "integrating" or infringing on the traditional autonomy of older departments; (2) the "integrated" ministries like Agriculture, Information, Health, and Transportation, whose finance, personnel, and housekeeping activities were centrally controlled by the ministry, while the constituent departments maintained their identity and operated their own action programs with little substantive guidance or control from ministry headquarters; (3) the "nonintegrated" ministries like Public Works and Finance where the constituent departments were within a minister's portfolio, but continued to operate their programs virtually independently and to deal directly with the Treasury and FEO on their financial and staffing requirements. The trend, however, was clearly toward greater "integration," more control by the ministries, and therefore by the MHFS over the departments, their activities, and their professional staffs.

A ministry was usually headed on the civil service side by a permanent secretary (or secretary of ministry) who might legally be a professional officer, but was almost always a member of the MHFS. In 1965 eighteen of nineteen secretaries of ministries were MHFS officers. In a larger ministry he was assisted by a deputy permanent secretary and small MHFS staffs handling finance, establishments and services (personnel), and administration (housekeeping). Few of these officers were trained in the policy fields for which the ministry was responsible, and they were transferred frequently from one ministry to another following the implications of the generalist doctrine. Very few had any training or expertise in modern personnel, financial, or supply management, and their capacities were based on knowledge of inherited personnel (general orders) and financial (treasury instructions) practices and experience. The departments thus complained that instead of assisting them, the ministries were bottlenecks, imposing controls without understanding, retarding the flow of work, and blocking their access to sources of funds and staff.

The major activities of MHFS officers are indicated in Table 8.[12]

Table 8. Major activities of MHFS officers

Administrative management, including personnel, finance, and housekeeping	223
Land and district administration and local government	118
Foreign affairs	136
Economic administration: planning, commerce and industry, inventory and fiscal, public works, transportation	80
Social administration: education, health, labor, welfare	14
Agriculture and rural development	23
Internal security and defense	35
Other	38
Total	667

[12] DAU and Staff Training Center, *Training for Development in West Malaysia*, p. 63. Data are from 1967. Braibanti and Associates (p. 654) have compiled a comparable table for the former British colonies in Asia as of 1963–1964. The main structural difference between Malaysia and India-Pakistan was the percentage of officers working in the states and districts. In India and Pakistan these totaled 55 and 40 percent respectively, in

81

Excluding those working in foreign affairs and in district, land, and local administration, there were more officers in the ministries concerned with traditional "administrative" work than with all substantive activities combined. Consequently, the ministry secretariats provided little substantive or management leadership or programmatic coordination for the operating departments and retarded rather than facilitated communication between them and the central guidance and control agencies.

The weaknesses of the ministries were partly the consequence of the central agencies. The key central agencies were the Treasury and the FEO. Their highly centralized patterns of detailed control inhibited the development of management initiative and responsibility in the departments and in the ministries. When government was small, the Treasury could maintain a rigid control of funds, but in a decade the national budget tripled and the territory and population doubled, while the staff in the supply division of the Treasury, which reviewed budget estimates and controlled budgetary expenditures, remained stationary at thirteen officers. Requests for authority to take numerous small actions—filling new positions, purchasing equipment and supplies, disposing of obsolete stores, minor shifts of expenditures between budget subheads (virement)—floated up to the Treasury for approval by officers who were both overworked and unfamiliar with the details of departmental business. No effort was made by the Treasury to decentralize these minor decisions to the ministries, even though the secretaries of ministries were high-ranking MHFS officers, or to train ministry staffs and financial officers in Treasury doctrine. This practice and similar controls exercised by the Federal Establishments Office on the grading and filling of jobs created a sense of futility in the ministries since there were few matters which they could actually decide. It reinforced a desire among the operating departments for the right once again to deal directly with the

---

Malaysia 18 percent. The differences can be traced to two factors: in Malaysia about half these positions are held by members of state civil services rather than by central cadres, and the foreign affairs staff in Malaysia have been amalgamated into the higher administrative service.

Treasury and the FEO and thus avoid the ineffectual ministerial level.

The central guidance and control agencies evolved from the Treasury, the classical repository of these functions in the British administrative system. The Treasury's monopoly was shattered prior to Independence both by the creation of an Establishments Office in the office of the Chief Secretary to handle personnel matters and by the setting up of a Prime Minister's Department in 1957. At that time, the FEO was assigned to the new Prime Minister's Department with the full range of personnel functions except for selection, promotion, and discipline, which the Constitution entrusted to a quasi-judicial Public Services Commission (PSC) to protect the services from political interference. The PSC was dominated by retired senior civil servants. In 1959 the development planning function, to which the Treasury had laid an ineffective claim, was committed to a new Economic Planning Unit (EPU) in the Prime Minister's Department with close links to the Deputy Prime Minister. A Cabinet secretariat was organized in 1956 to process documents for Cabinet consideration and follow up Cabinet decisions. The trend has been for the Prime Minister's Department to harbor a cluster of expanded central management organs,[13] leaving the Treasury under the Ministry of Finance to specialize in budgeting, expenditure control, and supply administration.

The Treasury was as much concerned with raising revenues and with monetary and fiscal policy as with budgeting and expenditure controls, but the latter accounted for its impressive power over administration. There were two budgets: an ordinary budget dealing with recurrent or operating expenditures (roughly two-thirds of the total) and a development or investment budget (roughly one-third of the total). The ordinary budget was entirely controlled by the Treasury. It was a line-item budget, based on objects of expenditure, such as personal emoluments, transport and travel, printing and stationery, office

[13] This trend was continued with the establishment in 1966 of a Development Administration Unit which is analyzed at length in Chapters 5, 6, and 7.

rentals, and special expenditures. For each administrative unit, and under each main category, all expenditures were listed, including each position by its specific salary grade as determined by the FEO, with the subsequent approval and often revision by the supply division of the Treasury.

It was difficult to determine from the budget what services were being provided and at what cost, the emphasis being entirely on objects of expenditures. The annual budget reviews for each department involved discussions primarily of proposed incremental expenditures, the justification for each new position or for each addition to such items as electricity, transportation and travel, or special expenditures. The original basis of the previous year's expenditures was seldom if ever challenged. Since the budget said little about the services a department proposed to provide with its money, it had little interest for key operating officials. Estimates were prepared by financial clerks in the departments and ministries and defended in the Treasury by middle-level officers, not by department heads or permanent secretaries. Void of programmatic or cost information, this budget was primarily an instrument of financial control rather than of fiscal analysis, program choice, or management guidance. Funds could be legally spent only as specifically authorized, and the Treasury endeavored to insure that the authorized budget was underspent, especially if revenue receipts were expected to be less during an expenditure period than estimated.

The development budget was drafted by the Economic Planning Unit of the Prime Minister's department. Every project appearing in that budget had to be approved by EPU to insure its consistency with the five-year development plan. Determination of the magnitude of the development budget caused an annual confrontation, pitting the stability-minded Treasury and its redoubtable Minister of Finance (with the help of the Central Bank) against the growth-minded EPU and its indomitable Minister (the Deputy Prime Minister), with final resolution by compromise in the Cabinet. What specific items were finally included was determined jointly by the Treasury and EPU officials.[14] Because foreign-aid funds were often uncertain and slow to arrive and solid projects were not available from many ministries, there were lags built into the development budget. Through its normal expenditure control, the Treasury attempted to insure that funds were carefully spent; the EPU, concerned with stimulating the economy, pressed the departments to spend the whole budget. The Treasury calculated that it was doing its job if development expenditures in any year were held to about two-thirds of the budget. Because the two separate budget operations failed to account systematically for operating costs in subsequent years, resulting from completed investment projects, funds sometimes had to be transferred from the "softer" development budget to the tighter and hard-pressed ordinary budget during the year to cover such shortfalls as the unanticipated operating costs of new hospitals or underestimated costs of the expanding education system.

The real powers of the EPU over administration were its influence over development funds, its control over foreign technical assistance, and its role in negotiating—in company with the Treasury—economic assistance with foreign donors and lenders. The EPU was a relative newcomer in the Malaysian administrative scene. Aside from drawing up and monitoring the progress of five-year development plans, it attempted to shape economic policy so as to facilitate economic growth and served as the economic brain trust and staff arm of the Deputy Prime Minister, performing numerous services at his request. The EPU was preoccupied with macrolevel analysis and with specific project reviews. The operating ministries and state governments developed no sectoral or regional planning capability, and the EPU provided no assistance in these areas. The range of the EPU's responsibilities was far too great for

---

[14] The group making these determinations was the estimates subcommittee of the National Development Planning Committee, a group of senior civil servants who are responsible for supervising the five-year plans. That such major allocations were made by a committee of civil servants is an indication of their power in the Malaysian political system.

its small and inexperienced staff of fifteen local professional officers, few of whom had received advanced training in the disciplines relevant to development planning. It therefore relied heavily on foreign advisors.

The Federal Establishments Office was a large staff agency which controlled the personnel system. It analyzed and recommended personnel policies and was the authoritative interpreter and amender of the General Orders, the rules governing personnel administration. It "established," that is, it set up and graded, all new jobs and approved the regrading of old jobs; in the absence of written job classification standards, its decisions in grading had a pronounced occult quality which often baffled the operating departments. The FEO's approval was required for any change in schemes of service—the qualifications, promotion ladders, and salaries of any group of positions. It was responsible for negotiating with organized staff unions through the British-model Whitley Council system— still so designated in Malaysia—which was a trial to officialdom but gave the organized employees an effective channel of influence on matters related to salaries and conditions of employment. The FEO controlled the pension system, which meant that it must approve the establishment and grading even of state government positions that were pensionable, and it adjudicated the pension rights of all employees benefiting from the government's noncontributory scheme.

The FEO was considered the employing department and managed the posting and assignment for "common-user" services, especially the MHFS and the general clerical service, this function being handled for other employees by their own departments, for example, for engineers by the Public Works Department, for postal clerks by the Post Office Department, and so on. The FEO also administered overseas training and scholarship activities and was responsible for the Government Officers Staff Training Center. Personnel administration was as tightly controlled at the Center by the FEO as was financial administration by the Treasury. FEO staff members had not been trained in modern personnel management concepts or practices any more than the Treasury staff had been trained in modern public financial practices. They learned their craft by experience and maintained the system which they inherited from the colonial period.

Selection for entry into the service was the responsibility of the Public Services Commission, a quasi-judicial constitutional agency whose purpose was to protect the civil service and "service standards" from political interference. Job qualifications and the number of vacancies were prescribed by the FEO. The PSC announced and conducted examinations, relying exclusively on academic performance records and brief interviews to determine relative suitability. No objective aptitude, achievement, or psychological tests had ever been used, even for clerical and mechanical positions. There was no "rule of three," and employing agencies were required to accept candidates selected by the PSC. This examining system caused allegations of informal racial criteria for selection and promotion to be frequently made by non-Malays, who tended to distribute their blame equally on the FEO which set policy and the PSC which made the specific decisions.[15]

The statutory corporations were another important part of the central government. These bodies were totally owned, financed, and controlled by the government. Though they performed public services, were responsible to a Cabinet minister, and governed by acts of Parliament, they were considered nongovernmental, a distinction with considerable importance. Nongovernmental meant that they were not subject to normal Treasury and FEO controls on finance and staffing,

[15] Until 1966 the PSC also adjudicated and made binding decisions on promotions and disciplinary actions for all services, receiving recommendations from the departments, but not necessarily accepting them. The PSC acquired the reputation of adhering rigidly to seniority criteria in promotion actions and of being dilatory, legalistic, and proemployee on disciplinary matters, both of which had the effect of undermining management's control of staff. To the great regret of the staff unions and employees generally, the government through a constitutional amendment in 1966 withdrew promotion and disciplinary matters from the PSC and transferred them to the operating departments.

their personnel did not have the status of government servants and did not participate in the noncontributory pension system. The government (or statutory) corporations had proliferated in recent years and used about 25 percent of the development budget. They were active in the following major areas: (1) commercial activities such as the National Electricity Board, the Port Swettenham Authority, the Rubber Research Institute, the Pineapple Marketing Board, the Employees Provident Fund (similar activities like the Telecommunications Department and the Post Office Department operated as regular government agencies, while the Malayan Railways was a hybrid); (2) developmental activities for the benefit of Malays like the Federal Land Development Authority, MARA (Council for the Benefit of Indigenous Peoples), and the Federal Agricultural Marketing Authority; and (3) miscellaneous activities that required a special push such as the Federal Industrial Development Authority, or that had special autonomous status, like the University of Malaya and the National Language and Culture Center.

The main reason for this proliferation of government corporations was to mitigate the rigors of normal financial, procurement, and personnel controls for activities which require energy, innovation, and dynamism and must respond quickly to changing situations, assuming that "government" and its ordinary procedures are (and must always be) slow, legalistic, and cumbersome. In resorting to government corporations, Malaysia has not been free of the problems that this form of enterprise has provoked in similar systems, notably the United Kingdom and India. What happens when they begin to pirate scarce technical and managerial personnel from regular government agencies? How much freedom can they be allowed in salary, wage, price, and major investment decisions without disturbing government economic policy? How can their activities be coordinated with those of related corporations and of regular government agencies? How much control must a minister and his staff be able to exercise so that they can accept public responsibility for these activities before

Parliament? Malaysia has attempted to deal with these problems by: (1) selecting key officials of these agencies from inside the civil service, a substantial percentage of whom prove to be MHFS officers chosen at an earlier age than they would otherwise be eligible for such senior posts; (2) placing government representatives, always including one from the Treasury and one from the responsible ministry on the board of each corporation; and (3) imposing wage standards and ceilings to prevent competitive salary escalation and the pirating of scarce personnel.

These measures have been reasonably successful in controlling salary escalation and providing opportunities for senior government officials to influence the major operating decisions of the corporation without controlling its routine operations. While some of the corporations have behaved very much like regular government agencies, several have generated administrative innovations (National Bank, Port Swettenham Authority), some have operated their programs with a high degree of technical competence (Rubber Research Institute, National Electricity Board), others have pursued their developmental activities aggressively (Federal Land Development Authority, Selangor State Development Authority). Their managers are unanimous in attributing their success to freedom from normal Treasury, FEO, and ministerial controls. While they have become enclaves of modernization, their innovations have not spread because they have few transactions with other government agencies and because the central control agencies and training institutions have not attempted to learn from their improved practices and to diffuse, extend, or adapt them to other operations.

TERRITORIAL STRUCTURES

Nine of Malaysia's thirteen states were headed by hereditary Malay sultans, the other four by governors appointed by the King and thus selected by the Prime Minister. Each of the four was a Malay even though the majority of the people in Penang, Malacca, Sabah, and Sarawak were non-Malays. In each state there was an elected unicameral assembly responsible for electing a Mentri Besar (or chief minister) and an executive council which shared the executive functions. Below this simple political structure was the administration headed by a state secretary, who was a senior MHFS officer, except in the former unfederated states (Johore, Kelantan, Trengganu, Kedah, and Peerlis) and in the Borneo states (Sabah and Sarawak), which had their own small state civil services. In addition to a small secretariat which handled personnel, housekeeping, local government, and miscellaneous functions and assisted the chief minister and the executive council, each state had two other senior officers, a state financial officer, and a state commissioner of lands and mines, staffed from the MHFS or a state civil service. There were also a series of departments responsible for functions assigned to the states by the Constitution, such as agriculture, veterinary, forests, fisheries, drainage and irrigation, and public works. The Division I officers who headed and manned these departments in West Malaysia were, in every case but religious affairs, drawn from federal services and posted from Kuala Lumpur. Their salaries and the operating expenses of their departments, however, were paid from the state treasury and their subordinate technical and clerical staffs were state employees, although they had to be approved by the Federal Establishments Office if they were to be eligible for pensions.

The pattern in Sabah and Sarawak was different. The state department heads were from the local civil service, actually British expatriates. They were a source of controversy, the federal Alliance leadership charging them with undermining federal authority and plotting against the Kuala Lumpur government. Yet these state governments preferred British expatriates to officers from West Malaysia, hoping optimistically that by 1973, when their contracts would expire, native Sabahans and Sarawakians, would be trained for these positions, and that these would not be predominantly Chinese, for in East Malaysia the Chinese were even further ahead of the other races in education than in West Malaysia. The pattern of relations between the center and the states of East Malaysia was still evolving, and it appeared likely that the Borneo states would retain greater autonomy than the states of West Malaysia. Though Sabah and Sarawak complained that they were neglected by Kuala Lumpur, that controls were too tight and decisions too slow, the federal government pointed out that it invested more per capita in East than in West Malaysia and that the net flow of funds ran strongly in favor of East Malaysia.[16] The state secretaries regarded themselves as administrators qualified in personnel, finance, housekeeping, and land activities, but not in "professional" or programmatic areas. They were not certain that their role permitted them to intervene in substantive areas or that they were competent to do so. The department heads belonged to federal services and were in regular communication with their chiefs in Kuala Lumpur. For these reasons, the departments effectively formulated and operated their own programs virtually independently of direction or coordination by the state government. Exceptions to this autonomy were their dependence on state government for junior personnel and operating budgets, usually a routine procedure, occasional interventions by the chief minister, and the

[16] Estimated by the Minister of Finance in his presentation of the 1967 budget at $140 million Malaysian dollars in 1966. The more fundamental tensions between the Kuala Lumpur government and the state governments of Sabah and Sarawak are not treated in this study. They involve the fear of many Borneo politicians that Kuala Lumpur is attempting to impose Malay domination over these territories whose populations are 75 percent non-Muslim and treat them like the state governments on the peninsula, without consideration of their special cultural, political, and economic interests which they believe were protected in the instruments that led to the formation of Malaysia. Aside from the inevitable problems of accommodation among politicians and administrators who had little contact before 1963, the interventions of the federal government and the Alliance Party in the politics of Sarawak has aggravated suspicion of Kuala Lumpur's motives, especially among the Iban who are the largest ethnic group. For an excellent discussion of these problems, see Michael Leigh, "Party Formation in Sarawak," *Indonesia* (Ithaca, N.Y.: Cornell Modern Indonesia Project, No. 9, 1970).

activities of the state development officers on "development projects." The smooth working relations between the states and the center that characterized West Malaysia since Independence can be attributed to two factors: the key position of the MHFS and members of other federal services in the state administrations and the control of all state governments save one by the Alliance Party.[17]

Thus the political and administrative lines of communication between center and states were smooth and effective in West Malaysia, although they had not been satisfactorily worked out in Sabah and Sarawak. The only significant area of conflict was the allocation of land for federal projects. States demanded a high price when asked to provide land, which they control constitutionally, for federal uses. They were often very slow to act and were frequently not responsive to the federal government's development priorities—especially when this involved the alienation of public lands to non-Malays.

Parallel to the state secretaries and the state departments were the state offices of agencies run directly by the federal government, such as police, health, education, MARA, and telecommunications. In some cases their clerks were assigned by the state governments, though their salaries were paid by the federal. Coordination among the state offices of these departments and between them and the state departments and the secretariats was informal, infrequent, and *ad hoc,* except

[17] While the Alliance leadership has repeatedly stated that it could not cooperate with a state government controlled by the opposition and that such a state could not expect a substantial share of federal attention or investments, available fiscal data did not indicate a pattern of discrimination against opposition-controlled Kelantan. In 1965 federal grants to Kalantan's budget were M$14.4 per capita, compared to an average for all of West Malaysia of M$12.2 Kelantan was ahead of such stalwart Alliance states as Johore and Negri Sembilan. Kelantan was discriminated against in allocations from the Federal Land Development Authority, but this is the only instance that I have seen documented. After the 1969 elections, the Alliance government in Kuala Lumpur worked out an effective relationship with the opposition- (Garakan Party) controlled government in the State of Penang.

for "development" activities. Unique coordinating instruments for development projects were the state development committees headed by the chief minister and assisted by the aforementioned state development officers.

Local government was controlled by district officers, lineal inheritors of the colonial structure. In West Malaysia there were seventy-one districts, each headed by a district officer directly responsible to the state secretary. The district officer was a member of the MHFS except in the former unfederated states where he belonged to a small state civil service. In his district he was the principal representative of government. He was neither guided nor restrained by representative or participative organs, but unlike colonial times he coexisted and attempted to accommodate with local politicians who made frequent demands on his office on their own behalf or on behalf of constituents and who cultivated links, which they did not hesitate to exploit, with party leaders at the state and even the national level. In this way local government was becoming politicized, and local people were finding the political channel often a more personalized and more efficacious approach to government than the administrative. Nevertheless, the District Officer was still the most important man in his area. He was, in most states, concurrently head of the land office, which collected land revenues, processed applications for state lands, registered the transfer of titles, and settled small estates. He or a junior member of his staff chaired the town councils and other units of local government within his district. After 1963, elections for these councils were suspended because a number of the larger councils fell into the hands of opposition parties and many had been characterized by administrative incompetence and corruption.

The structure of the district office remained substantially the same as during the colonial era, but its functions were changing. Specialized officers—police and magistrates—had relieved the district officer of most of his law-and-order duties. The land offices tended to be run by junior officers. The main role of the district officer was to promote rural development, to coordinate the development activities of the specialists—agriculture, public works, health, veterinary—and to stimulate, activate, and increase productivity and participative behavior among the residents of his district. No longer was he to be the remote and unapproachable representative of foreign authority, but rather the friend and counselor of the people, mingling with them, helping them to organize and use the resources provided by government for their own improvement. The modern district officer was thus asked to combine two roles: he was still the authoritative senior representative of government, but he was also expected to be the prime mover in rural development, a tutor, and an agent of social change. His training still prepared him only for the traditional role. Before he was confirmed in the MHFS, he sat for examinations in law, general orders, and finance. He had no training, unless he happened to take a relevant course at the university, in the disciplines and professional practices relevant to his new role as the animator and coordinator of rural development. He was expected to learn from experience, but experience offered him few guides.

His district was broken down into *mukims* or wards, each with a resident *penghulu,* a Division III officer responsible to the district officer for registration and other miscellaneous duties. He was a full-time officer selected in most states by examination but in a few by hereditary succession. The network was completed by the *ketua kompong,* the head man in each village, appointed by the chief minister as the government's representative. As a pillar of the ruling party, he was expected to represent authority as well as to be the spokesman for the villagers themselves, even though he was not responsible to them in any institutionalized way.

State government was the backwater in contemporary Malaysia. Modern change-oriented political leadership gravitated to the federal level; modern administrative and professional personnel belonged to federal cadres; financial resources were overwhelmingly in federal hands, and so were the main functional sectors either by constitutional provision or by virtue of the leadership, drive, and financial power of the federal government. Not a single policy, programmatic or administrative innovation, except for the Selangor State Development Authority and a low-cost method of land development in Kelantan, originated in the states. State government was the repository of tradition, the sultans and their courts and the Islamic religious establishment, of which each sultan was the head and which maintained close and conservative surveillance over the lives of Malays, especially in rural areas. The state civil services were inferior to the federal and in some cases were afflicted with nepotism and patronage. Thus the more able and ambitious young graduates gravitated to the more modern atmosphere and the greater opportunities provided by the MHFS, even though many of them were required first to serve in the state civil services as repayment for their scholarships. West Malaysia (formerly Malaya), about the size of Missouri, consisted of eleven states only because this was the price required to secure the support of the sultans, who symbolize Malay hegemony, and their retainers. The state government's policies regarding land and natural resources often retarded economic growth and encouraged corruption without contributing to social equity or enhancing the well-being of Malays.

The states, as instruments of economic development and modernization, were an anachronism in Malaya. They had not served as laboratories of experimentation, but they provided some opportunities for training and experience in small-scale political management and a secondary source of recruitment to positions of national political leadership. The federal form of government facilitated the accession of Singapore and the Borneo states when Malaysia was formed in 1963. The traditional system of deference and control symbolized by the sultans and the religious establishment has retarded the political mobilization of rural Malays. While this has probably slowed down modernization, it has also dampened communal conflict, which is the likely consequence of political mobilization in Malaysia.

Dimensions of Performance

One measure of the performance of an administrative system is its "extractive" capacity. This elegant term refers to its ability to mobilize domestic resources for the public sector. The federal government of Malaysia mobilized about 18 percent of GNP through taxation. If domestic borrowing is added, it extracted 21 percent of GNP from the economy, a very respectable figure by international standards.[18] It also extracted compliance. Its writ ran the length and breadth of West Malaysia, despite organized crime in the cities and Communist insurgents on the northern border. This is related to its "penetrative" capacity, another dimension of performance measured roughly by density of coverage. The figures indicated in Table 9 are suggestive.

Table 9. Dimension of performance by density of coverage

	Government employees per square mile	Government employees per 1000 population
West Malaysia	5.6	32
East Malaysia	.57	40

In West Malaysia coverage was comprehensive. Every community was served at a minimum by a teacher, policeman, postman, and *penghulu*. On the West Coast, every citizen had access to specialists, not always of adequate quality or service motivation, in agriculture, veterinary, health, public works, and other fields, and the East Coast was gradually improving in this respect. In East Malaysia, because of low population density, large areas were only lightly served and the quality of public services was generally considered to be in-

[18] This compares with 21 percent for France and 20.4 percent for the Netherlands, 17.8 for Japan and Thailand, 9.2 for the Philippines, and 7.5 per cent for Pakistan, all in 1959 (Russett, p. 62).

ferior to West Malaysia. The writ of the government was challenged, especially in Sarawak, by an aggressive, clandestine Communist organization operating in sparsely populated areas where government presence and services were few and infrequent.

The "penetrative" capacity of the Malaysian political system, its ability to employ and deploy 10 percent of the labor force, depended on its impressive extractive capacity which, in turn, reflected the export orientation of its modern economy, imports and exports yielding more than half of tax revenues. However, in comparison with other administrative systems which employ a similar percentage of the national labor force—most of them advanced industrialized countries—Malaysia appeared to be receiving a much lower return for its money. The low productivity of many Malaysian public services was due to four interrelated factors: (1) the relatively low level of managerial and technical skills in its labor force; (2) the inefficient systems and procedures employed in public agencies; (3) the misallocation of staff, including overstaffing in clerical and manual occupations and understaffing in such technical fields as agricultural research and extension; and, (4) the inability of the public to use government services effectively, to interact with and make demands on government personnel and agencies because of illiteracy, habits of deference, lack of organization, and suspicion of authority.

The Malaysian administrative system in 1965 can be evaluated according to four major dimensions of performance: system maintenance, integration, adaptation-innovation, and conflict management.[19]

[19] These dimensions of performance apply to the outputs of an administrative system. Thus they are not and should not be isomorphic with the roles (inputs) of development administrators as outlined in Chapter 1. The achievement of system maintenance, for example, is not emphasized as a function of a development administrator though this may be a consequence of his managerial role. On the other hand, the conflict management outputs of an administrative system may involve the policy, change agent, and political roles of a development administrator.

SYSTEM MAINTENANCE

Colonial administration was oriented to routine and control, and these dimensions of administration were still paramount. One could not live in Malaysia without admiring the reliable postal service, telephone system, and electricity supply, the excellent highway maintenance, the pure domestic water supply which more than any factor accounted for health standards and life expectancy which are exceeded by no other tropical country. One was also impressed by the perpetuation of routines that belonged to another era and had not changed since Independence, including the personnel, financial, and supply systems previously discussed and the files and office communications procedures straight from the pages of Charles Dickens. The social welfare system was designed for the needs of early twentieth-century England, not for a country in Malaysia's circumstances. The system of land administration had nearly collapsed because of inability to adapt to new conditions and rigid adherence to routines which had not changed since World War I. Even relatively new services like agricultural extension and town planning soon became victims of pale and unimaginative routine.

Order and regularity were the pride of the system. Precedent was highly prized. The administration was files-oriented, and few officers were prepared to take or recommend any action without first digging deeply into the files for precedents to determine and legitimatize their decision. The present generation of officers was taught by their expatriate mentors to respect and be guided by regulations and precedents and to perpetuate routines. They were not encouraged to deviate or to experiment. The purpose of administration was to keep things going along established and approved lines, not to change them, and this applied equally for administrators as for clerks. Officers knew only the substantive approaches and the operating procedures they learned by experience, and few had any training that provided alternative models. The public, too, knew only present procedures to which they had become accustomed and seldom made strong demands on government. The service was disciplined, the routines went on, they were reliable and predictable, but changes imposed from the outside quickly became routine and lost their innovative thrust. The great strength of the system was thus its capacity to sustain established routines. This conservative bias was system maintenance in its most fundamental sense; it was antithetical to all the elements of development administration specified in the first chapter.

INTEGRATION

The integrative capacity of an administrative system is its ability to interrelate the activities of its component parts in order to establish and maintain priorities, resolve conflicts, and achieve consistency and mutual support among diverse but related operating programs. Integration (or coordination) is a function of every level of management. It is essential to the managerial element of development administration where program aspirations run ahead of resources, new activities proliferate, and many programs designed to serve the same clienteles function independently of one another or work at cross purposes.

At its top levels the federal government was amply equipped with structures with high but unrealized integrative potential. The fundamental difficulty was the deficiency in this respect of the MHFS. The most convincing justification for an elite administrative service is its ability to transcend departmental parochialisms, to assess public problems in a larger systems context, to harmonize program priorities among diverse and competing agencies, and to guide program execution accordingly. This critical function was not being carried out by the MHFS because it was precluded by their role definition as administrative housekeepers, their lack of training, interest, and confidence in substantive policy areas, and their innocence of modern management practices. This is why the first priority in administrative modernization was to strengthen the capacity of the MHFS.

99

The budget system was not effective as an integrative mechanism because it did not deal explicitly with action programs but only with administrative units and objects of expenditures. The personnel system provided useful common standards for personnel actions, but it was broken down into watertight services and in the absence of manpower planning and of training that might enhance interservice communication, it was a force for fragmentation and programmatic provincialism rather than integration. The five-year development plans provided a rudimentary framework for program coordination by indicating to the various departments and agencies how their activities and major products fit into a national development program and what performance was expected of them. Yet the plans did not treat the specific problems of interprogram and interagency cooperation in a way that could be meaningful to operating personnel. State or regional planning, which might facilitate the integration of activities in geographic space, had not been initiated. In its reviews of functional programs in agriculture, industry, and education, preliminary efforts were made to identify major problems of coordination, but these were hampered by the very limited staff capability in the EPU and the higher value its leadership and especially its foreign advisors attached to economic policy analysis than to management problems.

There was a network of committee structures at the top management level composed of senior civil servants. The most important were the secretaries of ministries and the National Development Planning Committee (NDPC), which supported the EPU. These structures and the Cabinet itself were handicapped by a shortage of analytical inputs, particularly from the operating ministries, departments, and statutory corporations. This dearth of well-reasoned staff papers prevented these forums from fulfilling their potential as integrative structures.

The second level of integration was the ministries, in which program integration should be the main function. In a few ministries like Foreign Affairs, which were not burdened by pre-existing constituent departments, integration was an accomplished fact. In others hesitancy on the part of MHFS officers, the absence of coordinative structures like planning and management units in the secretariats, and the quest by the operating departments for maximum autonomy undermined progress. Departments preferred to protect their autonomy, neither initiating external contacts nor welcoming interference from others. Thus a veterinary station experimenting with growing animal fodder failed to ask the Department of Agriculture for an agronomist, even though they were both in the same ministry and the Veterinary Department had no trained staff agronomist. There was little cross communication among departments and to achieve a minimum of interference from the ministries and their MHFS cadres, departments avoided referring problems of program coordination to them. Clientele groups were not yet sufficiently organized or activated to compel interagency coordination on their behalf.

The third level of integration was regional, at the level of the state governments. As already indicated, the state secretaries were a poor vehicle for coordination because they took little interest in the action departments. So ineffective were they in this role that they were excluded from the newly organized state development committees, which were set up by the Deputy Prime Minister as part of the rural development–operations room system in 1959. Razak realized that the government agencies at the state and district levels were not working together and that their perverse independence was an obstacle to rural development. He also remembered the war emergency rooms which the British military had organized at the state level to insure interdepartmental cooperation in the battle against the insurgency. So he set up in each state a development committee headed by the chief minister and consisting of members of the state's executive council (politicians), the state-level representatives of federal departments (e.g., education, health, police), and state department heads (e.g., agriculture, public works, veterinary, forestry, town planning). The executive secretary was the state development officer, an MHFS officer selected by and responsible to Tun Razak. He maintained the state operations room, in which the schedules and current status of development projects were prominently displayed. He monitored and expedited projects and held weekly "morning prayers" meetings of the principal department heads. At these meetings problems in project coordination that involved more than one department or level of government could be identified and often solved on the spot. This device increased integration but unfortunately was limited to development projects, defined as construction activities financed from the development budget. The ongoing services of government, including the uses of facilities built with development funds, were not included in this system of coordination. Thus the construction of an irrigation scheme was monitored by the state development committee until the project became operational, but not the uses to which the water was later put. Cooperation between the Departments of Agriculture, Drainage and Irrigation, and Information and the Federal Agricultural Marketing Authority on behalf of a program to increase rice production was outside the province of the state development committees or of any group. For such activities there was no effective integrative machinery at the state level. Thus while the structure existed, it was put to only limited use.

The pattern of state development committees was replicated in each district by a district development committee chaired by the district officer. In each district office there was an operations room equipped with wall charts; for each development project there was a large "red book" with detailed drawings, financial and physical data, and current progress information. But again the emphasis was on spending the development budget on such minor construction projects as mosques, community halls, wells and piped water, and feeder roads. Most district officers were untrained in the management of rural development activities and their energies were dissipated on these minor projects, on the routines of overseeing land offices and local councils, on managing campaigns for National Language Week, and similar activities. They were also handicapped by the limited expertise of the specialist officers representing the functional departments at the district level, their negligible discretion for programmatic initiative, their preference for routine and control over service activities, and the strong communications bond that linked them with their state department chiefs. Again at the districts, the integrative structure was there, but it did not attend to the main programs that affect the economic or welfare needs of rural people. Increasingly the principal function of the district development committees was to permit resident federal parliamentarians and state assemblymen to claim small amenities and construction projects for their constituents and to pressure officials for their implementation.

ADAPTATION—INNOVATION

The third dimension of administrative performance is the capacity of the system to adapt and to innovate. Conceptually adaptation and innovation may be distinguished. Adaptation relates to the system's ability to anticipate and to respond to environmental change; innovation is its capacity to generate measures that improve its own performance or induce changes among clienteles. In this discussion adaptive and innovative elements of change are combined because they both deal with the ability of administrators to set goals, influence the course of future events, and manage change processes.

These combined capacities are critical to the assessment of an administration's role in development, which is its ability to accommodate and to guide change processes. In these respects Malaysia's administration tended to lag in adaptation to external pressures and showed little propensity to innovate. As of 1965, the baseline for this survey, it had not introduced even simple new management technologies, like modern files or records systems, into its internal operations. It had been slow to respond to chronic problems in its most familiar task environment, like the breakdown of land administration, not to mention more complex issues like stagnant productivity in rice or migrant squatters in urban areas. It had been ineffective in reaching out to work with clients and experiment with new programs that would be helpful to them, whether with Malay rice farmers, unemployed urban youth, or Chinese manufacturers. The professional departments had accepted new physical technologies. Thus the Telecommunications Department was introducing satellite communications, medical officers prescribed modern drugs, and the Ministry of Local Government and Housing was experimenting with large-scale prefabricated structures. They were far more receptive, however, to new developments in physical than to new social or management technologies.

Most of the adaptations sponsored by the professional departments were slow in pace and modest in scale. Because few departments provided continuing and specialized education for their staffs in changing technological developments and because the professionals had been taught to regard themselves as technicians and advisors, not as policy makers and administrators, they were expected to carry on existing programs through familiar methods rather than to initiate improvements. The limited avenues for exerting societal influence on government spared administrators from disturbing pressures that might have evoked the search for improvement and compelled experimentation and change. The system was not equipped with research, planning, and policy analysis resources which would increase its capability for timely responses to events, not to mention anticipating them. Thus decisions were often made in response to crisis and with inadequate information or analytical preparation, and adjustments represented the minimum feasible departure from the *status quo.*

Reinforcing this dearth of external pressures on the bureaucracy, this generation of senior officers lacked inner drive which, again, reflected their conservative role definition and their disinclination to deal with policy matters and management problems, the main responsibility of an administrative elite. Thus most of the adaptive and innovative thinking and action were provoked and sponsored by a handful of political leaders, notably Tun Razak, assisted by a small coterie of change-oriented civil servants and foreign advisors. The most far-reaching administrative innovation has been the aforementioned operations room–red book system. A set of procedures for installing the system was elaborated and vigorously installed in every district office and state government and exemplified by the national operations room in Kuala Lumpur. For several years Tun Razak made this system work by inexhaustible pressure—endless surprise visits to state and district operations rooms and dramatic intervention on the spot.[20] He exhorted officers to greater effort, to speed up performance, to work together, to concentrate on development activities, and he achieved results in speeding up action and in demonstrating to rural Malays the government's concern for their welfare. The system survived Razak's inability to supervise it intensively after he assumed additional responsibilities beginning with Indonesian confrontation in 1963. But the officers who had to work the system had not been involved in its design or trained in the management of rural development. It was "installed" and they were expected to conform. The officers on the ground tried to work the system because it was expected and demanded of them, but they developed no capacity to adapt or innovate further, and the expression of new or critical ideas was not encouraged. Officers were told repeatedly that they had an ideal system, internationally celebrated, and their job was to make it work. As a result the system froze. It became increasingly an end in itself rather than an evolving instrument of rural development. It remained locked into construction projects and minor amenities, even though the officers themselves were increasingly convinced that these were unimportant to the productivity and welfare of the rural people, had lost their political value, and no longer responded to felt

[20] Milne reports that in 1962 Razak attended 118 district rural development committee briefings in Malaya's 71 districts and traveled 43,000 miles through the countryside (pp. 157–158).

needs. They were carrying on the old system until the Deputy Prime Minister would tell them to change it. Thus a promising innovation had become ritualized. It had not only lost its innovative thrust but had even ceased to adapt. The senior MHFS officers who should have been evaluating this system and adapting a useful structure to new needs confined themselves to maintaining the system at a fixed point in its development.[21]

Adaptation and innovation did exist in Malaysian government and administration, but not enough to generate, sustain, and undergird ambitious development programs or to anticipate and mitigate communal conflict. There was very little adaptation or innovation in the main administrative structures. The successes of a few statutory corporations like the Rubber Research Institute, the Federal Land Development Authority, and the MARA Institute of Technology in these dimensions of administrative performance suggest that such behavior may be facilitated by autonomy and that pressures for integration may in fact retard or inhibit innovation because they imply the imposition of external controls. The cultivation of integrative and of adaptive-innovative capabilities may at any time be conflicting rather than mutually reinforcing objectives. Since both are necessary to development administration, reform policy must attempt to keep them in balance, trading one for the other depending on the problem at hand. Thus the establishment of two new statutory corporations—a Federal Agricultural Marketing Authority (FAMA) and an Agricultural Research and Development Institute (MARDI)—independent of one another and of existing agricultural service agencies was a clear decision to emphasize innovation over integration and, at least initially, to sacrifice the latter for the former.

CONFLICT MANAGEMENT

Prior to Independence, in the absence of politicians, conflicts that entered the public domain and could not be settled informally were resolved by administrators. For some classes

[21] This subject is treated in more detail in Chapter 7.

of disputes, such as land titles and mining rights, rules were established and applied by administrators. In others, particularly at the district level and for problems that were not highly structured or predictable, administrative discretion governed. With Independence and the appearance of politicians, the application of rules became the province of administrators, while discretionary matters were increasingly invaded by politicians. Some situations formally governed by regulations became subject to expedient political intervention.

There were two styles of conflict management among post-Independence Malaysian administrators. The first was the old district officer tradition, the guardian caring for his flock and dispensing even-handed justice. These paternalistic practices still prevailed in rural districts, but were being influenced and circumscribed by politicians. The second was the more sophisticated and bureaucratic rule-of-law procedure which prevailed at state and especially at federal ministerial levels. The range of discretion which most senior administrators permitted themselves in interpreting regulations varied according to the subject. The more the external public was involved, the more they limited themselves to strict adherence to rules and precedents. If there was limited public or politician interest, some senior administrators would exercise cosiderable discretion—as in budgeting allocations—but this was exceptional behavior, the majority of officers seeking refuge in rules and precedents.

Important issues of conflict—between trawlers and traditional fishermen, between private grain millers and government marketing agencies, between federal departments desiring land and state governments, between groups of squatters and local authorities, and especially in situations with important communal implications—floated up to senior state and federal politicians for negotiation and decision. Administrators usually preferred to play it safe by searching for rules and precedents or passing the buck to politicians. They could do this even in an administrative state, so long as relatively few controversies entered the public arena, competing interest groups made only modest demands on one another and on the resources of government, public initiatives in developmental areas were limited in scope and the conflicts they generated could be handled by a small group of senior politicians. Under such conditions, administrators could minimize their risks and limit their involvement in conflict management. In Malaysia, administrators thus took little initiative and made little contribution to important problems of conflict management, including those with communal implications.

Administrative performance is a function of the intensity of societal demands, the technical and economic capabilities of the system, and the values, beliefs, and role definitions of its leading actors. Since Malaysian administration is an elitist system, it can be better understood by an appreciation of the values and beliefs of its senior cadres. These are explored in the next chapter.

4

Changing Values and Belief Patterns of Malaysian Administrators

Every group of men who maintain continuous cooperative relationships share some values and beliefs. This sharing is essential to communication and to the predictability of response that makes cooperation possible. By values I refer to norms of conduct "held by individual human beings, of what human beings ought to desire, i.e., the desirable. They are supported by internalized sanctions and function as (a) imperatives in judging how one's social world ought to be structured and operated and (b) standards for evaluating and rationalizing the properties of individual and social choices." Beliefs are cognitive propositions about the nature of reality, "the structure and operation of the social and physical universe and one's place in it; vectors which bear upon an individual as he confronts a choice of conduct." Values and beliefs (together with impulses which are biologically generated drives or need-dispositions) help to orient man to the universe around him. They help him to screen information and attach meaning to it, and thus influence, though they do not fully determine, his behavior. Every man in a structured group like a bureaucracy is expected to play a social role which fosters and encourages some forms of behavior and frowns on others. This social role circumscribes the autonomy of any man who wishes to function effectively in the system. Values and beliefs produce attitude sets—orientations to reality and dispositions to behave. Attitude sets are part of the cement that holds a group together and helps to determine both individual and collective behavior.[1]

Appreciation of the attitude sets of any group helps to understand and explain behavior within the group and to predict responses not only to familiar but also to new situations. For persons interested in influencing public policy and for change agents, such information about client groups is useful in shaping tactics and priorities. Because of my interest in better understanding the determinants of behavior among Malaysian administrators and in shaping and implementing change strategies, I found it useful to attempt both to describe and to explain their behavior. This could be facilitated by an analysis of the modal value and belief patterns or attitude sets of this important component of the Malaysian governmental elite.

A few important cautions are in order, however. All the significant values and beliefs that influence the behavior of any group of men cannot be identified, especially those of sophisticated men functioning in complex organizations in a rapidly changing environment. Nor can it be said that particular values and belief patterns are held with the same relative intensity by individual members of the group; at best the descriptions characterize the average member, but there are likely to be deviants, some of whom point the way to future patterns. It is possible to identify relatively few but salient themes that are important in orienting members of this bureacracy to their jobs.

Another difficulty is the changing character of the attitude sets. While basic values and beliefs have great continuity and are a stable element in personality, they can and do change, men can and do learn. Changing environmental conditions and new ideas do feed back and modify beliefs and attitudes. They may change gradually for individuals and more

[1] Concepts and quotations are from Phillip Jacob's article, "Values and Their Function in Decision Making," *American Behavioral Scientist,* Supplement, 5 (May 1962).

rapidly for institutions in periods of accelerated generational succession, even though the continuity of institutions is itself a conservative influence on those whom it recruits and socializes. Because of the critical factor of change, I attempt to distinguish the major patterns found in the older and in the younger generation of Malaysian administrators and to use these insights in the next chapter to undergird change strategies.

The final problem is method—how to find out what these attitude sets really are, how conflicts among them are resolved, and in what directions they are changing. Fortunately, it was possible to draw on the work of scholars who have attempted recently to probe the behavioral and motivational dynamics of Malaysian administrators. Particularly helpful was the work of James C. Scott, who examined the views of a carefully selected group of senior Malaysian administrators through extended interviews as recently as 1965 and supplemented these interviews with several questionnaires administered to larger groups of civil servants.[2] Scott was attempting to identify political beliefs and to construct the modal ideology of senior Malaysian civil servants, but the orientations that he was probing are directly relevant to the purposes of this study. I have also drawn from William Siffin's perceptive analysis of the bureaucracy of Malaysia's neighbor, Thailand.[3] Acknowledging a very considerable debt to these scholars, I nevertheless relied primarily on unstructured interviews with dozens of Malaysian civil servants of all ages and racial backgrounds and from several services (administrative and professional) and on my observations from two years of participation in the Malaysian government. This means that I report inferences from what I have seen and heard, but most of them, fortunately, are supported by Scott's investigations.

Finally, I must dispel any tendency to look upon these

---

[2] James C. Scott, *Political Ideology in Malaysia* (New Haven: Yale University Press, 1968).

[3] William Siffin, *Thai Bureaucracy: Institutional Change and Development* (Honolulu: East-West Center Press, 1966).

attitude sets as uniquely Malay or Malaysian. Many of them, of course, derive from Malay tradition, but similar patterns are present in other preindustrial societies experiencing similar problems. I am impressed by Scott's proposition that many of these beliefs are based on rational expectations about the realities of a society that has known poverty, uncertainty, dependency, and ethnic tensions for long periods of time. They are not aberrations arising from identity crises or other personality strains associated with rapid change, but are reality-serving orientations, even though some are becoming outdated as the real environment changes. In conversations with Malays, I was struck by an almost universal tendency to ascribe any set of attitudes or behavior patterns that seem to depart from idealized British norms as peculiarly Malay. This is a consequence of limited personal and intellectual contact with other modernizing societies, the emphasis of the Malay Studies Department at the University of Malaya on the uniqueness of Malay culture, and the tendency of the colonial education system to treat British middle-class virtues as norms.

The Malaysian administrative culture is syncretic, combining elements from two major sources, Malay and British. Though they have held specialist positions for many years, Chinese and Indians are relative newcomers in administrative positions.[4] Consequently theirs has been a conforming and accommodating rather than a major influencing role. Modern administrative structures were set up by the British and governed by them directly until 1957 in Malaya and 1963 in Sabah and Sarawak. Malaysia's current stock of senior administrators was tutored by British officers and in British and British-model educational institutions. So were most of its leading politicians. Therefore, British administrative attitudes, beliefs, and styles have molded not only the structures but also the officers who man them. British influence on Malaysian administrators is a form of secondary socialization. It comes

[4] The first small detachments of non-Malays were admitted to the MCS (now the MHFS) only in 1953.

from formal education and from experience in the bureaucracy. The Malay tradition—and likewise the Chinese and Indian—provide a series of values and beliefs derived from the family and from childhood experience, with deep roots in enduring cultures. These values are attenuated, reinforced, or blended into others which are learned in secondary schools, the university, and the bureaucracy itself, where British models, standards, and styles prevail. The resulting attitude sets combining Malay and British elements and influences are widely shared and remarkably normative among senior civil servants of all races.

Despite the structural pluralism of Malaysian society, the similar values, beliefs, and behaviors of senior government officials of all ethnic groups can be explained by the following factors: (1) the prevalence of many common beliefs in their traditional cultures, including similar evaluations of the nature of the real world and of their fellow men and of requirements for survival; (2) the powerful influence of secondary socialization on persons who experienced British-style secondary and higher education and served under British officers; (3) the dominance of Malay styles in Malaysian government and administration and the need for non-Malay officials to accommodate to them. Scott reported few orientations that could be differentiated on ethnic grounds. Where I perceive differences associated with ethnic factors, I shall so indicate.

In order to emphasize the essential qualities of these attitude sets, I shall present them in exaggerated form as ideal types which apply especially to the older generation of serving officers. This will set the stage for a discussion of significant departures from this model among younger officers, which in turn points the way to strategies of reform. I have selected six major themes which help to orient men to their social roles, particularly to bureaucratic roles. They are a convenient way of organizing and presenting the modal attitude sets of senior Malaysian administrators.

Theme I. The Nature of the External World

In the belief system of Malaysian administrators, the essential feature of the real world is scarcity. There is not enough to go around, not enough wealth, income, prestige, power, security—not enough of any important value. Therefore, one man's benefit is by definition another man's loss, since they are competing for a fixed quantum of goods. Because of the intense competition for scarce items, every man must jealously guard what he has, for one man's gain in any value is necessarily at the expense of another. The result is generalized intergroup and interpersonal suspicion, corrosive of the social trust which is essential to effective individual and organizational cooperation.[5] In the Malaysian context this is exacerbated by intercommunal suspicion and distrust which interprets each community's gains, political or economic, as necessarily coming at the expense of the other.

The pervasive nature of scarcity extends beyond material values. Malaysian administrators are jealous about bestowing praise on colleagues, fearful that praise for the receiver will somehow detract from the donor. I recall a conference at which a young officer was presenting a proposal for reorganizing the administration of rural development programs. To illustrate the feasibility of his proposed reforms he cited the dramatic success achieved by a particular district officer, who had experimented with similar techniques and had thereby achieved dramatic increases in rice production. Since these reforms represented important departures from current practices, the young officer expected some hard questions. To his amazement, the two-hour meeting was almost void of reference to his substantive proposals. Instead the young officer was roundly rebuked for singling out one district officer for

[5] Scott reports that his sample of Malaysian administrators was significantly more pessimistic in their responses to the Rosenberg "Faith in People" scale than respondents in the U.S., U.K., Germany, Italy, and Mexico (pp. 65–66).

praise, while failing to mention the good work done by others, especially those attending this meeting. Praise and recognition were too scarce to be distributed generously.

Students of Malay society—and other cultures of poverty—have pointed to the presence of a perverse equalitarianism. A man who takes initiative and attempts to assume responsibility or leadership in his group is frequently cut down to size by ridicule. He is presumed to be asking something for himself at the expense of his peers and of his group. At the village level in Malaysia this has contributed to the difficulty of achieving or sustaining effective organization by local initiative. This pervasive mistrust makes it hard to maintain the cooperative behavior essential to goal-oriented group action, except for traditional religious activities which are highly institutionalized. Within the administration the effects are similar. Organizational patterns are tightly structured along formal hierarchical lines, and officers must be quite certain of their terms of reference before they interact with others, a condition that makes fluid cooperation and easy adaptation to new conditions rather difficult.

It is even more difficult to achieve cooperation across organizational lines because organizations are protective of their domains and suspicious of the motives of others. But while they defend what they have, Malaysian government organizations do not characteristically attempt to occupy new fields, for they are more concerned with keeping their existing share of the scarcity than in increasing their risks and responsibilities, even though opportunities for expansion have been plentiful.[6] There is no functional substitute in Malaysian bureaucracy for the extended family, which is the unit of mutual trust and obligation in Malay and especially in Chinese society.[7] Nor is there an equivalent to the vertical cliques which provide mutual service and obligation in the Thai

[6] One reason for the establishment of statutory corporations has been the sluggishness of government departments and their reluctance to expand into new but related activities.

[7] Chinese business firms deal with this problem by filling positions with

bureaucracy or similar patterns that create areas of trust in other systems. In the absence of broad patterns of trust, Malaysian bureaucracy thus appears to be an atomized community. This intense individualism is reinforced by the educational system, which puts enormous emphasis on competitive examinations and is attenuated only in part by associational ties from university days.

Throughout the administration there tends to be a greater awareness of scarcity and limitation of resources than of opportunities. MHFS resistance to lateral entry of qualified persons from other services can, racial factors aside, be attributed to the fear that this would automatically deprive MHFS officers of opportunities, even when there were many vacancies, promotions were rapid and frequent, the service was expanding, and there was a great demand for good MHFS officers in the burgeoning public corporations. So convinced were these officers that within a few years "normal conditions" would prevail, and consequently jobs would again be scarce and promotions slow, that their basic response has been instinctively protective. The pervasive image of scarcity also inhibits innovation in the bureaucracy and predisposes people to cleave to established routines and to vested interests, fearing that in the shuffle provoked by change they may end up with less of the constant pie than they now have.

In economic policy making there is a similar tendency to underestimate resources—tax revenues, external borrowing capacity—and to be satisfied with a lesser growth rate than the economy can achieve, to overestimate scarcity, and to underestimate opportunity.[8] Even a resource which is not scarce, like rural land in the East Coast states, is treated as though it were, on the assumption that the economic benefits to

members of the extended family which tends to insure a community of trust.

[8] This evaluation of the existential base has been strongly reinforced by secondary socialization. Colonial economic policy was thoroughly imparted to local officers by their expatriate mentors.

Chinese from the use of the land would necessarily be at the expense of Malays.

Theme II. The Nature of Man

These various attitude sets tend to reinforce one another. Reinforcing the concept of environmental scarcity is the view of man as essentially self-seeking, egoistic, opportunistic, and prone to socially destructive behavior. The prevailing scarcity compels him to pursue his own interests in order to survive economically and socially. But because of man's self-seeking nature—a product less of original sin than of a hard Malthusian and Hobbesian environment—instruments of social control are required. The main instruments are religion, the moral guide, and government, which maintains the means of coercion needed to check man's antisocial tendencies. Thus government is morally superior to man, a far cry from the main doctrine of Western liberal thought. Government is not a mere human artifact, but part of the natural order required to discipline man because he is not able to govern himself. From this it follows that those who govern must be beyond the reach of the interests and forces which create the basic need for authority. Thus the principles of governmental autonomy and responsibility take precedence over the principles of responsiveness and representation. Parliamentary government is, of course, good so long as it produces the right kind of leaders, who must then be left free to govern without nagging interference from self-seeking individuals and interest groups. But if it should produce the wrong kind of leaders or should contribute to political instability, Malaysian officials would be prepared to dispense, perhaps reluctantly, with parliamentary processes. This view is corroborated by Scott's research.[9] The communal tensions in Malaysia, the

[9] Scott (pp. 182–201) reports that the verbalized commitment of his sample of Malaysian administrators to democratic norms proved to be "formalistic" in that the commitment did not hold up when democratic

need to protect society from politicians who would incite and exploit communal discord, emphasize the need for strong government.

The main purpose of government, of course, is to maintain order. Where possible, it should also be benevolent, provide services, and stimulate economic growth. But the first objective is order, and this requires a firm presence. Malaysian administrators, and, I believe, all segments of Malaysian society perceive a deep need for a manifest, external authority and could not imagine a situation in which "government is best which governs least" or where the state would wither away, or where the cure for the evils of democracy is more democracy, or where an invisible political hand could allocate values fairly among competing group interests. Indeed public authority is needed, not only to control antisocial behavior, but also to guide behavior along the paths of rectitude. Officers today recall with great respect their idealized image of the firm and fair British civil servant. They comment that the current generation of officers is much too lax in dealing with the public. For this deterioration a number of reasons are given, including political interference, inadequate training, and an inclination to be "soft" with one's own people. Tun Razak admonishes his officers: "You must be tough to be kind." The people need to be told and shown what to do: to compensate for backwardness if they are Malay peasants, or for avarice if they are Chinese businessmen. To look for felt needs is regarded as dubious and futile at this stage of the game. The people need to be instructed and guided and where necessary controlled.

As public authority is required to control the public, so senior government officers must control their subordinates. Government officers and clerks, like other men, are prone to

---

practices might threaten the values of order and hierarchy which they consider more salient. This tendency was confirmed by a series of questionnaires (respondents were a group of 116 administrators) on various dimensions of democratic commitment adapted from Herbert McCloskey's work.

self-seeking behavior, to neglect their duty, to do things the easy way, and even to corruption. It is the duty of seniors to control their subordinates, and the most effective method is by surprise checks, dramatized by the behavior of Tun Razak, Malaysia's superadministrator. People are motivated to duty primarily by fear. Therefore the emphasis is on externalized discipline imposed by higher authority rather than on internalized norms of behavior, not that the latter are considered unimportant, but because they seem to be less reliable and less effective.[10] The need for externalized discipline in the service is, however, a source of pain to many Malay officials because they abhor personal confrontation and prefer to handle tension-producing situations by indirection or avoidance. While they admit the necessity of enforcing discipline within the service, they would prefer that someone else do it, and they thus do too little of it themselves.[11]

Though man is antisocial and requires externalized control through government, man is also weak; because he is weak, society ought not to impose too many demands on him, nor should legitimate government unduly restrain his personal needs. So long as he does not threaten the base values of the society or the regime, the security, institutions, and religion of the state, he is entitled to compassion and magnanimity from those in positions of authority. If a poor peasant cannot repay a loan—perhaps because he had to finance a festival to meet a religious obligation—or if a civil servant must, without warning, visit his village for unstipulated family reasons, the tendency is to respond with forbearance rather than discipline. Civil servants are readily forgiven such venal sins as incompetence and nonfeasance; time deadlines are rarely imposed and even more rarely enforced; high-ranking politicians have been redeemed after episodes of official corruption because—as Siffin observed in

[10] In other words, this is a "shame" culture rather than a "guilt" culture. Norms and discipline are essentially externalized.

[11] This does not apply to Chinese officers whose style tends to be more direct.

Thailand—the system is "suffused with tolerance" of the weaknesses and the backsliding of ordinary men and is disinclined to circumscribe their personal or family obligations. The former Prime Minister, a Malay aristocrat, takes specific account of this strain of Malay humanism which he describes as "kindness." [12] Achievement norms are thus constrained by norms which protect the dignity and autonomy of the individual. In the process they undermine organizational discipline and reduce the productivity of government. This strain of compassion, plus the inclination of senior officers to avoid confrontation, tend to minimize the actual impact of externalized discipline in the service. Coexisting attitudes are thus operationally in conflict, a not infrequent occurrence in complex belief systems. This incompatibility will probably be resolved in the next generation by the triumph of achievement over compassionate norms, but the system may lose in human values as it gains in productivity.

Theme III. The Nature of Interpersonal Relations

Malaysian administrators are not radical democrats. They are strong believers in the legitimacy of status differences and in the superiority of some men over others. In the bureaucracy this superiority is gained by formal qualifications (education) and experience and is measured by the rank one holds in the official hierarchy. Rank creates formal authority and expectations of deference, which are respected. Malaysian society in all its component communities is highly stratified along class lines. The higher civil servants have been part of the ruling class for nearly 100 years, and there has been no social revolution to disturb the present system of stratification, which has accommodated senior politicians without displacing senior administrators. Status hierarchy occurs in every bureaucracy, but its influence on behavior varies with the power of the bureaucracy in the society and the values attached to relative status.

[12] Such tolerance is far less prevalent among Chinese officers who regard it as a defect in Malay character and a residue of feudal behavior.

In Malaysia, official status is high status. In colonial days officials were the government; they had power, prestige, and comfortable incomes. Today they must share power with politicians. Careers are open in modern industry, especially in foreign-owned firms, which are said to pay more than government and there are the liberal professions, yet only one who knew the situation in colonial times could despair of the current or the prospective status of Malaysia's senior bureaucrats. They have lost their virtual monopoly of status, there are alternative routes to power, prestige, and income, but the administrators are still the core of the Malaysian establishment. Neither the increasing supply of university graduates nor increasing numbers of professional and management posts in the private sector are likely soon to erode the position of the higher civil service. Their power rests primarily on a universal appreciation of the need for strong government which they symbolize.

Officials of all ranks feel superior to most nonofficials, though they are aware of and take account of the influence exercised by wealthy businessmen and politicians. Officials expect a polite and deferential approach from the public, who have few effective avenues of protest, and whose expectations are still modest. Malaysia's public still does not impose heavy demands on the administration, and the politicians who benefit from the good will of administrators have not yet taken up the cry. The public still petitions for service and treats officials, especially of the MHFS, with courtesy and respect. Officials do not tend to seek out and learn the problems of their clients at first hand, to engage in meaningful and sustained dialogue, or to advocate new or improved services. The main pattern still usually is to prescribe well-trodden routines, a procedure which helps the official to maintain appropriate social distance from his clients.

Within the bureaucracy status differences are considered highly legitimate, despite the predictable grumbling of junior officers. Its effect is to inhibit initiative and problem-solving behavior. Problems tend to float to the heads of agencies for decisions with the familiar consequences—overloaded superiors, underutilized staffs, avoidance of responsibility, and discouragement of initiative. Delegation is difficult because of the reverse reinforcing effect of status, superiors feeling that even routine decisions can properly be made only by themselves.

Many middle-grade and even senior officers prefer to wait for instructions before they act, and it is not discreet to press seniors for instructions. Frequently, they ask for instructions, not by presenting an analysis of alternatives plus a recommended decision, but by presenting the raw problem and expecting their chiefs to provide the answer. While some senior officers grumble about this practice, there are few serious efforts to discourage it. The time-honored British colonial practice of "minuting" and passing files up the line with little value added at each successive level and closure only at the top of the tall hierarchy is slowly being eroded in Malaysia under Tun Razak's exhortations and the pressures of work load. The difficulty, of course, is that the proposed change in behavior is not merely a technical matter, but a modification of habits reinforced by deep-seated values and beliefs.

Passive obedience to superiors is one of the base values of Malay society. It is inculcated and enforced among children at home and at school. The great folk hero, Hang Tuah, serving a sultan who had grievously wronged him, killed his own brother who was trying to avenge this very injustice. There are no Robin Hoods in Malay tradition. The lack of opportunity for occupational mobility tends to commit people to a lifetime in a single small service, in which power is concentrated in a few senior officers. A serious mistake in interpersonal behavior, especially one that violates loyalty, obedience, or other status norms, may block an officer's career. Status factors are not taken casually in the Malaysian civil service. They are highly normative, and officers are not embarrassed or ashamed to discuss them.

This emphasis on hierarchy is detrimental to the development of informal, lateral communication between units of the same organization and especially among different organizations. It is, therefore, one of the main impediments to interagency cooperation and interprogram coordination. Communication is so bounded by hierarchical channels, so little authority is delegated, and subordinates are so disinclined to take initiative that any matter not of a routine character is delayed, particularly if it involves more than one agency. This problem is exacerbated by the inability of the MHFS officers to see their role as program coordinators. Siffin found in Thailand that the status system not only delayed, but also distorted the content of communication and made it difficult for staff agencies to function properly because to do so would challenge the strict principle of hierarchical communication. Junior staff officers were put in the position of reviewing the work of more senior line officers. Unlike Thailand, where the power of hierarchy prevented staff agencies from functioning properly, staff work in Malaysia is done primarily by the high-status MHFS. Staff services are less effective than they should be, not so much for status reasons as because the MHFS officers are not yet technically equipped for these activities and do not accept a managerial definition of their role.

Status relationships are highly normative in guiding behavior within the bureaucracy and between officials and the public. Status inheres in rank within the same service. Professional officers, of course, outrank subprofessional and clerical personnel, but MHFS officers enjoy higher status than professionals of the same grade. There is no evidence that this order is changing, but the fear that they may be losing power to the better trained professionals has prompted some younger MHFS officers to press for more rigorous and relevant substantive and management training for members of their service, while beginning to redefine the relative importance of status and achievement values.

Theme IV. The Nature of Causation

Many senior Malaysian officials display little confidence in their ability to influence the world about them. Events are governed mainly by forces beyond the control or even the effective influence of ordinary men.

This adds up to a sense of limited efficacy, little confidence that even high-status men can do much to manipulate, control, or change their physical or social environment.[13] The effects of limited efficacy can be corrosive to development administration. Under these conditions, men do not try, and many senior Malaysian administrators do not try to do more than watch over routines and cope with unexpected events. For if events are controlled by unpredictable forces, is it not foolhardy, even blasphemous to attempt to plan for the future or to remake institutions? If the future is as uncertain, dangerous, and unpredictable as the immediate past has been, obviously one must make the most of the present and discount the future. So what is the sense of planning ahead for the nation or for an organization when human plans can be so easily disrupted by contingencies? These short-time horizons, this resignation to superior power are further legacies of a pretechnological situation of scarcity, a fair assessment perhaps of man's realistic possibilities in these circumstances.[14] They no longer reflect Malaysia's real possibilities, their existential base is eroding, and they are inhibiting the pursuit of goals to which the national political leadership is increasingly committed.

Theme V. The Nature of Government and Administration

As an essential control agency, government is indispensable to the survival of society. It is not only part of the natural order, but next to religion it is the most precious human institution.

[13] While attitudes of limited efficacy characterize officers of all races, their reactions are visibly different. Malay officers especially of the older generation tend to be more passive and easily discouraged when confronted with frustration; Chinese respond more actively, recognizing that while the environment is hard, man is obligated at least to try. The differences in style between the more passive Malaysian and the more activist Singaporean administrations reflect the different senses of efficacy among the politicians and the officials who dominate and populate these structures.

[14] Scott attempted to demonstrate that in Malaysia constant pie thinking, social distrust, and lack of felt control over the future form a syndrome of mutually reinforcing attitudes. He cites Almond and Verba,

Administrators who run the government partake of its transcendent qualities. The dignity, perquisites, and salaries to which they are entitled derive not merely from the jobs they do, but also from their participation in an authoritative institution. This is one reason that many officials were unhappy with the market test for compensation applied by the recent Royal Commission on Government Salaries. Because it is the ruling institution, government's performance cannot be judged purely by instrumental standards and cannot be compared with business or other profane activities. The main test of government is its ability to maintain control and continuity, and for these purposes routines, precedents, pageantry, and monuments are self-justifying because they symbolize the continuity and majesty of government, though they may have little to do with efficiency or public service.

Politics and administration should be separate spheres of activity, though they inevitably and unfortunately overlap. There are two kinds of politics, one legitimate, the other corrupt. Legitimate politics concerns policy issues, parliamentary elections and debates, and ministerial responsibility to guide and protect the administration. Corrupt politics is the politics of interests, of politicians who badger administrators to pander to small groups of undeserving constituents or to line their own pockets. The danger civil servants see for Malaysia is that the petty and corrupt politics of aggressive individual and small-group interests may destroy both legitimate politics and administration, and in the hands of greedy, ambitious but ignorant politicians may even destroy the country. While they respect several of the senior politicians at the national and state levels, especially those who are well-educated and experienced as administrators, they have a profound contempt for politicians as a class and for most of the ones they observe. To the civil servants, not only are most politicians ill-educated

---

and Robert Lane to support the proposition that relative affluence is associated with higher levels of social trust and greater confidence in personal efficacy (pp. 147–148).

and ignorant of the proper ways of government—many hardly speak English—but their motives are selfish and their increasing "interference" with administrative decision making introduces self-serving criteria into what ought to be the impartial application of law, penalizes the honest citizen, and threatens the morale of the civil service. Like administrators universally, Malaysia's civil servants distrust the political processes of pressure, influence, and expedient bargaining, and they distrust as well the political role. Now that they must share public power with a new breed of grass-roots politician, they are apprehensive of how the country and the administration itself will fare.

Administrators, therefore, emphasize the separation of administration from politics—a doctrine readily available from familiar British sources—and the need for substantial autonomy, which has for the most part been respected by the present generation of political leaders. The core of autonomy concerns "service" matters, the management of the civil service itself, for which administrators claim the full right to self-government without political interference. This covers recruitment, assignment, performance evaluation, promotion, the grading of positions, and discipline—all aspects of personnel administration except assignments to important high-ranking posts, where the concurrence of the minister is required. Otherwise, politicians should interfere only by enacting general provisions of law, but never by interfering in individual personnel matters.

Administrative autonomy extends beyond service matters. It is the duty of politicians (ministers) to make policy after receiving advice from senior civil servants, and of the civil service to carry it out. The only politician to whom the bureaucrat feels responsible is his minister. No other parliamentarian or local politician has any right to intervene in any administrative decision or action by the exercise or the threat of political power. In a celebrated case in 1967, a young district officer was evicting two prosperous businessmen from state land which they were illegally occupying. When their member of Parliament, an assistant federal minister, attempted personally to stay the eviction at the last minute, the district officer snapped back in the presence of a battery of newspapermen: "I do not take orders from politicians," but only from his minister, in this case the Chief Minister of Selangor, who had not ordered him to stay the eviction. He was applauded by his colleagues in the service, less for tact than for courage. He was reiterating a principle to which the service is deeply committed and which has come under attack in recent years from Malaysia's emerging grass-roots politicians who do not accept the outsider role the administrators assign them in public decision making outside their legislative activities. They are not willing to see specific allocations of land, licenses, and other valuables or the fate of their constituents determined entirely by administrators.

The administrator's definition of his own social role is to maintain the service and execute routines according to law and precedent, but seldom to question or change them. The bureaucratic stratification prevents him from attempting to reorganize office routines—on which much of his operating efficiency and effectiveness depends—because this is the do-main of the clerks. He copes with problems as they arise, re-solving them where possible by precedent and by reference to specific established rules or he passes them up to his supe-riors. No longer can he make it a virtue to maintain appropri-ate social distance from the public, but how close he should be is not clear. He risks accusation either of partiality, or of being aloof and insensitive to popular feelings and "aspira-tions." [15] In any case it is proper that the public come to him for service rather than that he seek out opportunities to serve them. He stays within his own organization unit and takes care of today's problems, not tomorrow's, thus binding himself both spatially and temporally within a narrow arena of action. This profile of the role orientation of the colonially trained ad-

[15] Younger Malay officers are especially sensitive to the prominent theme in current Malay vernacular literature which pictures MHFS of-ficers in an unfavorable light as remote and alienated from their people.

ministrator, the system maintainer, has, however, begun to change, and it is being redrawn along lines which are more consistent with the development administration model.

Theme VI. The Nature of Intergroup Relations

Malaysia's civil servants are subjected to the same communal pressures that influence the attitude sets of other Malaysians. Their primary socialization, their identities, their religious and family associations link them indissolubly to an ethnic community. This is as much a concern to them, and they are as prone to discuss its implications as are men from other other walks of life. They are not above the struggle because ethnic tensions are reflected in the life of the bureaucracy, as well as in the larger society. Chinese officers are quick to complain about discrimination against non-Malays and the greater burden of work they must bear. Malays grumble about the unwillingness of non-Malays to use the national language and their inability to appreciate the deep aspirations of the Malay people for greater participation in the modern economy. Younger Malay officers are inclined to use the powers of government to redress the economic and educational imbalances between the races, at some cost to non-Malays. Chinese officers tend to emphasize equal rights, free competition, objective standards, and efficiency. The ethnic distrust which pervaded Malaysian society has not escaped the civil service.

Civil servants, however, are more sophisticated on racial matters than members of other groups and more aware of the need for accommodation. They have shared a common educational experience, either at secondary or university levels, often at both, and they have in any case followed the same British-designed curriculum, which enhances intercommunication. They partake of a common middle-class, western style of life, usually in government-provided housing where they are frequently neighbors. They meet and work together on common problems in government offices five and a half days a week. Both groups recognize that the stability of the society in which both have so large a stake depends on achieving and maintaining viable patterns of accommodation—though they may not agree on what specific patterns are feasible or even just. The Chinese in the civil service, working in an environment dominated by Malays, have far more sympathy with the deeply felt needs of most Malays to redress the existing economic and educational inequities through governmental action than do most Chinese outside government and are far more prone to accommodate on matters of language and style. Malays in the civil service have more appreciation than grass-roots Malay politicians or intellectuals of the danger to the society of disturbing Chinese economic activity or alienating Chinese from the political system. They tend to be moderate—albeit still partisan—on communal issues. Each group recognizes the legitimacy of some of the claims and even the demands of the other side, and they share an interest in maintaining the society and the state which has been generous to them.

Their attitudes thus are ambivalent, beyond the demands that most men face to reconcile competing loyalties, ethnic and national. More than any other group, excepting only the politicians active at the national level, the senior civil servants are the embodiment and the custodians of the concept of Malaysia, a modern nation, whose survival, order, and progress supersede the claims of any of its constituents, including the ethnic groups to which each remains attached and partisan. Potentially, therefore, they are a force favoring communal accommodation.

Generational Succession

Changes in the attitude sets of Malaysia's civil servants have been provoked by generational succession and the unremitting pressure by political leadership, especially by Tun Razak. Razak has attacked the inherited attitude sets, especially on the theme of efficacy. In a speech each week since 1956, he has tried to convince the civil servants that what they do really counts, that they must take initiative, and that the implemenation of development programs should be their chief concern. He has attempted to persuade them that the inherited routines of the colonial bureaucracy and its workways have no inherent validity, that they must be supplanted by attitudes and methods which eliminate needless paper work, reduce delays, and serve the public more efficiently and sympathetically. Most of all he has put his faith in the younger generation of university graduates. He has encouraged the more experienced nongraduate officers, those who floated to the top at the time of Malayanization, to retire at age fifty, the minimum age for pension eligibility, and has recently reduced the mandatory retirement age from sixty to fifty-five. In violation of service conventions he has interfered in the placement of officers, directing the posting of those whom he considers especially promising to key positions in the ministries and especially in the statutory corporations, with consequences which have been highly successful in some cases, disappointing in others, and have predictably aroused some resentment in the service. His main tactic has been to speed up and to capitalize on generational succession.

The younger administrative grade officers differ from their elders in four respects. A much smaller percentage are aristocrats. Educational opportunities provided by government subsidies have enabled young men from modest backgrounds, particularly the sons of teachers and minor officials, to enter the civil service, and they are far more representative of Malay society than were their seniors. They are tuned to the concepts, styles, and expectations conveyed by modern mass communications and urban living; their idiom and outlook are modern. Their youth and young adulthood have been spent in a politically independent rather than a colonial society. They are university graduates, while most of their seniors were not. These factors have modified and can be expected further to modify the basic attitude sets described above. The great division in the MHFS is between the older nongraduates and the younger graduates. The latter are far better educated than their seniors, but not yet trained in the concepts, analytical methods, and operational skills required for effective development administration.

The graduates have much greater confidence in their efficacy than do their seniors. Their exposure to secular and scientific thinking at the University of Malaya, even in its Malay Studies Department, has endowed them with some confidence that they can impress their influence on events and institutions and that it is their proper function to do so. A nucleus of able young officers do so behave when they find themselves in sympathetic situations, and many more would be prone to do so if they were better equipped with the necessary knowledge and skills. In many cases, however, this fledgling confidence fades in the face of frustration at the dreary process of socialization in the bureaucracy, where young officers are confronted with tedious and often meaningless routines in land offices and even in ministries, under supervisors who demand only dumb compliance with routines. Tun Razak inspires them "to make precedents, rather than follow them," but many of the chiefs who still govern their careers are not convinced. Instead of reinforcing a disposition to activism, this kind of experience tends to thwart it, except among the lucky minority whose early postings are more fortunate or the stalwarts whose activist inclinations survive initial frustration.

This disposition toward activism is a noticeable trend and not likely to be reversed. It is beginning to erode other attitudes, one of which is the inclination—never shared by Chinese officers—to be tolerant of personal weaknesses among officers and to make generous concessions to personal needs. As achievement values become more normative, younger officers tend to make more demands on one another, to impose and enforce time deadlines, and to attach greater importance to getting the job done.

This shift toward efficacy and changes in their role definition are beginning to change inherited attitudes toward rank and status. Here deeper levels of socialization are involved, and more obvious interests are threatened, but the trend is detectable in conversation and in behavior, albeit still fragile. Equalitarian doctrines which lurk in nationalism and in modern education and greater emphasis on achievement norms undermine the utility and legitimacy of deference to status which inheres in traditional Malay society and was reinforced by the norms of the colonial bureaucracy. Combined with the doctrine that government should help the citizen, especially the Malay peasant, to improve his living standards and to modernize his life styles, the appropriate relationship between official and public is being debated and redefined. The new official defines his role as the friend and tutor of the peasants. He is interested in knowing their needs and problems and in devoting himself to improving their welfare, even though he considers that officials quite properly should maintain status superiority by virtue of their higher education and association with government. The old aloofness and social distance toward the public are no longer considered desirable postures among younger officers who, incidentally, have little experience in how a really demanding clientele can behave.

Within the administration younger officers find the prevailing status ordering increasingly onerous because it is demeaning to them, it is old-fashioned in style, it slows down the flow of work, and its requirements conflict with new-found achievement values. Thus the younger officers echo the prescription of Tun Razak for greater decentralization to simplify and speed up action. But this impatience with the premises underlining the rigidity of the old status values of strict obedience, deference, and passivity is not yet reinforced by the system, which continues to expect and reward more traditional behavior. As a result the motivating effects of their new attitudes toward appropriate relations within the bureaucracy are still precarious. Younger officers often fail to take advantage of the opportunities for initiative and decentralized decision making that are available to them. To conform to established status expectations is safer, and few of the younger administrators yet take risks.

Their attitudes toward politicians and the political process are also undergoing change. Most of the younger officers do not look upon local politicians as attractive characters or upon politically induced pressures on administrative decision making as legitimate, but a minority now concede that politicians do enjoy a different relationship to constituents than is possible for civil servants and that most politicians can be "reasonable" if handled tactfully. They are searching for an accommodation between administrators and local politicians which would continue to exclude the latter from "service" (internal personnel) decisions, but would recognize their role as spokesmen for constituents on matters affecting relations with government, their need to take credit for many of the benefits that government bestows, and even their right to influence the allocation of specific benefits among individuals and groups.

The most decisive break from the older attitude sets is on the theme of efficacy, the much-enhanced confidence of the university graduates that man can and should influence his environment, that he is not totally constrained by metaphysical forces, inherited institutions, and established practices, nor should he be totally dependent on the authority and initiative of higher-status people. Thus he gropes for a new definition of his role as an administrator—active, efficient, technologically competent, modern in style, developmental in substance, socially meaningful, especially in fostering economic growth and in redeeming the Malay peasant from his poverty and backwardness. Of course, he values the civil service highly for its perquisites, security, and prestige, but his career should yield other satisfactions as well, the opportunity to impress the values of the modern Malay—economic progress, social and communal justice, technological efficiency—on the institutions of government and society.

This new-found confidence in their efficacy and the new role definition that it implies can be an important lever for a strategy of induced administrative change. An elite which knows that the world offers opportunities as well as constraints and considers the exploitation of these opportunities to be its appropriate role can be equipped with the cognitive and operational instruments to use its confidence. Economic growth and social opportunity promoted by such achievers can even attack the existential basis of the scarcity which breeds individual pessimism, aggravates social distrust, and contributes to ethnic conflict. They can help moderate politicians to manage the crises that inevitably accompany rapid social change.

5
Blueprint Strategy for Administrative Reform

Origins of Administrative Reform

After Independence in 1957 the Deputy Prime Minister mounted a patient and unremitting campaign to modernize the civil service. His main interest was to speed up the implementation of development projects. His targets were the old ways of the colonial bureaucracy, the ritual pushing of files, the commitment to routine at the expense of purpose, communication by elegant minuting on files through successive stages in the formal hierarchy, and delays in decision and action which thwarted the public and contributed to official corruption. Those practices which impeded the administration of rural development programs, particularly the failure to integrate specialized programs, he dramatized as "the seven deadly sins of bureaucracy." [1]

[1] The seven deadly sins were: (1) interdepartmental jealousy in the course of day-to-day execution of government functions and conflicting departmental policies on the ground in the rural areas; (2) lack of co-ordination between departments in what they are trying to do for the rural areas; (3) lack of complete day-to-day cooperation between government officers on the ground, mostly due to a lack of understanding of each other's task; (4) every department thinking its function is the most important, in other words, too many priorities all pulling at cross purposes and leading nowhere; (5) lack of proper planning in the departments aimed to fit into a master plan for the rural areas; (6) lack of a master plan at all levels for the purpose of achieving the maximum development in the rural areas; (7) lack of sufficient directive control at the top

Tun Razak is not by disposition a patient man; he wants practical, no-nonsense results, and he wants them fast. But he also knew that Malaysia's civil service could not be transformed overnight, and he did not intend to destroy it in order to secure reform. He was prepared for a long campaign. He never seriously entertained the alternative of substituting party politicians or other outsiders for civil servants. Not only did he respect the civil service as an institution, despite its shortcomings, but he feared the consequences of politicization both to the order-maintaining and to the service-providing functions of government. In Malaysia, politicizing the civil service at its higher reaches would also have constituted a social change, the displacement of educated men, many of them Malay aristocrats, by less-educated, grass-roots commoners, men less disciplined and less sophisticated in the ways of government and less moderate on communal issues.

Tun Razak's views on administration deserve mention because they have affected the processes of reform. To Razak what is important in administration is largely a matter of common sense and personal dedication. Reasonably intelligent men, such as those in the MHFS, who have enjoyed better than average educational opportunities, should be able to accomplish most of what modern administration requires if they are properly motivated. To him, deficiencies in the performance of most Malaysian administrators stem more from weakness of character than from inadequate knowledge or skills. There is no plausible reason for an officer in independent Malaysia to cling to colonial habits and work ways, when society requires more of him, except wrong attitudes and inertia which can and should be changed. Razak has attempted to change them by tireless exhortation from one end of the country to the other. He has combined inspiration with pressure and insisted, though with indifferent results, that other ministers, permanent secretaries, and department heads should emulate this

to ensure that government in the rural areas functions as an efficient machine manned by a purposeful, single-minded team, and driven toward one goal only, that of rural development.

136

form of externalized discipline to tighten up performance in the ranks. In the classes of change strategies which are discussed later in this chapter, Razak's exhortations, his attempts to change attitudes and develop a greater will to perform are cultural; his uses of discipline are political; his introduction of new procedures to plan and monitor rural development activities are technological.

He has improvised several tactics to circumvent the normal, sluggish channels of the civil service. One of them is associated with the operations room system previously outlined. The operations rooms represent a simple but ingenious technology for project planning, scheduling, and monitoring, emphasizing the imperatives of interagency coordination, the establishment and maintenance of time schedules, and the participation of elected legislators in the choice of minor projects.[2] Malaysian administrators have learned to use this system and to comply with its requirements; it has imposed an impressive scheduling discipline on construction projects and has forced interagency coordination in their implementation.[3] In this way, he has attempted to bypass the archaic machinery of state government and put his men in a position to ride herd on the functional departments, federal and state, which are responsible for implementing development projects at the state and district levels. To avoid Treasury and FEO controls and the sluggishness of many of the federal ministries and departments, he has set up statutory corporations and assigned them where possible to his own ministry, where he can watch over them. He also established the Economic Planning Unit, which reports to him

[2] Razak did not emphasize the organization of clients or constituents to impose greater responsiveness on civil servants. This would have been contrary to his basically technocratic view of administration. Moreover, it would not be easy to organize rural Malays for this purpose, and in any case he expected that locally elected parliamentarians and state assemblymen would "represent" their constituents in the operations room setting. In this respect his expectations were not realized, partly because the clients were not organized to communicate or press their needs on their representatives.

[3] See Ness, pp. 159–171.

on substantive matters and thus gives him direct control over medium-term planning and the annual development budgets and a strong voice on economic policy.

Malaysian administration has responded to pressures for change in the hectic years since Independence. In virtually every case Razak has been the moving and sanctioning force, so much so that other potential sources of innovation have yielded the field. The process has been complicated by Malaysianization—the rapid but remarkably smooth replacement of expatriates with local men who were, on the whole, far less educated, trained, or experienced in high-level decision making or in managing large-scale action programs than their predecessors.[4] They moved into their new responsibilities precisely when the functions of government were expanding rapidly into new areas of policy under the impulses of Independence, development, expansion of Malaya into Malaysia, and Confrontation with Indonesia. A service which was undergoing such pressures could hardly be expected to absorb more reform than the restless Razak had already attempted.

By 1965 Malaysianization was nearly complete in the public sector, but the performance of the civil service, with few exceptions, was still slower, less imaginative, less service-oriented, and less responsive to developmental priorities than Razak considered acceptable. His view was shared by some of his Cabinet colleagues who were picking up complaints of sluggishness, insensitivity, and corruption through political channels and by a small group of senior civil servants who gravitated around Razak's inner circle of advisors. Professional officers were complaining increasingly about the obstacles to action and to efficiency for which they blamed the MHFS officers who were taking control of the newly formed ministries. The time seemed appropriate for a new push in the direction of administrative reform.

Within the service officers were uneasy. They had become accustomed to Tun Razak's bombardments and felt they were

[4] See Tilman, Chapter 3. At Independence in 1957, expatriates held 61 percent of Division I positions. By 1965 only a handful remained.

complying and accommodating as well as they knew how. Certainly, they felt, they were the most competent, most honest, and best disciplined civil service in Southeast Asia. They had brought the country through insurrection and confrontation and had successfully executed two five-year development plans, but the criticisms were not stilled. They did not feel threatened, for there was no significant attack on the civil service as an institution, but they were becoming cynical about the motives of the politicians and intellectuals who continued to find fault with them. Above all they were confused. What did the critics really expect of them? They were aware of no administrative or policy alternatives to the way they were doing their jobs. Few were familiar with practices, systems, methods, and approaches to administration different from those which they had inherited from the colonial period and had been faithfully trying to maintain. British-inspired higher education in Malaya and Singapore provided no exposure to the study of administration or management and little to the policy issues in modern government. Only a handful of officers had enjoyed the opportunity to study them abroad. Though the service had been softened up by a decade of lectures from Tun Razak, officers were not certain what they ought to be doing differently. The few who had insight about the need for improvement felt they lacked the know-how. It was not easy for a proud and conservative service to be told repeatedly that they were falling short, but they had heard it so often that they began to suspect it might be true. While they were not clamoring for reform, they were prepared cautiously to listen, and a few of their number were even eager.

The groundwork had been laid quietly in 1963, when Professor Merle Fainsod of Harvard University was invited by the Ford Foundation to explore the opportunities for administrative reform in Malaysia. Fainsod's patient investigations and suggestions, stressing practical measures for improving the personnel system, yielded support in some quarters, hostility in others. By 1965, on the eve of the First Malaysia Plan—Malaysia having been formed in 1963—the country faced a minor problem in public finance which threatened the funding of its annual development budget, Tun Razak's special concern. An economy drive was set in motion, which implied the need for administrative reform and drew the powerful support of the Minister of Finance to administrative improvements that would reduce costs. A new Chief Secretary and head of the civil service had taken office who was a cautious supporter of reform. At the University of Malaya, a committee of inquiry, including highly placed representatives of government, was considering the establishment of a new faculty of economics and administration to provide professional instruction that would meet the needs of a modern developmentally oriented civil service. While Confrontation with Indonesia was still an annoying problem, the government was confident that it had the situation under control. Tun Razak was convinced that the time had come for another dose of reform. This time the auspices would be American.

Richard Dye, the Ford Foundation Director for Malaysia, asked Merle Fainsod to return for a more intensive study and to recommend the initiation of a program of action, perhaps along Hoover Commission lines. Fainsod, however, was ill and unavailable. So the Ford Foundation invited John Montgomery of Harvard, a colleague of Fainsod's, and me to undertake the mission.

The Montgomery-Esman Report

Neither Montgomery nor I knew much about Malaysia, having visited it only as tourists in the late 1950's. Our reconnaissance study was to be the kind of "parachute drop" which we would emphatically have deplored in our classes on technical assistance. I was available for four weeks, Montgomery for only two, but our venture into Malaysia was not quite the combination of innocence and effrontery that this short time period might suggest. We carried in our heads a model of post-British colonial administration—a product of accumulated recent scholarship in comparative administration—which served as a reliable orienting system.[5] Its main features, the stratified service dominated by generalist administrators, preoccupation with paperwork routines, precedents, and procedural rigidity at the expense of substantive performance, and the overpowering influence of Treasury controls, emerged quickly in Malaysia. Robert Tilman's recently published study sensitized us to some of the effects of communalism on the structure and behavior of Malayan administration.[6] We were not prepared for the degree of insularity that prevailed in the MHFS, their unfamiliarity with administrative thinking or practice outside the immediate system they had inherited; the impressive operational capabilities of the technical and professional departments; the remarkable dynamism of the private sector and the ability of Chinese contractors to perform virtually any kind of building or engineering job competently and promptly (a major factor in the implementation of successive development budgets); the degree of conservatism and deprivation among rural Malays; the severe lag in postsecondary education and the consequent dearth of high-level manpower, especially of research capability in all fields except rubber; nor for the ingenious patterns of federal-state administrative relations in Malaysia.

But with the help of this initial orienting model, skillful planning by our hosts in the Economic Planning Unit, highly publicized government support, and the openness and candor of most of our informants, we were able at the end of four busy weeks to present the draft of a report and a set of recommendations to Tun Razak. After a shirtsleeve evening session discussing its major ideas with Razak and a few of his close advisors— the Deputy Prime Minister enjoining us to "present the facts straight and forget the soft soap"—we took our leave, re-

[5] Braibanti and associates (pp. 662–666) list 76 major government reports from 1947 to 1964 on public administration in India, Pakistan, Burma, Ceylon, Malaysia, and Nepal. Included are such well-known reports by American scholars as Paul Appleby's on India, Rowland Egger's on Pakistan, and Merrill Goodall's on Nepal.

[6] Tilman, especially pp. 68–80.

drafted the report aboard a plane from Kuala Lumpur to Tokyo, had a fresh draft retyped by a public stenographer in Tokyo, and retouched it between Tokyo and Chicago. It was revised and put in final form by Montgomery in Cambridge, mailed to the Kuala Lumpur office of the Ford Foundation early in September, reproduced and transmitted to Tun Razak on October 15. To the astonishment of the authors, who had expected that their report might serve as a point of departure for further debate and more intensive investigation within the government and would in any case have to be softened and modified before publication, it was endorsed by Razak, approved in principle by the Cabinet, laid before Parliament, published, and distributed, all before mid-March 1966.[7]

Tun Razak's support was decisive. He wanted action and was not prepared to have the report and its recommendations talked to death in a Hoover Commission and ultimately buried by skeptical and cautious officers in the senior ranks of the civil service. Public response as expressed in the newspapers was uniformly favorable, as would be expected for recommendations which bore the imprimatur of the Ford Foundation and promised greater efficiency in the civil service. The public silence of the civil service was more a reflection of their professional self-discipline and their fear of Tun Razak than of genuine support.[8] Though on this as other issues the civil service is seldom unanimous and though a number of pro-

---

[7] John D. Montgomery and Milton J. Esman, *Development Administration in Malaysia: Report to the Government of Malaysia* (Kuala Lumpur: Government Printer, 1966).

[8] The Public Services Commission circulated within the government a lengthy and carefully drafted memorandum reacting to the report. They welcomed many of its proposals, especially those calling for enhanced staff training, but rejected others as based on incorrect factual premises or as unfeasible. The underlying tone was a warning against precipitate acceptance of American reforms that would be disruptive and unworkable in Malaysia. The young officer who drafted this memorandum was subsequently assigned to the new DAU and became an enthusiastic reformer.

fessionals and younger MHFS officers welcomed the report, the prevailing reaction among senior MHFS officers was apprehensive. They feared the report would usher in a spate of radical "American" reforms that would disrupt a basically sound administrative system. The service was not prepared for and did not understand many of the proposed reforms, but it feared that Razak and a new group of American "experts" would install them with excessive zeal and haste. While Razak's decisiveness assured formal acceptance of the report, it also tended to cut off debate and further exploration of its implications among those who were apprehensive without knowing exactly why, but would be most affected by its proposals and could have the power to facilitate or hamper their implementation.

Razak was sold on the report as a practical action document. It was short, decisive, and unambiguous. It sedulously avoided any mention of communal issues which would have been considered presumptuous for foreign advisors and might have generated opposition on those grounds alone. It did not dilate over theory but came directly to the point: Malaysia's administrative system, while honest and effective in providing routine services, is not an adequate instrument of development administration. The "Summary" that follows embodies the tone and major recommendations of the twenty-three–page report:

This report presents a number of recommendations for improving administrative systems in the Federal Government of Malaysia. They are intended to increase the speed, reduce the costs, and improve the quality of governmental services. Our most important proposals call for three major governmental actions:

(1) The creation of a Development Administration Unit in the Prime Minister's Department, staffed by professional management analysts. This Unit would plan and guide the major programs of administrative improvement. It would focus on such government-wide systems as those involving personnel and career development, budgeting and expenditure control, procurement, and contracting. It would also help the departments plan and implement their own

management improvement activities. A contract relationship with a public management consulting firm should be undertaken at once in order to implement this recommendation.

(2) Improvement of the government's education and training programs for all levels of the civil service. This includes first, creating and supporting a graduate program in development administration in the University of Malaya to be used primarily for the post-entry training of Malayan Civil Service (MCS) officers. For this purpose the University will require adequate staffing, both Malaysian and foreign; sufficient advance program-building time; and ready access to governmental agencies. A relationship with a foreign university will be necessary to provide institutional and professional support during the formative years. Secondly, it will be necessary to provide mid-career university-level education for the professional cadres, expanded in-service training activities for the technical and clerical staffs, and periodic staff seminars for top-level officials.

(3) Strengthening the professional competence of the MCS so that it can provide the necessary administrative leadership for this rapidly developing country. Such action will require first the initiation of a rigorous post-entry university course in development administration for all newly selected officers; second, the creation of opportunities for MCS officers to fulfill their careers in specialized areas of government activity; and third, a policy of extended postings for MCS officers in a single ministry or program so that they may become masters of the substantive programs for which they are responsible.

Since the first two of these recommendations involve the use of external personnel, we suggest that conversations be undertaken in the near future with representatives of agencies that might be prepared to assist in making the necessary arrangements for the institutional or personal contracts that will be involved.

Other detailed recommendations regarding improvements in the Malaysian administrative systems and procedures are suggested. Some are stated in general terms, in the expectation that continued study and analysis and an active program of in-service training will provide the necessary details and modes of implementation.

Modernization of administrative systems and procedures in

Malaysia should begin immediately but it should be regarded as a long-term, continuing process.

Four Strategies of Action

The report incorporated four principles which were so fundamental to the subsequent action strategy that they deserve lengthy discussion.

The first principle was to work within the existing structure. This had two major consequences: to accept the legitimacy of an elite corps of officers recruited directly into the service as policy officers and generalist administrators, superior in power and status to other groups of officials; and to acquiesce in Malay control of this elite corps through the existing quota system. As a practical matter, the report would not have been accepted or even seriously considered if it had challenged either of these arrangements. Some quarters had expected that a team of American scholars, drawing on American experience and values, might attack the concept of an administrative class as a barrier to in-service mobility and as a misconception of the administrative function. According to the dominant American model, men in government and industry should begin their careers as professionals or as specialists in a program area or a set of technical skills. As they advance, they either remain specialists or they move gradually into administrative roles. They are anchored in an established profession or program field and while changes from one program to another are not uncommon, they are not the norm.[9] No group of men are tapped as elites from the moment they enter the public service and guaranteed a monopoly of the most powerful and prestigious posts. Men from any professional background or functional specialty can compete for senior administrative positions. To have recommended this pattern would have called for an administrative revolution in Malaysia, and its elites, of whom the

[9] John Corson and R. Shale Paul, *Men Near the Top* (Baltimore: Johns Hopkins Press, 1966).

administrators comprise an important element in this still stable system, were prepared to consider moderate reforms, but not revolution.

More fundamentally, we saw positive merit for Malaysia in a well-trained and motivated administrative class. The abuses which can be attributed to modern "guardians" or "mandarins" have been exhaustively detailed, and Malaysia is not immune to them.[10] In the absence of specific program commitments or instrumental management skills this elite may become pure careerists or sinecurists, consuming themselves in bureaucratic politics, plundering the economy, and hovering superficially and arbitrarily above the substantive activities of government. To protect their high status, they may insulate themselves from public influences and from effective interchange with subordinates. While fully aware of these possibilities, we concluded that they were not inevitable and that the possible benefits for Malaysia of an effective administrative elite far outweighed the risks.

As previously noted, the Malaysian administrative system is deficient in integrative, adaptive-innovative, and conflict-management capabilities. One of the principal strengths of an adequately trained administrative elite is its capacity to communicate freely across organizational lines and among program fields. Since its members are not committed to specific organizations or programs, but are identified with a government-wide service, they find it easier to think of priorities and requirements for programmatic coordination than can officers whose training and experience have been confined to a single specialized field. If members of the administrative elite can be trained and experienced in substantive policy fields and equipped with management skills, they are likely to be oriented to program integration. Moreover, the conservatism inherent in professional and program specialization is less likely to occur among men whose role is to see public problems in

[10] A recent statement of this position is Fred Riggs, *Thailand: The Modernization of a Bureaucratic Polity* (Honolulu: East-West Center Press, 1966).

146

system-wide dimensions, who are explicitly concerned with policy decisions, who are sensitive to political demands and thus to the need for continuing change.

The British model has no provision for political administrators drawn from the ranks of the ruling political party or coalition. Immediately below the ministers are the senior civil servants. Given the available distribution of talents, the prospects for developing competent integrative and adaptive-innovative political administrators and conflict managers in Malaysia are better through the civil service then the political route. Adding politicians to the interstices between the ministers and the senior civil servants would not eliminate the functions of the administrative class unless the civil service was politicized at all levels—which would probably destroy the effectiveness of government. Such reasons, aside from racial politics, which will be treated in the next paragraph, provided a convincing rationale for achieving administrative and programmatic leadership in Malaysia by strengthening the administrative class rather than by dismantling it and replacing it either with politicians or with program specialists. Accepting the existing structure enabled us to propose far-reaching internal reforms— functional specialization in the MHFS, longer postings, intensified training and career development, and selective entry of outstanding men from other services and from outside government at grades appropriate to their experience. Several of these proposals would still have to be battled out because they were perceived as inappropriate and even threatening by a majority of MHFS officers. Accepting the structure and emphasizing measures to strengthen its performance capabilities was nevertheless an approach that might succeed. Attacking the structure would probably abort the reform enterprise entirely.

The closely related problem of the racial quota was even more sensitive. Non-Malays continue to expect that objective and fair-minded foreigners analyzing their civil service will share their own sense of grievance and frustration at a policy which they consider fundamentally wrong. Other foreign observers have condemned Malay privileges, of which the MHFS quota is the most categorical example, as both inequitable in its denial of free and fair competition for public employment and as inefficient, denying the government the services of many able citizens and thus reducing the productivity and morale of the public services. While fully cognizant of these problems, we were equally aware of the political function performed by Malay control of the MHFS. So long as the non-Malays maintain a long lead in education and in every sector of the modern economy, the maintenance of a precarious communal equilibrium requires that Malays, the largest ethnic body, control the government. One instrument of this control is the higher civil service. Four to one is a higher ratio than needed to maintain effective control. The quota distributes severe dissatisfactions to educated non-Malays and it reduces government efficiency in an operating sense, but it does represent an element of rough justice on the scale of intercommunal power. Had we challenged the quota arrangements we would have opened a political sore that could have overwhelmed the report and resulted in its summary burial.

Accepting the existing distribution of power within the bureaucracy protected opportunities for influence. In some situations this might have involved unacceptable costs in other values. Here we did not feel this was the case.

The second major change strategy was to give priority to central government-wide processes rather than to specific operating programs. Central government-wide processes include: the manpower or personnel system—recruitment, placement, training, promotion, incentives, rewards, discipline, and other elements by which public personnel matters are governed; the financial system—the methods and criteria for mobilizing, allocating, controlling, and accounting for government funds; the logistics system—the procurement of supplies and equipment relating to government functions and their maintenance, control, and disposition; and the organization system, the major structural patterns, and management processes. We searched for a feasible method of attacking a fifth process, the production, conversion, and channeling of information, but found no available technologies to deal with these needs on a government-wide rather than a program-by-program basis. The four central systems identified for priority attention involve the availability, deployment, and control of the traditional management resources of men, money, materials, and organization. The practices which governed these systems derived primarily from the British tradition of rigid and centralized Treasury control designed for a small colonial administration operating under *laissez-faire* principles. The dysfunctions of these systems impaired every operating program, particularly those that required flexibility, speed, and competence in large-scale management. The modernizers were resorting increasingly to independent corporations to break away from the constrictions of Treasury controls, but such independence provided only the opportunity, not the assurance that better management practices would be introduced. Experience on this score had not been conclusive. Moreover, the proliferation of independent corporations exacerbated the difficult problem of programmatic integration already plaguing administration.

Development administration focuses on the outputs of government to society. These are embodied in substantive action programs which enhance growth, induce structural and behavioral changes, and manage conflict. It is thus ironic that a reform program concerned with development administration should have to begin with activities which are essentially internal to the machinery of government. Yet these internal processes are critical to the capacity of the operating departments to deliver services to their publics. Improving the performance of these influential internal systems could "loosen up" the entire structure of government and thus enable it to handle a greater volume of more complex demands with greater flexibility, speed, and efficiency. This initial assignment of priority to the central systems precluded the alternative strategy of selecting critical operating programs and attempting to build enclaves of development within them. While this policy had already yielded some success, it was becoming increasingly evident that *the inadequacies of in-*

ternal machinery were severely hampering operating programs. It was our judgment that the first few years of the reform program should concentrate on the government-wide systems. This would not be an absolute priority, and some energy and resources could be simultaneously committed to improving specific operating programs in such sectors as industry, health, education, and rural development. After the initial concentration on modernizing the central systems, priority would gradually shift to strengthening the administration of substantive action programs. This, in turn, would probably extend administrative reforms to building or strengthening participative organizations that would improve the capacity of the public to interact with government agencies and take advantage of public services. As we shall see, this strategy was actually attempted in the organization and the activities of the Development Administration Unit.

Another consequence of the concentration on government-wide systems was to reinforce concern with the most salient group in the civil service, the MHFS. Once it was decided to accept the elite role of the administrative class, any fundamental change in the performance of government-wide systems would involve the MHFS officers controlling the major systems of manpower, finance, supply, and organization. Their role perceptions and operational skills would have to expand to include substantive policy making and the guidance and coordination of action programs. As a logical prerequisite, the government-wide processes which they have traditionally controlled would be reshaped and reoriented so that they might contribute to the implementation of these same developmental activities.

The third strategy incorporated an approach to induced social change which has been identified in recent years as institution building.[11] The institution-building approach as-

[11] The basic model on which this strategy is based is outlined in Milton J. Esman and Hans Blaise, "Institution Building—The Gulding Concepts," Interuniversity Research Program in Institution Building, mimeo., University of Pittsburgh, 1965.

sociates induced social change with new or restructured organizations which develop the capacity to embody, promote, and protect innovations. Change-producing organizations must not only survive in their environment, but also transmit new beliefs and action patterns successfully to other organizations with which they must accommodate and establish compatible linkage relationships. The innovations then become institutionalized, meaningful, and prized within society. The organization also achieves acceptance, becomes an institution, and subsequently faces the problem of maintaining a continuing innovative capacity.

This model of induced reform, an approach that was then being analyzed in depth by a major interuniversity research program, was reflected in the strategic emphasis on a new organization in the Prime Minister's Department. The recommended Development Administration Unit would be a staff agency parallel to the existing Economic Planning Unit. The two organizations would work in tandem to promote and protect developmental innovations, the EPU concentrating on economic policy, the DAU on administrative action. Both could draw on the authority of the Prime Minister's Department to support their innovations. But unlike the EPU, which controls the development budget and foreign technical assistance, the DAU would control no resources. It would rely ordinarily on intellectual initiatives, technical skills, and persuasion, with the power of the Chief Secretary and of Tun Razak available as a latent resource, well known to all parties but to be drawn on parsimoniously.

The institution-building approach meant that the administrative innovators in Malaysia would be concerned not merely with building the new DAU on a firm foundation—though this would be an important concern especially in the early years—but also with managing the interorganizational linkages that would enable them to extend innovative attitudes and practices throughout the government and adapt reforms to the technical and political realities of Malaysian government and society.

The fourth basic strategy was to emphasize technological instruments for inducing organizational and behavioral changes, but to support technological with cultural and political methods. This strategy calls for fundamental exposition. There are three main methods for inducing systems changes: technological (by introducing new methods, work flows, equipment, processing devices, and cognitive information); cultural (by modifying ideas, attitude sets, and role definitions); and political (by allocating rewards and sanctions and by redistributing or threatening to redistribute power). Change strategies which affect large and complex sets of structures and wide ranges of behavior like the Malaysian administrative system must utilize all three approaches, usually in combination.

There are two elements in technological change strategies: the systems or techniques and the understanding or commitment of users to those techniques. If one relies exclusively on installing techniques—a computer, an inventory control procedure, a promotion system—without insuring the users' understanding and commitment, the technical innovations may not achieve their intended objectives. Employees may accept the changes formalistically, acquiescing in the required routines without understanding their purposes, or they may sabotage the new system or use it to produce results identical with the old. Such behavior could reflect disagreement, misunderstanding, fear of consequences, or lack of confidence in their ability to use it for its intended purposes or to adapt it to unanticipated conditions. These have been the fate of many administrative innovations, including an expensive computer installation in Malaysia, position classification in the Philippines, and program budgeting in Korea. To insure the successful use of technologically induced changes, change agents must work simultaneously to introduce the techniques and insure understanding and commitment of influential persons among the groups affected. The latter become the internal adopters and legitimizers of the changes, but the changes they accept may not be identical with those originally visualized by the change agents, who must be prepared to modify them accordingly.

If cultural instruments only are used, changing the behavior of men by the conversion of their beliefs and attitudes, the results will be very slow over long periods of time with no assurance that the conversion will ever take place. The sad experience of nearly every community development program which relied primarily on changing men testifies to this prospect. To attempt to produce motivation to innovate or to change behavior—assuming one knows how to do so— without first providing the instrumental technological resources is a sure prescription for failure, especially in social structures so conditioned as bureaucracies to technological discipline and in societies where change processes have not become institutionalized.[12] Political-change tactics which would reorganize agencies, redistribute responsibility, or shift personnel provide the opportunity for the acceptance of innovations and facilitate consequent behavioral changes, but they may prove futile if the rewards go to persons no different in attitudes or basic motivation from their predecessors or if they lack the knowledge or technical capacity required to effectuate organizational or operational changes.

In the Malaysian situation, as in others involving relatively stable but complex, noninnovative systems, it was our hypothe-

[12] See Lawrence S. Mohr's formulation of the relationships to innovative performance in large organizations of motivation, resources, and obstacles, "Determinants of Innovation in Organization," *American Political Science Review*, 63 (March 1969), 111–126. Much of Tun Razak's inspirational exhortations to Malaysian civil servants have suffered this fate. He attempted to combine cultural and political change tactics, but assumed, often incorrectly, that the officers had as much basic know-how as they required. The officers did not, however, know how to instrument the inspiration that Razak conveyed or to take advantage of the political opportunities. The proposition that their main problem was one of character rather than know-how proved to be incomplete. One reason that Razak decided to call in the Americans and to organize the DAU was his recognition that cultural and political methods of changing administrative behavior unsupported by a strong technological element cannot work.

sis that the most effective thrust is likely to come from an emphasis on technological instruments. This is especially true for foreign-sponsored change processes. Technologically based changes are both more tangible and acceptable to internal change agents and their clients than cultural or political methods. Technological instruments can, moreover, provide the opportunities and the incentives to induce or compel attitudinal changes, even when not directly supported by cultural or political methods.

The hostility of many social scientists to technologically based social change results from their fear that technology implies technocracy, that change agents will inevitably attempt to install prepackaged technologies in societies and among groups which are unable or unwilling to assimilate them or for which they are inappropriate. Since the world of technical assistance is replete with efforts at direct installation or imposition of foreign models, some skepticism is warranted, but technological innovations need not be crudely imposed or installed. They can be adapted while complementary and supportive attitudes and structures are fostered and cultivated. The affected persons can be involved, and a learning experience can occur both for the change agents and their clients. This approach to guided change does not relieve the innovators of responsibility for initiative, for pressure when necessary, for improvising and adapting new methods, for the entire panoply of incentives, pressures, compromises, and concessions which are indispensable to organized action. Technological methods can be supported and reinforced by cultural and political methods with the caveat that the latter can facilitate but not substitute for a primarily technological and thus cognitively based learning process. That technologically based change strategies require learning and local adaptation is not easy to demonstrate to self-assured and zealous foreign experts or to impatient local clients who practice externalized discipline, demand quick results, and expect that methods tested and proved in "advanced" countries can be installed with a minimum of delay to "streamline" local practices. It does, however, comport with the most reliable knowledge available about induced social change in stable bureaucratic systems.[13] Chapters 6 and 7 illustrate some of the problems of working with this doctrine in a society accustomed to externalized initiative and discipline.

Establishing the DAU

After the Montgomery-Esman Report had been accepted in principle and published by the government of Malaysia, the Ford Foundation was asked to provide assistance to set up the new DAU and to launch its program. At the same time, negotiations were near completion for the Ford Foundation, which had been supplying individual specialists for the EPU, to increase its commitment and entrust future technical assistance to the Development Advisory Service (DAS) of Harvard University. The DAS had conducted similar advisory activities in economic planning in Iran, Pakistan, Colombia, Argentina, Ghana, and Greece. The government of Malaysia was eager to draw on the intellectual resources and the reputation of Harvard in the further development of their central planning and economic policy-making capabilities. The leadership of the DAS examined the Malaysian situation in January 1966 and found the prospects unusually promising for a long-term assistance effort in economic planning.

The Ford Foundation and the Malaysians strongly wanted the prestigious DAS to assist the new DAU as well as the EPU, the two activities being considered closely related instruments of economic development. Previously the DAS had not undertaken work in administration, since it had neither interest nor expertise in that field. In this case the pressure of the Ford Foundation, the preference of the government of Malaysia, and their own increasing interest in "implementation" persuaded them to take the plunge. Instead of turning to a

[13] For a discussion of organizational change strategies, see Jeremiah J. O'Connell, *Managing Organizational Innovation* (Homewood, Ill.: Richard D. Irwin, 1968).

management consulting firm with overseas experience, as the Montgomery-Esman Report had proposed, this solution committed assistance to an academically related organization. Instead of bringing in a team to initiate the reform program, it was decided to begin more cautiously with a single advisor who would help the Malaysians to formulate their reform program, expanding its scope and bringing in additional specialized advisors as needs were identified. The DAS asked me to be that advisor.[14]

In retrospect the decision to begin with a single senior advisor knowledgeable in development and comparative administration was a wise one. It was less threatening to the Malaysians, and it avoided the technocratic bias which so often characterizes management firms.

The DAU was formally activated on July 1, 1966. A director was selected from the senior, but not the top ranks of the MHFS. For reasons of interbureaucratic equity, the DAU directorship could not be ranked higher than the top position in the EPU which, at that time, was undergraded. From the beginning the DAU suffered from the modest grading of its top position since every subordinate position was graded proportionately. An officer who had attended a management course in the British Treasury was appointed deputy director. The small organization and methods unit in the Treasury to which he had been attached was transferred intact with its three trained technicians. An enthusiastic young officer who had just returned with a master's degree in public administration from the University of Pittsburgh was assigned to the DAU and was subsequently appointed chief of its personnel and training division.

[14] Since the DAS had no expertise in development administration, it was agreed that the Graduate School of Public and International Affairs of the University of Pittsburgh, which specializes in this field, would backstop the DAU component of this joint project. Backstopping meant research and documentary support, recruiting short-term and long-term specialist advisors, and developing study programs for DAU staff members sent to the United States on fellowships made available by the Ford Foundation.

Shortly after the organization was established and housed in commercial space in downtown Kuala Lumpur pending the construction of a building in the Prime Minister's compound, Professor Fainsod arrived for a month's consultation. He was well acquainted with Malaysian administration from his previous visit in 1963, and he knew several of the key personalities. In a month he helped the new director to design his organization. It would have four operating branches following the main priority areas recommended by Montgomery and Esman: personnel administration and training; planning, budgetary, and financial administration; management services, incorporating the former organization and methods technicians; and state and local administration. Assignment of officers would be flexible depending on work load. Each branch would be headed by an officer at the bottom rank of the senior scale (superscale H) and would have two junior staff members (timescale officers) except for the management services branch which would be initially staffed by the three organization and methods technicians transferred from the Treasury. Except for these latter personnel, the professional staffing would be entirely from the MHFS, and it would be a predominantly Malay agency. Generous leave provisions were established to permit DAU officers, once recruited, to be trained overseas in the specialized areas of modern public administration which had not previously been available to Malaysian students or public officials. The Ford Foundation grant to the Harvard DAS contained generous funding for overseas study fellowships.

A major innovation was a high-level standing committee on development administration. This committee would provide the same guidance, sanctioning, and legitimatizing function for the DAU and for administrative reform as a similarly constituted National Development Planning Committee had for several years provided the EPU in its area. The National Committee for Development Administration (NCDA) would provide policy guidance for the DAU, consider recommendations made by it, authorize the implementation of such recommendations as it approved, and report progress to the Cabinet. The establishment of this prestigious committee composed of the highest ranking civil servants in the country had the effect of reassuring those officers who feared that the DAU might impose hasty and inappropriate foreign-inspired reforms. The Chief Secretary of government (concurrently head of the civil service and secretary of the Cabinet) was designated chairman of the NCDA.

6

Launching the Reforms

Initiating the process of induced social change comprised three interrelated tasks: building a competent and viable organization, designing and managing an action program, and gaining acceptance and influence in the environment. This campaign, as previously noted, was explicitly influenced by the institution-building model of social change. This model postulates an organization (or group of organizations) as the vehicle of innovation carrying on transactions with other organizations and groups in its task environment. Through these linkages it attempts to secure their acceptance of the services it produces and the related innovations. As the environment accommodates to these innovations, the organization which sponsors them and the new norms or action patterns become valued and thus institutionalized. Establishing a change-producing and change-protecting organization is the first step.

Building a Competent and Viable Organization

The organization must be both competent to perform its technical tasks and committed to innovative goals. Since the organization is the principal resource of change agents, they must be prepared to invest in it both materially and normatively. According to the institution-building model, competent and committed *leadership* is a critical determinant of success. Leadership formulates and diffuses a *doctrine,* a statement of the purposes, priorities, and styles of the new organization; translates this doctrine into an action *program,* taking into account change readiness and change resistances in the environment; procures, develops and deploys *resources* in staff, finances, facilities, and information required to maintain the organization and induce supportive behavior in its linkages; and develops and manages a *structure* of production, authority, and communication (internal governance) that enables the organization to act effectively and to manage its external linkages. The structure must incorporate a system of material and psychic incentives and rewards sufficient to maintain staff commitment in the face of frustrations which inevitably accompany efforts at induced and guided change.

The critical variable is leadership. The more innovative its activities, the more it departs from established behavior and norms, the more the organization is likely to encounter skepticism and resistance and the more technically and politically competent and normatively committed its leaders must be. There is no guarantee that such leadership will be available to any organization. After Tun Razak secured the acceptance of the Montgomery-Esman Report and the decision to establish a DAU, he turned to other problems and left the organization of the new unit and the selection of its leaders—following normal conventions—to the civil service itself. The man selected to be first director of the DAU was an intelligent, experienced, and conscientious MHFS officer. He was, however, not an innovator, and like most of his MHFS colleagues, he had little previous contact with modern social thought or administrative practice. He was sensitive to his senior colleagues who desired to protect a tried and true system from hasty and radical reforms.

It was incongruous that so conservative a man should be selected to lead a reform program from which so much was expected so soon from the informed public and from Tun Razak himself. Their hopes were in any case destined to be disappointed for two reasons: they oversimplified the processes of administrative reform with the optimistic hope that the magic of "reorganization" or "streamlining" could quickly and surely "break bottlenecks," given will and drive; and the new organization had painfully little trained capacity to undertake substantial reform. Malaysian education did not include the study of modern administrative concepts or practices, and the job experience of young officers socialized them into the existing conservative pattern. There was no reservoir of trained talent available outside government and even if there had been, it probably would not have been tapped. A more rational policy would have been to select a group of promising younger officers and send them overseas for two years of intensive professional education so that trained cadres would be available when the organization was launched. Such forbearance, however, seldom guides institution building, for the claims required to sell such activities create their own demands for an immediate manifest presence.

The need to balance great expectations against limited capacity would have challenged imaginative, dynamic, and committed leadership. It imposed an unwelcome burden on a director who regarded the DAU job as another assignment that falls to a civil servant during a long career. After a year, he transferred to another post. He had completed the basic staffing of the DAU, had established the framework of an ambitious overseas training program for its staff, and presided over the inauguration of the initial group of projects. His successor, selected this time by Tun Razak, was an energetic, moderate reformer who had studied public administration overseas and had organized the Government Officers Staff Training Center.

Much of the burden of leadership during this initial period fell by default to the advisor to the new unit. To the public and to Tun Razak I was effectively in charge of the experiment. Malaysia was still an open system, and Malaysians were accustomed to having foreigners serve in operational roles. As a man primarily interested in results, Razak made no fine distinctions between advisors and operators. When visiting the DAU early in its career to demonstrate his interest and inspire its staff and with the director present, Razak turned to me and exclaimed: "Professor, you will have to toughen up your officers!" I had visualized my role as a resource person. I would advise the director on matters of organization, program choice, and tactics; I would help the officers to define their problems, design their research, consult with them as they conducted their inquiries and review their results; I would intervene with outsiders—the Ford Foundation, the Harvard Advisory Service—and even with senior Malaysian government officials when this could be effective. I would not be operationally responsible, for I had seen too many organizations that failed to become institutions because foreign "experts" did the work, while the local people failed to develop commitment to an organization in which they were not making the important decisions and taking responsibility for results. In this situation, however, I was coopted, like many foreign advisors, into an informal leadership role, providing intellectual support to the formal leadership and helping them to decide what to do and how to do it. Above all, I was to develop the younger staff members, the oncoming generation of leadership.

Interpreting the vocation of the DAU, formulating and enunciating its doctrine internally and even outside fell by default to me as one of the authors of the report that inspired it. The function of doctrine is to develop common understandings and cohesiveness within the organization and to project favorable images of its purposes and expected behavior to the external public. The doctrine which evolved combined the themes of development, efficiency, and public service. The doctrinal statement that was published and circulated throughout the government emphasized the importance of long-term and overall improvements in the government's administrative machinery, their contribution to successful economic and social development, and the importance of the DAU's cooperating with other departments both in the development and implementation of changes. This statement of operational style, designed in part to reduce the threat to client agencies, disturbed some DAU officers who feared that the absence of "executive authority" would deny it real influence. They wanted authority to compel operating departments to adopt the DAU's recommendations. This attitude, springing from the tradition of centralized control and externalized discipline, conflicted with the innovative theme that imposed solutions to management problems tend to undermine administrative responsibility, can in any event be subverted at operating levels, and cannot develop a commitment to continuing self-improvement, which is the enduring value of administrative reform in a stable bureaucracy.

The diffusion of doctrine to the public during the first year was an inconclusive process because the leadership did not forcefully exemplify or interpret it. Within the unit, the small staff of less than a dozen professional officers also had difficulty interpreting some elements of this doctrine. On the question of basic orientation they split into two groups, one primarily committed to innovation and change, the other, including the director and the former technicians, concerned primarily with improving efficiency within established patterns. As already noted, that part of the doctrine which involved operational styles was a source of discomfort to many of the younger officers, who were eager for quick and fundamental changes. Some ambiguity in doctrine can be useful to an innovating organization since it permits varying emphases to coexist and allows leadership to draw on a choice of themes in appealing to different external publics and even in program development. Under the circumstances, the DAU's original doctrine, focusing on the need for and the benefits of administrative innovation and reform, provided a combination of themes that could appeal to a broad set of publics and sanction program feasibility. Despite some reservations, the staff could identify—many enthusiastically—with the main elements of doctrine and new staff could be recruited according to their willingness to accept it.

The first problem of the DAU was to assemble and train a staff and to form an effective organization. Its staff had to be drawn from the younger ranks of the MHFS. Fortunately the young officer who had just returned with an American master of arts degree had served with the Public Services Commission and the Federal Establishments Office and knew personally most of the younger officers in the service. He was able to persuade the director of establishments that the DAU needed officers with some operating experience and thus, unlike other agencies including even the EPU, should not have to accept raw recruits direct from the university, and more important, the DAU's work required a special kind of officer with strong analytical capabilities and preferably with continuing interest in administrative problems. Therefore the DAU would not be assigned officers at random, but could bid for those who seemed intellectually and personally most suitable, including men who had outstanding academic records or overseas training in administration, preferably both. Such officers were hard to find, and several attractive candidates could not be pried away from other departments. The roster of MHFS officers studying overseas was scrutinized and from this list were selected three whose positions were kept vacant until they returned. Indeed two of them were directed to remain abroad for several additional months to take courses specifically related to the jobs they were expected to fill in the DAU when they returned.

Over the first year of its life, the DAU assembled a group of young, enthusiastic, change-oriented, and well-educated officers without peer in the Malaysian civil service. The opportunity to break out of routine roles and to innovate and the prospect of advanced training overseas provided them with plentiful psychic and material incentives. But their enthusiasm was not matched by technical competence. The officers themselves recognized this and it inhibited their initiative and undermined their credibility among clientele agencies throughout the government. This deficiency could be mitigated only partly by a judicious choice of activities requiring minimum technical skills. It was imperative that first priority be assigned to training these officers at the postgraduate level in public administration, preferably in degree programs, so that they would return both with solid training and with impressive credentials. It was also clear that general training in modern public administration—behavioral, quantitative, and institutional—would not suffice. Though it was important that the officers have this conceptual and analytical equipment, it was equally important that each returning officer also bring back a set of technical or programmatic skills which he could begin to adapt and put to use, for there were no other officers yet in Malaysia from whom he could acquire these skills on the job. Thus it was agreed that each DAU officer would be sent to the United States as rapidly as resources would permit—actually at the rate of three or four a year—for degree study in public administration, plus a specialized subfield of administration such as public finance, project management, intergovernmental relations, job evaluation, personnel incentives and staff relations, rural development, and computer applications. They would receive specialized training in class and in specially arranged intern assignments.

In many organizations, there is a trade-off between long-term investment in staff training and short-term operational performance. With the DAU this was only partly true. It was virtually impossible for the DAU group assigned to financial administration, for example, to have any influence with the proud and hard-nosed Treasury officers until they could demonstrate at least an equivalent knowledge of modern financial administration. For the DAU staff there was a deep uneasiness that they were expected to deal with such problems as technical management methods without the requisite knowledge. The first priority, therefore, was to build the professional equipment of the young staff and thus their competence and confidence. In the first year of operations three officers were sent abroad and two already overseas were coopted and assigned for further training. The second year three others were sent to the United States for degree training in public administration plus a selected administrative specialty, and it was expected that this pattern would continue for another four years. As a short-term expedient, an American specialist in management analysis was added to the DAS advisory component to assist DAU officers in analyzing simple problems in management operations.[1]

The government was generous in releasing DAU officers for training on full-pay leave, but it was not clear how generous

[1] David Harner's main purpose was to conduct a nine-month training program in basic management technologies for selected officials, who would then be assigned as the nuclei of management staff units which the DAU was urging the major ministries to establish.

they would be in allowing the DAU to retain its trained staff. Implicit in the government's agreement to accept assistance from the Ford Foundation, for both the DAU and the EPU, was a commitment to invest in these units over an extended time period so that they might become centers of expertise and innovation. Therefore officers drawn from these agencies and trained abroad should have been permitted to return, combine their skills with other officers similarly oriented, and remain with the same agency for several years. This doctrine ran afoul of a longstanding personnel practice, under which MHFS officers were not only transferable to any position within their service, but at promotion time they must be transferred since their original agency had no job for them at the higher grade. For the DAU this meant that as its young and highly trained officers became available for promotion, they would either be transferred out or their promotion sacrificed. Ultimately neither the DAU nor EPU could expect to retain all the officers they had trained. As they advanced they would move to positions within the area of their specialization in other agencies. This could provide the innovating agencies the opportunity to "colonize" linked organizations in critical posts with their own men. In the short run, however, these units must be allowed to keep their trained officers if they were to develop the institutional capacity to promote and protect the innovations for which they were established. To achieve even short-term staff continuity would thus require changes in the larger personnel system.

Gaining Acceptance and Influence in the Environment [2]

In managing a program of reform it would not be enough to build a strong change-promoting and change-protecting organization or to launch a series of far-ranging developmental or

[2] This section owes much to John Hanson's study, *Education, Nsukka: A Study of Institution Building among the Modern Ibo* (East Lansing: Michigan State University African Studies Center and Institute for International Studies in Education, 1968.)

reform activities. It was also necessary to cultivate and maintain a favorable climate of reform among those groups in the environment on whom short-run success might depend or who could facilitate future progress. Since these reforms were government-wide in their implications and could be blocked or facilitated at numerous points, it was important to identify linkages beyond specific activity relationships which might influence the program and to scan the environment continuously for signals that might indicate opportunities or trouble. While the DAU relied heavily on technological change tactics, any far-reaching reform is also a political process. In dealing with the larger environment, institutional leadership can respond defensively to pressures or it can attempt to assume the initiative in reaching out for contacts. Institution builders tend to be sensitive to their dependence on a favorable external environment and thus to reach out for supports. Five broad strategies were attempted.

The first was to identify with popular change-oriented slogans or themes which evoke sympathetic responses and would identify the DAU, its doctrine, and its activities with the forward-looking spirit of the times. Beginning with the Montgomery-Esman Report, the doctrine of the DAU, including the speeches written for high officials like the Chief Secretary of Government, attempted to relate administrative reform to "decolonization," "development," "modernization," "efficiency." Because of hesitant leadership and reluctance to arouse excessive expectations, the organization's initial information output was modest. What there was, however, attempted to relate administrative reform to popular, forward-looking themes and slogans.

Second was to establish normative links with the oncoming generation and speed generational changes. A board of studies composed of influential government officials and educators had recently recommended the establishment of a new faculty of economics and administration at the University of Malaya. The main purpose of this new faculty was to prepare young men and women for modern roles in government and industry. It would provide more rigorous and relevant training than the arts sub-

167

jects, particularly Malay and Islamic studies, which were the main routes for entry into the public services. Within the new faculty there would be a division of public administration providing both degree and diploma instruction and ultimately postgraduate study. This teaching program was a natural link for the DAU, and it was cultivated intensively. It was important that the teaching staff and the students in the new faculty, especially its department of public administration, sympathize with reforms. There were strains in the institutional relationships between university and government, for most of the teaching staff and their students of all races shared an antigovernment bias. Opposition personalities who tended to be more articulate than government spokesmen were far more popular on the campus. The two worlds were sharply differentiated and mutually distrustful. Many academics did not see service to government as a legitimate role, and many politicians and administrators were not unhappy to keep the academics (whom Tun Razak dubbed the "theory men") at arm's length. The DAU would undertake to change that.

Shortly after my arrival, I was asked by the Ford Foundation and the dean of the faculty of economics and administration to help the latter shape a curriculum and design a long-term development plan for the proposed division of public administration. The curriculum and the development plan which were worked out and adopted would influence the teaching programs of future administrators. Any teaching in political science or administration would be innovations in the local university curriculum, but administration oriented to development was a double innovation. Moreover, the program included an internship for students in a government agency, another innovation which would be regarded with suspicion by government because it threatened to open the hitherto protected precincts to outsiders who might not "understand," or might misuse information or violate the Official Secrets Act. Members of the DAU staff, particularly its advisors and its staff members returning from the United States with graduate degrees, have been close to the division of public administration, have participated in its teaching programs, and thus begun to shape the outlook of students and future civil servants. This preservice instruction was in addition to the diploma in public administration for serving officers—a program which was piloted through government by the DAU.

A related element in this strategy of identifying with the oncoming generation was the organization of a professional association, the Malaysian Society for Public Administration (MASPA). Its objective was to establish a continuing pattern of communication among members of the administrative class and the professional services, appealing particularly to the younger, better-educated, and more change-oriented officers. "Its formation was also spurred by the recognition of the need to promote development consciousness in the public service, to orient it from a colonial administrative system to one which emphasizes positive action for national growth and development." [3] DAU officers took the initiative in organizing the MASPA and provided most of its initial leadership.

On the premise that younger, better-educated officers would be more likely to sympathize with, accommodate to, and even sponsor the innovations associated with this long-range reform effort, the DAU used its influence to maintain the early optional retirement age of fifty for civil servants. Rapid generational turnover provides the opportunity for better-educated and better-trained younger officers with modernizing ideas and skills and an enhanced sense of efficacy to move more rapidly into positions of influence.

Third was to cultivate legitimatizing channels to sanction change proposals. One important way to attenuate the threat of innovations and to bring the weight of established authority behind them is to have them sanctioned by processes regarded as highly legitimate within the system. This was the wisdom of the decision to set up a National Committee for Development Administration composed of the most senior officers in the

[3] *Persatuan Pentadbiran Awam Malaysia—MASPA* (Kuala Lumpur: 1968), p. 1. Volume 1, number 1, of its semiannual journal, *Tadbiran Awam,* appeared in November 1970.

service and charged with the responsibility of reviewing and appraising every major reform measure proposed by the DAU before it is approved for implementation. This committee, comprising mature and responsible officers, met faithfully at least one full morning each month under the chairmanship of the Chief Secretary, reviewing the DAU's work program and specific recommendations. Their approval meant that no outrageous, exotic, or unworkable schemes were likely to be perpetrated on an unwary and hapless service. It also reinforced the DAU doctrine that those most directly concerned should not only be consulted, but where possible should participate in analyses leading to the framing of action proposals. That this approach provides at least a suspensive veto to those who may be resistant to changes cannot be denied. But since few permanent changes can be imposed on stable structures and since DAU doctrine conceives of change as fundamentally a process of induced and guided organizational learning, nothing was lost by this procedure. The sanctioning of the NCDA was a powerful persuader to change-resistant groups to rethink their interests and begin to accommodate to the inevitable.

Another legitimatizing channel for reform was the program of weekend seminars for sixty top officials of government, the permanent secretaries, department heads, and key senior officials in staff roles. Once before the reform program began a weekend seminar occurred, but, lacking a carefully prepared agenda and an agency to give it continuity, the practice lapsed. After the DAU was established, the Chief Secretary agreed to reinstate the weekend seminars. Each session would be confined to twenty selected officers from the top management group of sixty. The seminars would be held away from Kuala Lumpur where the participants would be beyond the reach of normal office pressures and have a set of carefully drafted papers around an important administrative theme to guide the discussions. Seminar sessions were to be held every two months so that three separate groups would meet on each topic and two different topics could be covered each year. The staging of the seminars and the preparation of problem papers in the name of the Chief Secretary would be done by the DAU. Because of unanticipated events, a turnover in the office of Chief Secretary, and inevitable religious holidays, only one cycle was held the first year, which the DAU considered insufficiently intense to have a sustaining or reinforcing effect on the thinking of the top managers. The officers themselves requested more frequent conferences as the sole opportunity for senior officers, particularly MHFS and professionals, to review common problems. The reformers looked upon these seminars as opportunities to gain greater insight into the concerns of the top officials, to influence their attitudes along lines compatible with reform, and to sanction innovational and reform proposals by exposing them to this influential forum.

The early success of the weekend seminars led to another proposal which would have expanded and institutionalized this process. It called for a conference center for senior officers—a Tun Razak center for development administration—where senior officers would meet with politicians, educators, businessmen, and other leadership groups to study nationally significant policy or management problems. Each conference, a few days to a few weeks in duration, would be guided by carefully prepared research. The capablity to produce policy research would have to be built into the institution. These conferences would not merely educate senior officers and sanction reforms through their approval, but would serve as an adjunct to the national policy-shaping process. This proposal would provide another important avenue for intercommunal communication at top levels as well as for participation from different institutional sectors in reviewing major national problems. The Tun Razak Institute was incorporated in the training report as approved by Cabinet, but at the time of writing had not received the go-ahead sign from the man after whom it was to be named.[4]

The fourth strategy was to cultivate nongovernmental organizations. Though such groups exert little effective pressure on government except through political parties, the maintenance of a favorable climate for reform required some modest attention to these linkages. The employee unions were virtually ignored because of the poor communication between the MHFS

[4] The training report is treated in detail in Chapter 7.

officers who control staff relations and the unions dominated by lower-status, non-Malay officers. The newly formed Malaysian Institute of Management, drawing on senior management personnel from the foreign (but not from the Chinese-owned) corporations and from government enterprises, had a natural interest in the DAU and in government administration, which was cultivated by DAU officials. The United Malay National Organization, as the senior partner in the Alliance government, was interested in the DAU's accomplishments in order to fend off expected criticism from the opposition, to take credit for the DAU's successes, and to feed information about its achievements into the party. An informal flow of information developed between the young executive secretary of the UMNO and a group of his former schoolmates among the DAU officers. In addition, the DAU officers attempted to induce the UMNO executive secretary to use his influence to initiate seminars among Alliance Party politicians—perhaps jointly with civil servants—to review the appropriate pattern of relationships between civil servants and politicians which the former felt were being violated by aggressive political interference in administrative operations.

Fifth was to establish and maintain close links and visible public association with power centers, especially the Prime Minister's Department and the Deputy Prime Minister.

A new, innovative organization must look to its enabling linkages—to those individuals and bodies that can insure and protect its authority to operate, its access to resources, and its power to achieve results. Institution-building research has demonstrated that leadership must avoid cultivating enabling linkages to the exclusion of other groups in the environment because enablers tend to pass on or to be superseded. An organization which has developed no other compatible linkages may not survive the departure of its enabler.[5] While the DAU was

[5] See Gilbert Siegal's study, "Development of the Institution Building Model: Administrative Department of Public Service in Brazil (DASP)," mimeo. University of Pittsburgh, Interuniversity Research Program in Institution Building, 1966.

conscious of the need to build supports broadly and attempted to do so, it also needed enablers, and in Malaysia there were two—the Chief Secretary who controlled the Prime Minister's Department in which the fledgling DAU was a unit and the Deputy Prime Minister, Tun Razak.

Fruitful linkages with two successive Chief Secretaries were established and maintained without strain. In each case the Chief Secretary who first feared that the DAU might initiate radical (American) changes too rapidly was soon mollified. Tun Razak approved their apparent support of reform measures, and soon DAU officers were writing their major speeches on administrative matters. The DAU also added to their resources, for unlike the Economic Planning Unit, which reported directly to Tun Razak on substantive matters, the directors of the DAU reported faithfully to the Chief Secretary. The first two Chief Secretaries were not enthusiastic reformers, but they listened to the DAU's proposals. In most cases they endorsed and supported its initiatives; in one dispute with the Treasury the first Chief Secretary intervened critically and decisively. His successor followed suit in an even more important case involving the FEO. On a few matters they were unable or were unprepared to translate their support into effective action, but for the most part their relationship to the DAU was supportive.

With Tun Razak, the problem was more complex. He was impatient for results, which meant primarily the elimination of delays in the implementation of action programs. He was not opposed to longer-term, more fundamental systems changes, but he also wanted early tangible results. The Montgomery-Esman Report anticipated this problem and advocated the establishment of a small group of expediters in Razak's office to break operational bottlenecks and to follow through on complaints. These men would be installed in the national operations room to monitor and act on shortfalls in project implementation. One such officer was actually assigned an expediting role in the Prime Minister's Department, but he got no effective results. Tun Razak hoped that the DAU might identify and deal with such problems on its own initiative, but this did not happen.

173

Partly for lack of staff capability, partly to protect longer-term relations with operating agencies, the DAU's leaders did not feel free to conduct inquests into administrative performance unless invited into specific situations. Its analytical capacity was confined during its first year to three former organization and methods officers, and they were heavily engaged. Moreover, several delays that seemed easy to solve on the surface proved to involve far-reaching and controversial organizational and procedural changes.

It was Razak's hypothesis that a principal cause of increasing complaints about petty corruption resulted from the slow movement of paper in government offices. This facilitated extortion by officials and induced the public to pay dilatory clerks and technical assistants for speedier service. When the DAU failed to solve this problem by its own initiative, Razak established an anticorruption agency under a young and zealous legal officer assisted by a corps of full-time investigators. This measure took some of the heat off the DAU. Though Razak continued to refer procedural complaints to the director of the DAU and to press for immediate results, he was increasingly reconciled to the longer-term nature of results that might be expected from the DAU. He loyally participated in events it sponsored, identified himself with its purposes, and conveyed the clear impression that it must be treated liberally in its quest for resources.

It appeared to the DAU staff that Razak, whose support they craved, did not regard the unit as a prime contributor to development activities; the director of DAU was never included in Razak's intimate circle of advisors; Razak did not boast as much to foreign visitors of the reforms associated with the DAU as he did of the well-publicized operations-room system which DAU officers knew had long since ceased to innovate; nor did he ask DAU personnel to write his speeches on administrative matters. To the DAU staff this was a source of regret and anxiety and of some relief. Perhaps he was leaving them alone, waiting for the agency to pay off on longer-range reforms, to enter more directly into development activities, while its officers gained greater experience and training and thus greater capacity to produce results. Meanwhile his support seemed solid enough, and the unit was building functional and normative links at multiple points in its environment—the Treasury, FEO, permanent secretaries, and state governments.

Designing and Managing an Action Program

Programming the activities of the DAU was a matter of the continual balancing of four key variables: priorities, pressures, opportunities, and capabilities. *Priorities,* as already indicated, were the central government-wide systems, but these were not absolute, for a gradual shift was expected in the direction of substantive developmental activities. Both the senior advisor and some of the younger officers occasionally displayed what may have been undue impatience in prematurely shifting these priorities in the absence of strong pressures, attractive opportunities, or special capabilities. The priorities not being absolute tended to drift toward the preferences of some staff members, but in the main they held reasonably firm during the first few years. *Pressures* were the demands from the environment for the DAU's attention, which varied enormously in their intensity and saliency. A request from Tun Razak would supersede every other claim on the DAU's resources. The Chief Secretary could also exercise a strong influence on its program and so could the NCDA. Casual requests from less powerful sources—which came in at the rate of several a month—could be ignored with impunity if they registered low on the scales of priority, opportunity, and capability. *Opportunity* reflected the difference between change readiness and change resistance among key participants in institutions that would be affected by a proposed DAU activity. Where the DAU's intelligence indicated that change resistance greatly exceeded change readiness, opportunity was considered negative. Sometimes this required preliminary testing during which the tactics used by the DAU might enhance clientele receptivity. The DAU was surprised at the change receptivity of the state governments, those citadels of administrative conservatism, to proposals for modernizing many features of land administration. There are several indicators of favorable opportunity. Among them are the perceived ratio among affected clienteles of benefits to costs, the prospects for quick and painless results, and the provision of useful services. *Capability* is a measure of the technical resources available to an organization to undertake a commitment. In the DAU's early history, priorities, pressures, and opportunities were continuously outrunning its capabilities. It was necessary to turn projects away or to undertake only those where capabilities at a minimum level matched requirements, or to resort to expedients like additional foreign advisors to supplement inadequate expertise, while the organization was training its staff in the conceptual and analytical equipment necessary for their jobs.

In deciding to take on an activity, the DAU's leaders weighed each of these variables. If all of them were positive, the project was a strong candidate for choice; if all were negative, rejection was indicated. But choices were never that simple. Seldom could the factors be weighted equally. Thus strong pressure from an enabling linkage might outweigh negative evaluations of all the other factors, and lack of capability might be in absolute constraint even when all other factors were favorable. The processes of choice derive from the imperatives of steering or guiding an organization through uncertainty, rather than any possibility of maximizing or optimizing a single value.[6] The number of variables was too great to deal with in maximizing logic. So choice was made by judgmental weighing of the four variables, plus others not stipulated in this analysis (like the strong interest of a staff member) and by evaluating the consequences of the available choices to the entire reform program and to the DAU as an institution. One of the recognizable distinctions between an organization which is on its way to becoming institutionalized and one that is not is the degree of autonomy it can exercise in the choice of its activities. In this respect the DAU scored well in its early years.

[6] Sir Geoffrey Vickers, *The Art of Judgment* (New York: Basic Books, 1965).

A subtle factor of choice, already mentioned, was the relative emphasis on innovation and efficiency. One group in the DAU's staff and in its significant linkages visualized the unit primarily as an organization and methods shop, concerned with procedural problems and with squeezing greater efficiency from existing structures and systems. The other group expected the DAU to emphasize major systems changes and innovations in the outputs of government. The two trends coexisted, competing for influence in the choice of activities and in the image the unit projected to its clients. Which approach was taken in a particular case depended partly on the disposition of the DAU's leadership, but more fundamentally on the change receptivity of affected clienteles and the models and techniques of reform that the DAU could muster. The latter may have been the more significant.

Two of the DAU's major ventures were the contrasting cases of program budgeting and land administration. In the first case the DAU had a plausible and tested technology of financial management to replace the prevailing system, which by common agreement was no longer functional. Simultaneously a few key Treasury officials became convinced that the inherited system might be beyond repair. With land administration, involving complex issues of agriculture, land use, and revenue policy, the DAU had no alternative set of policies or practices, nor were state officials in charge of land administration convinced of the need for far-reaching systems change. So the DAU opted for organizational and procedural improvements that would rationalize the existing system, hoping that these measures might be preludes to more far-ranging but undefined systems changes in the future. In some cases there was no such choice, like an order from Tun Razak to clean up the long queues in the registration department, a classical organization and methods job. But should the Treasury accounting system be changed or should new procedures and machines be installed to patch up the existing system? Should the procedures for determining industrial tariffs be speeded up, or should a new approach to tariff protection be explored?

A change agent must do more than recognize a problem. He must have a plausible alternative to offer a client in place of present arrangements. Plausible alternatives are a necessary but not sufficient condition to insuring the acceptance of innovations, for they may generate conflicts and resistances where vital interests seem threatened. In the absence of plausible alternatives, the change agent must rely on experimentation—which many line administrators are not prepared to accept—or fall back on incremental improvements in the form of greater efficiency, which in many cases is both less disturbing and quite sufficient. One limitation to the DAU's capabilities in the face of opportunities in its early years was the paucity of plausible alternatives that its untrained staff could muster or even understand. This virtually insured—even if it had not been reinforced by cautious leadership and conservative clienteles—that the weight of choice would favor approaches to increased efficiency rather than innovations and systems change.

Linkage Management

Before analyzing the main lines of the DAU's action program, it might be useful to indicate how the managers of such an innovating organization orient themselves to the environment they are attempting to alter. While institution builders must look inward and invest in their organization so that it may develop the capacity to carry out action programs, their ultimate payoff is their ability to make an impact on the environment. Thus they must focus on their external relations. Their relevant environment is not an undifferentiated mass, but rather a set of structures and sometimes individuals which control certain values, have interests of their own, and with which the change-oriented institution must attempt to establish and maintain compatible relationships. Different organizations have different degrees of saliency to the subject institution at any point in time.

In Diagram 1, I have attempted to map these relationships. This is a simplified, graphic presentation of the environment as it might be visualized by those responsible for guiding an innovating institution like the DAU. In the inner circle are the organizations or individuals who comprise the *critical linkages,* those which can vitally affect the outcomes of the institution's fundamental purposes and even its survival. For the DAU these were Tun Razak, the Chief Secretary, the Treasury, the Federal Establishments Office, and the Economic Planning Unit. On the outer circle are *secondary linkages,* those structures or groups which the innovating organization must influence and with which it carries on some transactions. Their degrees of saliency vary and shift over time. For the DAU an operating ministry like Commerce and Industry might be more important than

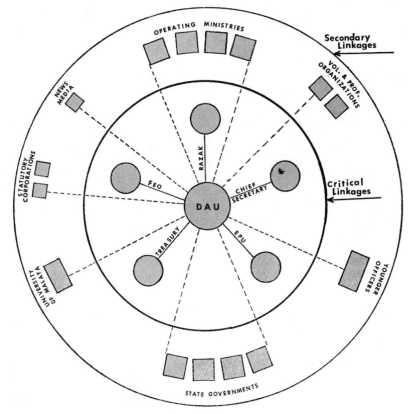

Diagram 1. Linkage map of DAU, 1966–1968

the state government of Trengganu. The degrees of difference, though not indicated in this simple map, are important to the leaders and are included in their own more detailed intellectual maps.

The linkages are live channels through which flow information or other elements of value by which the parties attempt to fulfill their own objectives and exert influence upon the behavior of others. Four major purposes of the innovating organization are served by these linkage relationships:

First, they transfer new norms and patterns of action. Thus the DAU attempted to induce the Treasury and ultimately the operating ministries and departments to accept radically new approaches to the processes of allocating and controlling financial resources.

Second, to gain and maintain support and to overcome resistance and thus insure continuing access to resources, authority to operate, and compatible relationships. The DAU was vitally interested, for example, in protecting its relations with Tun Razak and in overcoming resistance in the FEO to the idea of specialization in the MHFS.

Its third purpose is to expand its scope of action. The EPU was successfully induced to relinquish to the DAU its control over project management. The DAU was less successful in its efforts to expand into the field of rural development.

Last, they insure inputs for its operational requirements and outlets for its products or services. The DAU was thus concerned with insuring recruitment through the FEO of able officers and inducing operating ministries to set up new management staff units employing graduates of its training courses in management analysis.

It is strategically important that the initiative in these transactions be assumed and maintained by the organization which desires to exert predominant influence. Depending upon the resources available, it can deploy a number of persuaders—new ideas, legal authority, financial benefits—to induce the linked organization to accommodate to its purposes. In the case of the DAU, its chief persuaders were the latent support of Tun

Razak, its ideas, and its ability to present them and convince others that their interests lay in accepting its proposals. Influences inevitably flow in both directions, since the linked organizations also have interests and the capacity to assert them. At times the innovating organization must respond to unexpected developments and may find itself forced to react to unfriendly initiative or even to go on the defensive. This happened to the DAU when the FEO suddenly attempted to absorb the unit wholesale, but one of their enabling linkages, the Chief Secretary, was induced to protect them. An organization which is on the defensive or in retreat for an extended time soon loses its capacity to innovate in its struggle to survive. To maintain an innovative thrust it must retain preponderant initiative in its linkage relationships, even though it occasionally adjusts and accommodates.

The managers of an institution which continues to innovate must maintain surveillance of the condition of its critical linkages. They must also scan the environment for opportunities and dangers in its secondary linkages and in relationships which have not yet been identified as linkages. This feedback affects both the planning and the adjustment of action programs. A linkage relationship which is not working signifies trouble and draws the attention of leadership. Such problems may be met by: (1) *technical corrections or additional resources* without programmatic changes, when the dispute is about means, not objectives (thus the DAU increased its staff commitment to a computerized employee records project to compensate for the failure of the FEO to provide its share of project personnel); (2) *compromise,* as when the DAU accepted a lesser relaxation of Treasury controls on interfund transfers than it had originally proposed; (3) *mutual accommodation,* like the DAU's agreement with the EPU that the two agencies would cooperate on matters of project administration, with the EPU having the major voice over project choice and the DAU over project execution; (4) *withdrawal,* as when the DAU pulled in its horns, at least temporarily, rather than risk what it considered an unpromising conflict with the Ministry of Rural Development over proposed changes in the administration of rural development; and (5) *combat,* as when the DAU mounted conflict strategies offensively to compel the Ministry of Commerce and Industry to accept its proposal to reorganize the administration of industrial development programs and defensively to fend off the efforts of the FEO to encroach on its control of the management analysis function. The more innovative the organization's purposes, the more its leadership will be engaged in strategic decisions regarding external relations and the more energy it must devote to the planning and surveillance of its linkages. The surveillance process, fortunately, yields both difficulties and opportunities, like the aforementioned unexpected receptivity of state governments to its package of reforms in land administration.

As in any system of action, the external linkages are not only bilateral; they may be shifting coalitions and other cross-cutting patterns which produce varying combinations over time and over specific issues. Leaders not only must regulate relations within their organization, but must also be prepared to manage these dynamic external bilateral and coalition linkages. Some they initiate, others they react to. Some may be essentially supportive like the DAU's relation with the EPU; others like its relations with the Ministry of Rural Development contained elements of tension; others varied with the issue and the requirements of coalition politics. Organizations committed to innovation and reform must expect some conflicts in their linkage relationships, many of which their activities generate, and the dimensions frequently cannot be accurately predicted. So far as they initiate contacts, they must make tactical judgments by weighing their estimates of priority, pressures, opportunity, and capability and then learn and adjust with experience. If they press their priorities too far, they may outrun their capabilities or embroil themselves in unmanageable conflicts. If they are too cautious and too prone to accommodate, they may betray their innovative purposes as the easy price of survival.

7

The Initial Action Program

For a new and modestly staffed organization, the DAU in its first three years spread widely, if not always deeply, into government operations. It paved the way for centralized procurement and supply management in the Treasury, with specialists from New Zealand playing the key technical assistance role. It provided a full-time American advisor to train officers to staff new management units which it hoped to activate in the major ministries. It produced the first organizational and functional handbook of the Malaysian government.[1] At the invitation of a royal commission, it explored the organization and management of the vast national education system. At the request of the Cabinet it examined the structure of ministries and experience since Independence with ministerial organization. It conducted forty studies of organization, procedures, work simplification, and computer installations in specific government operations, the majority of which were accepted and implemented. These ranged from a computerized central staff records system to the reorganization of the Institute of Medical Research, the maintenance of government vehicles in the Public Works Department, the issuance of identity cards in the Registration Depart-

---

[1] Government of Malaysia, Development Administration Unit, *Organization of the Government of Malaysia* (Kuala Lumpur: Government Printer, 1967). This handbook provided a useful public service. Its main value to the DAU itself was in compiling the detailed information which represented the first systematic increment in its major resource of information.

ment, and a revised accounting system for the Army's paymaster general.

This chapter reviews five major projects illustrating the kinds of problems the reform movement encountered in its early years. These projects attempted to improve performance along the integrative and the adaptive-innovative dimensions of administration. They were directed at four basic classes of administrative problems: (1) those concerned with increasing the effectiveness of bureaucracy in administrative management activities, such as training for development and program budgeting; (2) those attempting to produce and guide behavioral changes in large and dispersed constituencies, like rural development; (3) those attempting to provide additional incentives to small and specialized clienteles, like industrial promotion; and (4) those attempting to improve the effectiveness of developmental services provided directly by government, such as land development. Combinations of technological, cultural, and political change tactics were employed, with primary reliance on technological methods, but with considerable attention to cultural and to political tactics in classes (2) and (3) respectively.

While the DAU maintained its priority on government-wide systems, it involved itself also in major policy areas and in procedural studies. Earlier than its blueprint anticipated, it faced a crisis on the priority question, which was related directly to the effectiveness of its linkage management. This, in turn, involved the relative status and power of its leadership in relation to the leadership of linked institutions, the resources it could deploy in these relationships, and the accuracy of its initial assumptions about the responses of linked organizations to the DAU's reforms. In fact, the responses of some of them were predictably passive or negative. Others were so much more sophisticated than the blueprint anticipated that, by embracing at least verbally the substance of reform, they threatened the premature obsolescence of the fledgling sponsoring organization. These unexpected contingencies in its institution-building strategy are discussed in this and in the final chapter.

The thin slice of time that this experience covers—little more than three years—in introducing changes into a stable bureaucratic system in a nonrevolutionary society precludes any claims for major impact on the behavior or the outputs of government. The substantive outcomes of these efforts for the cohesion of the polity or the effectiveness of government as they might be felt by Malaysian citizens in the quality of their lives or in their opportunities or satisfactions cannot yet be evident. The more reasonable test of these first few years is whether a significant program of administrative reform and development was launched and whether the prospects that it can be sustained are good.

Training for Development

This was perhaps the fundamental project undertaken by the DAU in its early years. It was at the top of the priority list, since staff training and development had been strongly emphasized in the Montgomery-Esman Report as esssential to modernizing public personnel, one of the central government-wide systems. Though there was no pressure for expanded staff training, there was no significant opposition or resistance. Regarding opportunity, the large prospective clienteles were likely to be favorable since training promised civil servants a wide margin of benefits over costs. Moreover, the DAU's capabilities to undertake this project were favorable. It required relatively less technical skill than many other projects; a young officer recently returned with an American masters degree in public administration was available as chief investigator and an experienced New Zealand advisor in the Government Officer's Staff Training Center was recruited to work on the project.

The project began by gathering facts from questionnaires and intensive interviews of senior administrators and officers responsible for training in central government ministries, departments, statutory corporations, and state governments. More than two years passed between the initiation of the study and its final approval, virtually without amendment, by the Cabinet. The three-hundred-page, tightly reasoned report was the most comprehensive survey and analysis of public service training ever conducted in Malaysia.[2]

Its diagnosis emphasized the prevailing neglect of post-entry training and staff development, except in such technical specialized services as telecommunications, customs, and police. There was virtually no formal or organized training in supervisory or administrative activities at any stage in any officer's career. Specialized education in all but a few professional fields was unavailable, and the same was true of opportunities to upgrade or update pre-entry education. Training had little relationship to career development, since many officers returning from overseas study were assigned to posts unrelated to their training and a high proportion of overseas training opportunities were accepted because courses were offered by foreign governments or institutions on a grant basis, not because they met the specific needs of the Malaysian service. There were few incentives to officers for self-improvement through education. There was no effective central government leadership to establish policies or to supervise programs which would help to increase the productivity of staff or officers to improve their career opportunities. Recent government efforts to provide a central training facility through the Staff Training Center had been inadequate in scale and insufficient in quality to meet current, not to mention future, requirements. The net effect was a growing lag in the capacity of the civil service to perform as the policy and management problems of government became more complex, the rate of change accelerated, and technologies became more and more specialized. The report found these deficiencies to be particularly dangerous in the administrative areas—in policy shaping, program development, and management at all levels of government.

The report then pronounced a doctrine for staff training. Among the themes it reiterated were (1) the need for training

[2] Government of Malaysia, Prime Minister's Department, "Training for Development in West Malaysia," Joint report of the Development Administration Unit and the Staff Training Center, mimeo., Kuala Lumpur, October 1968.

and retraining at multiple points in an officer's career in the substantive knowledge and operational technologies required by modern government; (2) the imperative of specialization within both professional and administrative services and of keeping abreast of new developments in all fields; (3) the importance of relating post-entry education and training directly to the management of each officer's career; and (4) the necessity of establishing clear government responsibility to effectuate the high priority that post-entry training must be accorded in Malaysia's administrative future.

The underlying intention of these innovations was to produce behavioral change—to replace the dilettantism, immobilism, and anti-intellectualism that dominate much of the civil service, especially its administrative class, with policy-relevant knowledge, professional skills, and developmental commitment that could capitalize on the increasing sense of efficacy among the younger generation of officers. Relying primarily on cognitive knowledge and operational skills is essentially a technological approach to behavioral change, but there was also the expectation that post-entry education and training would foster value changes and shifts in role definition, thus reinforcing technological with cultural change processes. An evaluation and promotion system that rewards performance more than seniority would add a political dimension to this change strategy.

These principles were applied to each main group of officials: the administrators, the professionals and other program specialists, and the technical and clerical services. The most dramatic chapter dealt with the administrative (MHFS) group. Because it contained the most intensive analysis ever published of this elite corps and because its recommendations were more far-reaching than any previous attempt to reform a post-Independence administrative service derived from British colonial tradition, extensive extracts from that chapter are reproduced in the Appendix. It pleaded for (1) a three-week induction course for all new entrants into the MHFS; (2) an eight-month diploma course in development administration at the university in the third year

187

of service prior to confirmation; (3) specialization within the MHFS and midcareer training in their field in courses extending from four months to a year or more in Malaysia or overseas; (4) advanced management training for all senior officers except those selected for advanced training in a substantive specialty, the latter to become masters of an important area of public policy; and (5) periodic policy-management conference programs for senior officers until their retirement.

Prominent in these proposals were recommendations for specialization or concentration within the MHFS. A detailed analysis of the activities currently performed by MHFS officers, a projection of the functions likely to accrue to the MHFS in the future, and the aggregation of these into broad combinations to permit meaningful concentration and still provide ample mobility and paths of advancement yielded seven areas of career concentration or specialization: administrative management, foreign affairs, economic administration, social development, rural and agricultural development, urban affairs and local government, and internal security and defense. These recommendations were designed to achieve concentration and expertise in these broad functional or program areas, while retaining the policy emphasis, systems-wide orientation, integrative capacity, ease of communication, and flexibility of assignment characteristic of an administrative elite.

Each officer, upon completion of his diploma course at the university, would select an area of specialization. His subsequent assignments and future academic training would ordinarily be within one of these seven broad fields, so that successive postings and academic opportunities would build upon previous experience and produce officers who would be masters of a broad functional or program area. This would equip them to gain the confidence of the more specialized professional departments and thus provide more effective administrative leadership. The venerable concept of the administrative generalist would be modified and the pattern of frequent and aimless shifting from job to job eliminated. At the most senior levels, including permanent secretary, assignments would depend less on previous specializations than on demonstrated high-level policy judgment and managerial leadership.

The report demonstrated that the government had provided no post-entry training whatever for more than 75 percent of its Division I officers and that from 1964–1967 only 10 percent of the superscale officers in the professional services had any training opportunities, mostly in the medical and police services. The report recommended a pattern of training and career development for each professional service similar to the one proposed for the MHFS. It advocated increased specialization within the professional services so that engineering, medical, agricultural, and other professional officers who preferred to specialize within these fields should not be discouraged or discriminated against, as previously, in promotional opportunities. Indeed the explosion of knowledge and the speed of technological change make it essential that intensive specialist and refresher training be available at several points in their careers. For the estimated 58 percent of the professional officers in superscale (middle and upper-grade) posts who were performing in administrative roles ("programming, planning, directing, coordinating and policy development") in large installations, state offices, or departmental headquarters, a succession of management and policy-related training experiences were recommended.

To make training productive, the report recommended that "measures be undertaken that would meaningfully relate training to career development of an individual officer . . . to the processes of recruitment, posting, promotion and other terms and conditions of service such as probationary period and examinations." This implied important changes in the personnel system, particularly more thoughtful periodic evaluation of employee performance and aptitude, de-emphasis on seniority as a criterion in personnel actions, job assignments based on careful identification and assessment of officers' aptitudes, capabilities, and potentials, provision of training where possible before the officer assumed a new post, and postings of sufficient duration (e.g., five years) to permit employees to master their jobs. Post-entry training and educational opportunities would be explicitly related to an employee's career development. Because of the growing interdependence of government and the private sector, opportunities should be provided for employees to be detailed to universities, research institutions, and especially private-sector enterprises in order to broaden their experience. To provide more opportunity for upward mobility and to encourage more lateral movement among various services as new technologies create new job requirements, the existing structure of the civil service (its "schemes of service") should be reviewed and made more flexible

The priority assigned to training and career development to fundamentally alter the traditional environment of the civil service would require organizational changes. At the center would be a new directorate of training and career development in the FEO, responsible for (1) manpower planning in the public sector and the relationship of training to projected manpower needs; (2) supervision of all departmental training programs and assistance to them in training resources and methods; (3) supervision of all government-wide training programs and institutions; (4) research into training methods and programs; and (5) external (overseas) training requirements and arrangements. In the latter, the Directorate would be responsible for insuring that overseas training and educational facilities used by the Malaysian government were suitable to Malaysia's requirements, rather than following the previous passive but costly policy of using such facilities as were offered "free", regardless of the relevance of their content. Every ministry and major department would be required to set up a training committee to reinforce and redirect, as proposed by the report, the training activities of existing services.

To effectuate these recommendations, the report proposed the strengthening and expansion of existing departmental training facilities dealing with technical and professional skills and sharing underutilized facilities. It called for radical expansion and upgrading of the Staff Training Center, sloughing off its existing clerical and induction training to state centers and to departmental facilities, and concentrating on two activities—

training the training officers for state and departmental installations and, more importantly, providing midcareer and advanced training in administrative management and certain policy fields. Its physical facilities would be greatly expanded, course content radically upgraded, length of courses increased, and staff specially trained overseas at the postgraduate level in major subjects of instruction, such as project management, planning, finance, personnel, management methods, rural development, and data processing. The Center would be renamed the National Institute for Development Administration (NIDA) and would work closely with the new division of public administration at the University of Malaya, which would concentrate on undergraduate and postgraduate degree education and on the diploma program for junior MHFS officers.

The capstone of this new training structure would be another innovation, previously mentioned—a conference center for senior officers to expand and intensify the experiment in weekend seminars. The Tun Razak Center would not be a staff college in the Henley-on-Thames tradition nor a U.S.-type executive development program, but a forum where senior administrative and professional civil servants, in association with political, business, and educational leaders would consider the country's current and future problems, including communal issues, and review alternative policy and administrative proposals for dealing with them:

What is required for these senior officers is not a conventional educational or training institute where knowledge will be imparted or shared in formal courses. These officers, in most cases, are beyond the stage in their careers where formal courses are required; in any event they can seldom be spared from their posts for the extended periods of time that useful formal courses require. What they need is a centre which can help them to do a better job of formulating and carrying out decisions on complex problems involving public policies, programme implementation, or the improvement of the government's administrative system. Such a centre would help them to anticipate and keep abreast of new problems confronting the country, new technological developments, and new management methods and to participate in discussions which will help to shape policy and action programmes affecting the main lines of the country's development.[3]

This brief summary of the training report suggests its far-reaching implications for public personnel administration in Malaysia and for the effectiveness of government. Specialization in the MHFS, a planned succession of educational experiences and postings consciously designed to develop subject-matter expertise and administrative leadership, management training for some professional officers, and intensive specialization for others were all breakthroughs in the Malaysian administrative context. That the report was accepted by the NCDA after

[3] "The Tun Razak Centre will have the following features: (a) The Centre will be dedicated to national development. Its deliberations will be concerned not only with the present, but with the nation's future. It will search for innovations, changes, and improvements in government policies and operations, changes that contribute to economic growth, social development and political integration of all the communities and regions of the country and to more efficient use of the nation's resources. (b) The Centre must be close to the Prime Minister's Department and the Cabinet. Officers participating in the conferences and seminars organized by the Centre will know that their work will be available to and may influence the thinking of the main decision makers of government. The Cabinet should regard the Centre and its activities as a major resource to which it can assign policy problems and a major source of advice resulting from the combined analysis of senior officials, scholars and leading members of the community. (c) Senior officers will be associated with members of other leadership groups, including politicians, private sector executives, educators, and other community leaders. The co-operation of all these leadership groups is essential to the solution of the problems the country will face in the decades ahead. (d) The conferences and seminars which will take place at this Centre will ordinarily be of short duration. They will be problem oriented and focused by carefully prepared studies or briefs based on research conducted by specialists in the subject under discussion. These specialists will be drawn from government, universities, foreign countries, and from the Centre itself and in some cases will be organized into task forces to develop the working papers. (e) The Centre will employ methods of study and of group interaction that stimulate creative thinking and provide deeper insights into public issues and the leadership role of senior officers."

lengthy deliberation, that the cautious Treasury after agonizing over the financial implications endorsed it as a sound investment, that the Cabinet adopted it as national policy meant that a consensus of influential and authoritative opinion had been convinced of its logic and utility. That its major thrust was consistent with the values of an administrative state and that its emphasis on strengthening the leadership of the MHFS reinforced existing communal patterns in government facilitated its acceptance.[4]

Throughout this clearance and review process, no significant opposition was expressed, but if the report had been exposed broadly in the ranks of the MHFS, resistance would probably have developed to the concept of specialization. For this contingency, the DAU was ready with a program to spare officers already in superscale positions the necessity of specializing, but would institute the process among younger officers who were less threatened and were eager for additional academic training. The main problem was implementation, and here the DAU's blueprint met a powerful obstacle—a linkage that failed to accommodate.

The report recommended that the planning and implementation should be the responsibility of the Federal Establishments Office which "in consultation with the DAU should be given the responsibility of designing and installing the new training system." The DAU looked upon this "consultation" relationship as a continuing opportunity over the next few years to influence the modernization of the personnel system in conjunction with the FEO. But the new and dynamic director of the FEO had other ideas. He had accepted the report with enthusiasm. It provided him with a ready-made framework for making his mark by modernizing the personnel system. Months before Cab-

---

[4] There are many parallels with the far-reaching recommendations of the report of The Royal Commission on the Civil Service (Fulton Committee, Command 3638, London: H. M. Stationery Office, June 1968). The DAU report was sent to the Cabinet before the publication of the Fulton report and few ripples of the radical thinking in the Fulton report reached Kuala Lumpur before actual publication.

inet approval, he had effected a key organizational recommendation, the creation of a new directorate of training and career development which would oversee the implementation of the report.

When this was accomplished, however, the FEO director saw no further need for the DAU's services, including the participation of the DAU officer who was the principal author of the report and two recently returned juniors with American masters degrees. He was a close associate of Tun Razak's and one of the three most powerful MHFS officers. Once the report was accepted he saw no need for an outside agency to participate in an activity within the purview of his organization. If further help was needed, the DAU might be invited, but since the FEO now had its own directorate of training and career development, which was not eager to accept outside tutelage, this was not likely. The director of the FEO was several steps senior in the MHFS hierarchy to the director of the DAU, and the Chief Secretary, to whom the latter could turn for support, was not inclined to challenge the director of the FEO on an issue clearly within the latter's jurisdiction.

Having embraced the DAU's innovations, the director of the still very conservative FEO decided to dispense with the DAU and implement the report on his own. The convention that a management staff agency should be involved in the installation of its recommendations had not been accepted, and the DAU was not politically strong enough to establish the precedent. Paradoxically, the DAU's first great success exposed its greatest vulnerability. It lacked the power to manipulate a critical linkage. It had no confidence that the FEO, unaided, would be able to implement this far-reaching set of reforms, especially such a major systems change as specialization in the MHFS, yet for the moment it had no capacity to intervene. It had been frozen out. Its option to arrange for the transfer of one of its trained officers to help the FEO implement the training report —and thus "colonize" a key linkage with one of its trained products—was not initially pursued. If the FEO proved unable to implement this major reform, the reform program itself would be jeopardized; if it did succeed, the DAU would have no further role in personnel administration, a key government-wide system, its first priority. Was its institution-building strategy coming apart?

Program Budgeting

According to the Mongomery-Esman Report, "revision of the budget system should be a first priority of the new DAU." The inherited system of budgeting provided tight central control of trivia, while large issues of resource allocation, program effectiveness, and operational efficiency were virtually ignored. The annual budget, tightly controlled by the Treasury, was organized by administrative units and by objects of expenditure. Every position from permanent secretaries to gardeners and night watchmen had to be listed specifically in a budget line item. In addition to pages and pages of line items on such "personal emoluments" were sections on "other charges annually recurrent" including travel, stationery, rent, electricity, and maintenance and on "special expenditures," mostly for supplies and durables, including office furniture, vehicles, and laboratory equipment. The budget was not organized according to programs of activity so that the input items could be related to the cost of any product or service the government was providing. Nor could the budget be used to evaluate even the most rudimentary cost effectiveness since unit costs were neither required by the Treasury nor volunteered by the agencies. The agencies did not think quantitatively, nor could they relate staffing to units of performance or output. The central Treasury maintained over-all control of total government expenses—so far as the heavily backlogged cash expenditures accounting system permitted—by setting ceilings for individual departments based on over-all ceilings fixed by the Cabinet, following the inevitable debate between a stability-minded Treasury and the growth-oriented EPU.

Once ceilings were fixed, budgetary deliberations were mostly a poker game. Previous years' estimates were regarded as fixed, and the Treasury concentrated on holding down increases. For most agencies the discussion hinged about the need for additional staff, position by position, or for increments in travel, or for new automobiles or typewriters. Some extremely large items —for defense, education, or MARA—were passed with minimum scrutiny because they were politically potent and the Treasury lacked the capacity to scrutinize them critically and in detail. The entire supply division consisted of thirteen officers, only two-thirds of whose time could be devoted to budgetary matters. Some of them were recent university graduates with little government experience, yet they were expected to pass judgment on the estimates of large, controversial, and complex operating programs. In no case could any officer—except in the case of defense—concentrate on only one department, nor could the budget officers find time to familiarize themselves in depth with the organization, operations, or specific problems of their client agencies. Since the budgeting process in most ministries and departments was handled primarily by clerks—the financial officers being MHFS generalists untrained in finance and subject to frequent rotation—the Treasury officers had little professional support in the operating agencies on whom they could rely for reliable information on costs or on needs for resources.

Once the budget was marked up following Treasury judgment of what was "reasonable," including Cabinet decisions on a few sensitive items, it was presented to Parliament by the Minister of Finance on budget day. Following British Parliament practice, the budget is an issue of "confidence," on which party discipline is invoked and the government stands or falls. It is debated for several days in Parliament as part of a review of the major outlines of government policy and performance with no committee review and virtually no scrutiny of the document itself, let alone its detailed provisions, and is then enacted into law. Once funds are voted, Treasury warrants are issued and departments may spend against specific "votes" (budgeted items), except those for which the Treasury requires prior approval. At the time of the Montgomery-Esman Report, prior approval was required to fill any new position, even if it was included in the budget enacted by Parliament. It was required for any switch of funds (virement) between items of the budget no matter how small or for purchase of any equipment. These controls were justified by the Treasury because of the alleged financial carelessness of many spending departments and because of the need for economy, specifically to retard the rate of expenditure if revenues were accruing at a lower rate than expected or if sudden increases in some budget items required the government to go slow in others. The consequences were not only inflexibility in the execution of programs, but also undermining of the responsibility of line management, where virtually no discretion remained. The Treasury's distrust of line management thus included their senior MHFS colleagues who were permanent secretaries of ministries. This venerable pattern of centralized Treasury controls had worked during the colonial period when government was relatively small and simple. By 1965, the budget having tripled since 1957, it threatened the public administration of the country with paralysis. It was partially in revolt against these practices that statutory corporations independent of Treasury controls had been created.

A further complication was the existence of two separate budgets, the "ordinary" and the "development" estimates. The procedure just described referred to the ordinary estimates— two-thirds of total public expenditures. The development budget was a separate and subsequent exercise. It was determined by the estimates subcommittee of the National Development Planning Committee, chaired by a Treasury man, but it was strongly influenced by the EPU. The EPU, however, was no better equipped than the Treasury to evaluate the technical feasibility or the cost estimates of departmental proposals for capital expenditures. So the rules of political pressure and of "reason" prevailed. The results, however, were pernicious. Development projects were regularly authorized without reference to their implications for ordinary budget expenditures in subsequent years. This resulted in serious misallocations of resources. The Treasury made strenuous and often self-defeating efforts to hold down annual increases in the ordinary budget. But development funds—since "development" was good and could be measured by the magnitude of its expenditures—were relatively easy to get, and the capacity of the Treasury and EPU to scrutinize them technically was quite limited.[5]

The consequences of this built-in bias were predictable. Development projects tended to be built prematurely, elaborately, at excessive cost, and without adequate consideration of the organizational, manpower, or budgetary resources to operate and maintain them. While Chinese contractors could construct facilities efficiently, hospitals, clinics, schools, and elaborate public buildings were used to a fraction of their capacity because trained staff were not available, and irrigation works were idle because state budgets could not finance their operation and maintenance. Even more serious than the low returns and the high capital-output ratios resulting from underutilization, the procedure was starving expenditures that were considered "ordinary" but were essential to the efficient utilization of existing facilities or to the expansion of services really vital to development, such as agricultural research, extension, and marketing. The separation of the two budgets thus tended to underfinance the development of human skills and institutions, neglect development activities that did not involve construction, reduce the utilization of existing facilities, and overfinance construction activities which were doomed to low rates of utilization. While this phenomenon was not unique to Malaysia or confined to underdeveloped countries, the dual budget system tended to exaggerate the bias.

The time was ripe for extensive budgetary reform and the emphasis in the Montgomery-Esman Report helped to sell it, particularly to the Minister of Finance who was hoping for more effective methods of cost control than the frequent, tedious "economy drives" which usually only delayed the filling of jobs and the purchase of supplies. This latent source of pressure was not considered in the DAU's early programming,

[5] For an analysis of this process and its implications, see Douglas H. Keare, "The (Mis)Allocation of Investment in Malaysia," mimeo. (Kuala Lumpur: Economic Planning Unit, August 1968).

though it proved an unexpected asset. The main factor in the DAU's decision to press ahead was the priority it attached to financial management as a key government-wide system directly affecting both the programming and the management of every activity of government. Indeed, it was inconceivable that programs of administrative reform could get very far unless they engaged the financial area.

The DAU's early attempts to recruit an officer experienced or knowledgeable even in the existing pattern of financial administration were thwarted by the Treasury's inability to release such an officer and the lack of alternative sources of such skill. The DAU was compelled to recruit bright officers who could partially compensate in aptitude for their lack of relevant experience or training. But since such officers could have little influence on the proud and conservative Treasury cadre, who were also the most capable group of MHFS officers in the government, it would be necessary to supplement the DAU's capability with prestigious and fully qualified foreign advisors. Meanwhile, the DAU arranged to train its officers overseas in modern financial administration.

Apprehensiveness about the opportunity or change-readiness factor proved unjustified. True, Treasury officers were not accustomed nor would they welcome having outsiders examine their budgetary operations, for they had long been a law unto themselves and their decisions were accepted docilely and with finality by the operating departments. Most of them saw no fundamental problems in the current system of financial controls, and few were aware of alternatives. They were not high in change readiness and would not on their own have invited innovations. But they were sensitive, more than outsiders, to the growing dissatisfaction of their minister with the results of the inherited system, and they recognized that reform was in the air, the Montgomery-Esman Report had been accepted, and it might be time for a cautious look at improving the system. Fortunately the new controller of supply was a man of more than average intellectual curiosity and psychological security, and he was highly respected in the service.

A few weeks after my arrival, he invited me to his office to advise me that he had been reflecting on the financial management recommendations in the Montgomery-Esman Report and thought the problem needed further exploration. Would it be possible, he asked, to engage an expert who might spend a few months with the Treasury, examining their financial procedures and suggesting how they might be improved, recognizing that it would have to be a gradual process over several years, rather than a violent change. The Secretary of the Treasury and his other senior colleagues concurred and so had the minister. Shortly thereafter the process of recruiting an expert began. Thus high priority and an unexpected opportunity initiated a program that may have far-reaching implications for Malaysian Administration.

While recruitment of the expert was under way, another break occurred. The secretaries of ministries—the top civil servants of all the ministries—interrupted their normally uneventful monthly meeting with sharp words about the harassing and hampering effects of Treasury controls and requested that the DAU look into relationships between the Treasury and the operating ministries. To be thus invited was unexpected sweet music to the new unit. The director began cautiously by exploring with the Treasury the problems which were key factors in the ministries' complaints. The result was the selection of four aspects of Treasury control which appeared to be most aggravating to the operating departments: (1) virements—the requirement of Treasury approval for any shifting of funds between subheads of expenditures, however minor; (2) Treasury approval for filling any new position, even when already established and included in the approved budget; (3) the disposal of obsolete and worn-out supplies and equipment; and (4) minor purchases. The actual investigations were conducted by a tough-minded, analytically acute, but financially inexperienced young officer who had recently been put in charge of the financial administration branch of the DAU and was eager to produce results.

Through arduous research in the Treasury's files, he discovered that 90 percent of all virement requests in 1965 were under

M$10,000 and 95 percent were ultimately approved by the Treasury. Concluding that the procedure was an example of control for control's sake, wasted both departmental and Treasury time, delayed action needlessly, diverted Treasury officers from more important matters, and usurped the administrative discretion of line management, he recommended that the Treasury release control of virement actions under $M10,000 to the permanent secretaries of the ministries. The Treasury could withdraw this delegated power from any ministry which misused it. At the NCDA, the Treasury appeared to accept the report, less than enthusiastically and with the proviso that the maximum figure be reduced to $M5,000 to prevent the use of virements to purchase expensive automobiles at the end of the fiscal year ("Christmas shopping"). Delighted at the prospect of the Treasury loosening its control on any subject, the NCDA approved the revision. But implementation did not follow. This was the first instance within living memory that the Treasury had been successfully prodded by an outside force, and the Treasury were sulking in their tents. Unaccustomed pressure from the Chief Secretary was required to induce the Treasury, after several months' delay, to issue the circular that implemented this change in virement procedure.

At the height of tensions over this assault on Treasury autonomy, the advisor on financial administration arrived for his four-month survey. Since his retirement as director of finance for the state of California, Thomas Mugford had served in Indonesia and Jordan and had thus been exposed to non-American financial practices. Soft-spoken and patient, he set about methodically learning the details of the existing system. His task was not simplified by the prevailing tensions over the virements report and later over similar pressure against the Treasury's prior approval of new appointments. Fortunately, Mugford's low-key style surmounted these problems, and after four months, in July 1967, he submitted his brief report (sixteen typed pages and seven pages of appendices) to the Secretary of the Treasury.

This report was a minor landmark in the history of administrative reform in Malaysia. In substance, Mugford the expert confirmed the diagnosis and prescriptions of Montgomery and Esman, the generalists. He advocated immediate doubling in size of the supply division, a movement toward program and performance budgeting beginning with a pilot study and installation in one major ministry, increased coordination between the development and ordinary budgets, training and longer posting for ministry finance personnel and, what Montgomery and Esman had neglected to advise, the overhauling of the accounting system. He proposed that the controller of supply go abroad for a study-orientation tour to observe modern financial management methods and that foreign advisors in budgeting and accounting be recruited to help design and implement changes in procedures and practices. The Treasury accepted the Mugford report in principle, Mugford departed a happy man, but once again nothing happened.

Counsels were divided in the Treasury, and the organization was not to be pushed into precipitate action. Negotiation having proved unfruitful, the DAU faced the unpleasant task of referring this issue to Tun Razak and thus compromising its long-term relationships with the Treasury when an unexpected and critical break occurred. The annual visit of the director of the Harvard Development Advisory Service led to a meeting with the Minister of Finance. The Mugford report was discussed, and two days later the Minister instructed the Treasury to proceed with its implementation. His intervention was decisive. The DAU was asked to recruit an advisor on budgeting, and arrangements were made with the Canadian High Commission to provide an advisor on government accounting. The controller of supply asked for a study tour after completion of the 1968 budget exercise.

It was difficult to recruit a senior advisor in public budgeting at the very time that the Planning-Programming-Budgeting System (PPBS) was sweeping the United States and absorbing skilled personnel in this field. Max Medley, who accepted the appointment, had many years of public financial management experience, culminating in the controllership of the large and sprawling United States General Services Administration. While he was acquainting himself with the local situation and with the officers with whom he would work in the Treasury and the DAU, the controller of supply undertook his three-month study tour to Pakistan, the United Kingdom, the United States, and the Philippines. Upon his return it was clear that he had made his decision. The financial management practices which he had observed in the United States were feasible for Malaysia if introduced and adapted gradually to local conditions. He was prepared to move ahead deliberately, realizing that his main constraint was the unfamiliarity of his staff with the theory and techniques of modern financial management and even greater deficiencies among the officers handling finance in the ministries and departments. Initially he would send members of his own staff, beginning in 1968, to the United States for postgraduate study in public administration, specializing in public finance. He would support in the NCDA the efforts of the DAU and the FEO to upgrade the Staff Training Center and to introduce more advanced instruction in financial administration. He would use his foreign advisor to train his staff and to initiate training conferences with financial officers in the ministries, and he proposed that the next cycle of weekend conferences for permanent secretaries and department heads be devoted to the "financial management functions of top administrators." Clearly he was moving and carrying the Treasury with him, but he was also determined that the Treasury should retain control. He thus proposed that the Treasury establish a financial management systems unit staffed by its own officers and that, by inference, the DAU should terminate its work in this field. The advisor provided by the Harvard DAS should be attached to the Treasury rather than to the DAU. The Treasury was now committed to reform, but on its own steam, at its own pace, and with no outside interference.

To an institution builder, this was a puzzle. Had norm transfer proceeded so far that the DAU, which considered itself the promoter and protector of innovation, could abandon its work in financial management and move on to other subjects? Was the Treasury really converted, and could the changes be sustained without external assistance and pressure? Or was the Treasury attempting to recapture its former autonomy, with no assurance of sustaining the reform momentum? As the Treasury perceived it, they needed no further help (interference). To the DAU, this sudden commitment to reform might freeze as fast as it was generated; external influence and surveillance were still required; and a number of elements in administrative development—the relationship of planning to budgeting, of staffing to work load, of budgeting to day-to-day management— would depend directly on improved financial management so that the DAU could not abandon its concern and active interest. It was the FEO story once again—total acceptance, at least in principle, of DAU-sponsored reforms combined with an effort to exclude it organizationally from their implementation.

The Minister of Finance made it known that he expected tangible progress in budget reform. The Treasury officers felt they must and could move ahead at a faster pace than Mugford had recommended. A single ministry pilot study would not be enough. Striking while the iron was hot, the Treasury issued Circular No. 5 of 1969 which unveiled its first version of the "new budget system":

In accordance with Government policy, the Federal Government is gradually converting its system of budget formulation and execution from the existing system to the "programme and performance budget" system. Initial efforts in this respect for the 1969 budget will include the following:

(a) The major emphasis of the budget examination will be directed to the Ministries/Departments' programmes, and activities thereunder, with less emphasis on the various classes of expenditure employed to carry out the programmes.

(b) The knowledge and expertise of all central staff agencies will be utilized in the budget examinations. Accordingly, the Economic Planning Unit, the Development Administration Unit and the Malaysian Establishment Office and others as well as the Treasury will contribute to the budget examinations.

(c) In order to obtain an integrated and coordinated budget review, the 1969 Development Estimates and the 1969 Annual Operating Expense Estimates will be examined together for each Ministry/Department.

(d) In accordance with (c) above, long term planning and forecasting will be instituted by each Ministry/Department for Annual Operating Expenses. Thus, the Annual Operating Expenses will be projected on a yearly basis through 1973. In making such projections, care must be exercised to provide for built-in increases in annual operating expenses caused by the completion of development projects.

(e) With the major emphasis and focus on programmes, equal consideration must be given to the legislation which authorises and supports such programmes. Therefore, an integral part of the new budget system is the submission by each Ministry/Department annually of a "legislative programme."

(f) A limited number of Ministry/Department estimates will be included in the 1969 budget on a "programme" basis.

This circular also contained an appendix describing the program and performance budgeting system in technical terms and demonstrating how it could be applied to a single agency with identifiable and measurable outputs. The actual reforms accepted by the Treasury went even further than these statements. The Treasury agreed for the first time not to review the gradings of individual posts, but to accept the judgments of the FEO. This decision, relinquishing a detailed traditional control to which the Treasury had clung for more than a decade, despite FEO objection, in turn prompted the director of establishments to request help from the DAU in selecting a training program in the United States where he could send a group of his officers to study job evaluation scientifically because he realized no officers in the FEO were prepared to do more than apply arbitrary and intuitive judgments to the grading of posts. Thus a breakthrough in one area of administrative reform facilitated progress in another.

Each provision in the 1969 budget circular represented a radical change in budgetary behavior in the Treasury itself and among financial officers throughout the government. None were technically or psychologically prepared for these changes. Officers in the ministries and departments had no idea how to proceed, and there were neither detailed instructions nor training conferences to guide them. The Treasury officers who should have been the main missionaries for this new gospel and their colleagues in the DAU were equally confused, for they too had not been introduced to the new system. Instead of following Mugford's advice to concentrate initially on training Treasury officers and departmental financial officials in the elements of program budgeting and to operate concurrently an experiment in one ministry to adapt program budgeting to Malaysian conditions, the Treasury was hurried into introducing elements of a new system, broadcast, without adaptive experimentation, prior training, or even adequate instructions. It was a risky venture into a major systems change, for everyone concerned felt inadequate, uneasy, and threatened. The actual budget hearings differed little from hearings held in previous years because the departments were not able to present data in the newly requested form and the Treasury, FEO, and DAU officers were not certain what different kinds of questions to raise. The departments proved unable to project their annual operating expenditures ahead for five years or to review their legislative requirements, and these provisions were quietly dropped from the 1969 exercise.

Despite this precipitate movement into program budgeting, with its suggestion of manipulative installation rather than adaptive and participative experimentation, the first year of budgetary reform was eventful and promising. For the first time the development and operating budgets of each department were reviewed simultaneously in relationship to each other, even though the double budget was maintained because Tun Razak wanted a separate development budget to dramatize the government's commitment to economic growth and Malay progress. Each department was forced, in most cases ineptly for lack of time and understanding, to attempt to relate its requests for funds to outputs or activities which it was required for the first time to specify. Inevitably this drew higher-level administrators into the unfamiliar tasks of formulating and defending their financial requests and into difficult questions of choice, especially on their operating budgets. Eight departments were assisted in presenting the estimates for their programs broken down into workload and unit costs, the first approach to performance budgeting. And the staff of the Treasury's renamed budget division was increased by 50 percent.

The capstone of this exercise was the *1969 Budget Summary,* in which the entire budget was presented according to major programs of activity and thus made intelligible for the first time to members of Parliament, the press, and the interested public. It analyzed the budget in a form that could be understood by laymen, according to major functional and economic classifications and the action programs of each operating department. This prodigious effort was the product of a small working party in the Treasury, and though it was crude and rudimentary by technical budget standards, it was a breakthrough for Malaysia. The 367-page printed document, issued at the same time as the traditional budget, was hailed by the Minister of Finance as the beginning of a broad reform in financial administration that would control costs, improve the rationality of allocative decisions, and make accurate financial information available to Parliament and the public. The conservative old Treasury was reforming itself and was winning kudos from ministers, parliamentarians, and the press.

The first year's accomplishments were largely mechanical. The logic of program budgeting and the necessary operating skills were still a mystery to all but a handful of officials in the Treasury and their American advisor. An extended learning process was in order, but Treasury officials were slow and hesitant in developing guides for financial officers and operating personnel in the departments and in teaching them to participate in the new system. Treasury officers did not yet consider themselves sufficiently masters of the new system to instruct others. To be praised as reformers, however, was a new and pleasant experience for them, and it was clear in government circles that they were determined to move ahead with financial systems reforms and that the rest of the government would have to conform. Enough momentum had been generated for budgetary reform that the techniques of the new system would surely be in place within the next few years.

The DAU's leadership was thrown off balance by the Treasury's unexpected enthusiasm for financial systems reform, which forced a premature shift in the DAU's priorities, but offered unexpected opportunities to pursue other important objectives. While the Treasury wished the DAU to relinquish financial management reform, they were willing, in turn, to admit the DAU into the budget examining process and to use this process to compel ministries and departments to review and justify their policies, programs, organization, and methods. With its limited power base, the DAU could thus enlist the Treasury's formidable power over funds on behalf of its interest in administrative development and reform. In order to capitalize on this unexpected opportunity in its linkage management, the DAU would have to reorder its priorities and relax its pressure on the Treasury in the field of financial management.

Land Administration

Land administration is a major and complex problem in Malaysia. West Malaysia is fortunate in that it has more good unexploited arable land (about seven million acres) than is currently under cultivation.[6] Despite limited research data on alternative efficient uses of agricultural land—resulting largely from the overwhelming emphasis during colonial days on one highly profitable crop, natural rubber—and despite limited managerial skills, economists estimate that the capital-labor ratio for land development (the amount of capital required to create a single job) is about one-third that needed to create a job in industry. Thus combining plentiful land resources with

[6] In East Malaysia there is an actual labor shortage. Land is plentiful, but much of it cannot be made available for modern agriculture because of traditional tribal claims to large areas where low-productivity, shifting culture still prevails. Moreover, the indigenous peoples do not like to work in modern commercial agriculture.

abundant labor resulting from a rapidly growing unemployed and underemployed labor force would achieve the most efficient use of scarce capital in terms of economic growth and job creation.

There have been serious obstacles to this development. Not the least important is communal. Much of the unused land is reserved constitutionally for Malays. Moreover, the Malay-dominated state governments control the allocation and administration of land and natural resources. They are reluctant to alienate additional agricultural land to non-Malays, either foreigners or Malaysians, which is a chronic source of irritation to non-Malays. It nearly destroyed the Alliance Party in the state of Pahang in 1968, the MCA and MIC threatening to withdraw unless some state land—none of which had been alienated to non-Malays since 1961—could be made available to them. Few Malays have sufficient capital to develop land even on a small scale, particularly tree crops—rubber and palm oil—which require four to seven years before they yield a crop. The federal government through the Federal Land Development Authority (FLDA) has in recent years developed about 220,000 acres accommodating 16,000 families (about 99,000 people), mostly landless laborers, and a number of state schemes have been attempted, with less success but at a fraction of the FLDA cost, which exceeds U.S. $700 per acre. The FLDA operates on too small a scale to make a dent in unemployment; in the past few years new jobs in agriculture from all sources have been sufficient to absorb only 75 percent of new entrants into the rural labor force. Only a few blocks of rural land have been released to the private (foreign or Chinese) sector in recent years. How to satisfy the Malay-controlled state govenments that sufficient benefits will accrue to Malays to warrant alienating "their" land to non-Malay enterprises is an unresolved issue. Some Malays ask why they should share their land with Chinese when Chinese will not share their banks or factories with Malays! [7]

[7] A recently completed comprehensive land capability classification survey conducted for the Malaysian government with Canadian assistance and a recently established Malaysian Agricultural Research and Develop-

There are other obstacles as well. Land administration has been the most neglected area of government. The procedures are anachronistic and in many instances absurd; professional staffs are untrained and buildings and equipment decrepit, reflecting the low priority assigned to this work. Backlogs of unprocessed applications exceeded 150,000 in 1966—30,000 in one state alone—and increase annually. Squatting—illegal occupation of land—has increased in recent years as land administration has broken down. The squatters are not only land-hungry peasants of both races, but also prosperous Chinese businessmen and "syndicates" which exploit the land commercially, often by growing "illegal" crops. Efforts to limit individual applications for land since 1962 and the publication of a new national land code in 1965 have not materially dealt with this problem. Land use is circumscribed by express conditions stipulating which crops can be grown on any parcel of land, so as to enforce a rigid system of tax assessment and to protect farmers from unwise land use by prohibiting the growing of crops which deplete the soils. The effect is to prevent farmers

---

ment Institute should, within the next decade, contribute technologically and economically feasible alternatives to the present overwhelming emphasis on rubber, oil palm, and low-yielding paddy. A very imaginative unpublished paper, "The Role of Land in the Economic Development of West Malaysia, 1966–1968," prepared in 1967 for the EPU by my Harvard DAS colleagues, William Gates and T. J. Goering, developed a full-employment, minimum-income growth model for West Malaysia. It would provide 935,000 new agricultural jobs in twenty years (thus reducing national unemployment to 4 percent of the labor force) on economic sized holdings by bringing 6.9 million acres of currently unused land into production. The total investment cost would be US $4.5 billion, half public, half private, a not unrealizable figure for a strong economy like Malaysia. Aside from formidable managerial, technical, and financial problems, the authors point to the present incompetent system of land administration and especially to the reluctance of state governments to alienate land to private (non-Malay) interests as grave obstacles to the implementation of this program. The logic of this model has evoked frequent pleas by Tun Razak to state governments to open up land for estate development by the private sector, but the response has been reluctant and very slow.

from shifting land use to higher-value crops. Since requests for changes in express conditions follow such cumbersome procedures—requiring a year and a half to be processed—many farmers disregard these provisions and grow illegally such valuable crops as tapioca which the colonial agricultural officers, before the days of chemical fertilizers, proscribed because they deplete the soil. Finally, the decision process has been retarded and corrupted by the centralization of decisions in the executive councils of the state governments, which have taken over the very considerable power over minor land transactions formerly exercised by district and land officers and by state commissioners of lands and mines. They have thus politicized land administration—even on such small transactions as temporary occupation licenses valid only for a year—because they want for themselves the power to allocate the most valuable resource at the disposal of state government. The system not only has failed to respond to changing needs; through politicization, administrative sluggishness, and neglect it has deteriorated and in many areas has virtually broken down. A DAU study revealed the situation shown in Table 10.

Land administration impinges directly on agricultural development, employment, state finance, local and district government, industrial location, and mining, not to mention urban land use. Nevertheless, it was not originally on the DAU's priority list, not having been considered a critical government-wide system. It was, however, a source of deep concern to the Chief Secretary of Government, the DAU's first-level boss. His frequent visits to state governments and district offices and numerous complaints which he and Cabinet members received on the subject of land administration convinced him that the problem was approaching a crisis and that the DAU, his new instrument for administrative reform, should consider it. His interest provoked the DAU's first venture into this subject, a conference of state secretaries, state commissioners of land and mines, and state financial officers. This conference, in turn, revealed an existing area of opportunity, of mild change readiness generated by dissatisfaction with the existing situation, great uncertainty

Table 10. Average time distribution in dealing with certain types of land applications *

Type of Application	Average time taken by land office	Average time taken by other departments	Average time taken by state land commissioners and executive councils	Total average time taken until approval
State land	167	375	22	564
Change of conditions	170	86	45	301
Prospecting permits	256	99	74	429
Mining leases	123	82	65	270
Renewal of mining leases	143	117	74	344
In percentages	45%	40%	15%	100%

Source: DAU: Land Administration: A Study on Some Critical Areas, Kuala Lumpur, Mimeo, 1968.
* All figures in number of days.

about how to correct it, and appreciation that the central government might be able to offer technical assistance without encroaching on the state's jurisdiction over land. At this time an officer with recent experience in land administration and great enthusiasm for management improvement joined the DAU, creating a staff capability to deal with the subject. The initial low priority was thus transformed into a major field of interest.

The April 1967 conference was billed as a "Seminar on Land and District Administration." It explored broadly the changing role of the district officer, the organization and staffing of district and land offices, their relationship with state government and the state secretaries, problems arising from illegal occupation of land, and the current impasse in processing transactions in land offices. The seminar exposed a number of opportunities for further investigation by the DAU. The choice was to concentrate initially on improving management within the main though limited lines of present land organization and policy.

This is where the DAU's comparative advantage lay, where much could be done to increase the capacity of the existing structure to process transactions by minor policy adjustments and relatively simple applications of office management practices, and where the state government clienteles would be receptive to assistance. As these investigations built up a stock of detailed knowledge, points of leverage might be found to influence more complex policy issues where the EPU and the Department of Agriculture could participate jointly on inquiries involving agrotechnical, economic, and political as well as management factors.

The officer in charge of this project began with two operating premises: he would stick primarily to management problems, and he would involve state officials at all stages of his research, since land administration constitutionally was a state responsibility and could not be modified without state consent. He selected as a laboratory and testing station a land office near Kuala Lumpur where the district officer was sympathetic to reform. He asked the recently arrived DAU advisor on management analysis to help design the research. He methodically charted every procedure in the land office and by random sampling determined the average elapsed time for each major type of transaction. He then experimented with a reorganization of the clerical staff in the land office, abandoning the assembly-line system, which condemned every clerk to an endlessly repetitive set of mechanical functions, and substituted a unit assembly system in which small teams of clerks were made fully responsible for the complete handling of a category of transactions. He found that productivity increased by 20 percent as a result of this minor reorganization. He induced a district officer in another state to try the same reform and found that similar results were achieved. By applying work simplification methods to each set of procedures and subject to a few management innovations like simultaneous rather than sequential clearance procedures, improved standard forms, limited delegations by the executive councils to land officers, and a few minor policy changes, he was able to propose revised work flow patterns which would drastically reduce processing time.[8] He also proposed that land office clerks be specialized and not be transferable at random to other work, that land officers be relieved of all other responsibilities and report directly on substantive matters to the state commissioners of land and mines, that the state governments provide the land offices with decent, modern, well-lighted, air-conditioned buildings with modern furniture, office layout, and equipment. He proposed reserving any action on additional staffing, for which land officers had clamored for many years, expecting that increased productivity would make additional staffing unneccessary. He also devised, with the aid of two experienced land officers, an ingenious scheme for eliminating the existing backlogs in the land offices and bringing their work up to date. These recommendations do not represent innovations in management technology. In the Malaysian context, however, they were highly innovative because elementary management technologies had not previously been applied to this field of work.

He frequently tested his ideas with groups of district officers and state commissioners of land and mines and modified them accordingly. When his first draft was ready the director of the DAU called a two-day meeting of representatives of state governments to review his proposals. A few proposals did not sur-

8 Type of Action	Present no. of steps	DAU-proposed no. of steps	Present no. of days	Proposed no. of days
1. Changes in express conditions	66	23	301	35
2. Applications for prospecting permits	88	25	429	64
3. Alienation of state land (group alienation)	28	17	700	190
4. Pocket land alienation *	–	–	564	30

Source: DAU *Land Administration.*

* Procedures not standardized among states or even districts within states.

vive their intense scrutiny, including one that would substitute the title of "land administrator" for the colonial designation of "collector of land revenue," which the officers preferred to retain. These state representatives agreed that each state should set up a small management unit whose officers should be trained by the DAU and which should work with it to improve the management of state and district government, first priority being reserved for land administration. These methods had inadvertently helped to arouse interest in the managerially backward state governments for simple management improvements.

The DAU officer followed up this meeting by trips to each state capital to review the land administration report in detail and to solidify linkages with state secretaries and their staffs and with selected district and land officers. In some cases the chief minister joined the discussions. These visits produced more than eight hundred requests for the DAU's land administration report, which surprisingly became a best seller. Preliminary steps to implement the report, particularly the unit assembly system, were initiated in more than half the states.

Less than two years after the birth of the DAU, a widely diffused process of management reform in land administration was under way. Much remained to be done within the DAU to test and improve the proposed procedures, by the individual state governments to implement them and the implicated revised policies, and by the National Land Council to modify some provisions of the land code and put political weight behind reforms in the functions of politicians on the executive councils. These initial management reforms laid the groundwork for further participation and initiative by the DAU on land policy, now that they had established their credentials and successful linkages with the main clientele in this field, the state governments. The report, for example, recommended a joint DAU-EPU-Department of Agriculture-Federal Land Commissioner study group to review the question of express conditions in land titles. The first tangible product of their work was a new procedure permitting district officers with the advice of district agricultural officers to act on requests to modify express conditions, avoiding referral to the state capital and to the executive councils. The DAU was to be included in future working groups on the organization of large land development schemes, like the 150,000 acre Jenka Triangle project in Pahang and the mammoth 1.2 million-acre Tenggara project which will require twenty years to develop. The problem of land taxation beckoned and beyond was the politically exposive problem of land reform and the communally sensitive issues of access to and uses of publicly held land.

The absence on study leave of the officer in charge retarded at least for a year the momentum of these reforms. The rate of implementation by the state governments varied, but two of the more advanced ones, Selangor and Johore, put them into effect on their own. The latter state reported a substantial reduction in its backlog of land applications and a sufficient increase in land revenue collections to more than finance the modernization of its dilapidated land offices. What had begun as a nonpriority in the DAU's scheme of things had become an important forward thrust, largely because an energetic young officer had moved imaginatively into an area of opportunity.

Rural Development

Rural development was the euphemism for a politically charged, high-priority national goal of uplifting the Malays. Eighty percent of Malays are rural dwellers, and 70 percent of rural dwellers are Malays. Though they dominate the politics of the country, by every other standard rural Malays are the have-nots—in per-capita income, in health conditions, in educational opportunities and attainment, and in modern motivational patterns. The disappointingly narrow margin by which the Alliance Party won the 1959 Parliamentary elections convinced the UMNO leadership that a big push was required to improve the conditions of rural Malays and to convey to this critical constituency an impression of deep governmental concern and manifest forward movement.

The Malaysian apparatus of rural development as improvised

by Tun Razak and his associates has been widely publicized as a highly successful set of innovations in development administration.[9] The operations room and red book system, previously outlined, has been widely praised by visiting dignitaries and highly commended in a book-length study by an American sociologist.[10] The government of Malaysia, through a Development Studies Center in the Prime Minister's Department has invited and paid for groups of administrators from African and Asian countries to exchange ideas on development experience, much of it devoted to expounding the virtues of the Malaysian methods of administering rural development. Malaysia's political leadership, especially Tun Razak, had a heavy psychological and reputational investment in this system.

The announced purposes of the system were to plan rural development projects reflecting the felt needs of the *kampong* people, to speed up their implementation, and to coordinate the specialized activities of the several government departments serving rural people. At each level of government—district, state, and federal—there was an operations room where a development committee, consisting of government officials and elected representatives, met regularly to plan and review the progress of development projects, with the emphasis on implementation.[11] The progress of all projects was charted in large red books and on maps and wall charts so that members of the committee and visiting dignitaries, particularly Tun Razak himself, could determine whether a project was on schedule or was lagging and should be corrected. Razak repeatedly emphasized that the operations room system could not work effectively unless civil servants radically changed their colonial bureaucratic habits, but that the system was slowly having a major effect on administrative behavior, "changing the hearts and the minds" of the civil service away from colonial attitudes and practices

[9] The most authoritative statement appears in "Techniques Used for Developing Malaysia," a pamphlet published in 1967 by the Ministry of National and Rural Development.

[10] Gayl Ness, Chapters 7–8, pp. 142–221.

[11] There are also village development committees, but no operations rooms at that level.

and toward the requirements of dynamic and service-oriented development administration. To facilitate these changes, Razak practiced externalized discipline—surprise visits to district operations rooms, on-the-spot visits to project sites to check actual against claimed progress, reports from state development officers, public rebukes to officers whose projects were lagging, punishment for those who misrepresented their progress, praise and promotions for those who appeared to be conspicuously successful.

Large projects and certain national aggregate data were handled in the national operations room in Kuala Lumpur. The state operations rooms controlled medium-size projects, including those financed by the state governments. The district operations rooms were concerned with small projects, which were supposed to reflect the felt needs of the people and could be completed relatively quickly. The felt needs were expected to be brought to the district rural development committee in its monthly meetings by locally resident Alliance Party parliamentarians and state assemblymen. The projects they proposed were examined for feasibility and costed out by the appropriate technical officer, such as the district engineer or veterinary assistant. If feasible, they were written up, included in an annual "plan," and forwarded to the Ministry of National and Rural Development in Kuala Lumpur through the state development officer. Some projects were accepted by the state governments for financing, but the great majority were sent to the national ministry and there sanctioned—technically and politically cleared—for financing and action.[12] Implementation became the responsibility of the district rural development committee, without having to pass through either national ministries or state government departments. Informally, each district committee was allotted a minimum of M$50,000 per year, but this was no ceiling,

---

[12] An underlying objective of the program, of course, was to maintain the position of the UMNO with its critical rural constituency, and projects were believed to be allocated partly with this objective in mind. In addition to this form of patronage, the rural development program employed a group of "adult education officers" in rural areas, outside civil service. These were invariably UMNO stalwarts.

and district committees were urged to submit more. The fund which financed those minor projects represented less that 1 percent of total development expenditures and was supplemented by a slightly larger fund drawn from receipts of the social and welfare lottery. To the district officer responsible for implementation, rural development represented a new role. He was assisted by the twenty or so technical officers representing functionally specialized departments operating in his district, whose activities he was required to coordinate. Each approved project was included in a "Red Book" and placed on a wall chart; implementation was planned, scheduled, and monitored through this system.

In the district operations rooms emphasis was entirely on small construction projects and amenities—mosques, religious schools, wells, feeder roads, community halls. Tables 11 and 12 indicate their distribution.[13]

Table 11. Minor rural development schemes financed from development budget

Project	1961–1965	1966	1967	Total
Community halls	$11,579,201 *	$ 590,800	$ 461,400	$12,631,401
Rural roads	12,765,356	3,132,151	1,405,174	17,302,681
Rural bridges	4,694,811	1,725,206	596,330	7,016,347
Playing fields	4,331,794	378,210	330,410	5,040,414
Wells and water supplies	5,558,953	600,180	185,937	6,345,070
Jetties	1,092,567	183,610	145,820	1,421,997
Drainage and irrigation works	2,790,858	353,676	229,764	3,374,298
Total	42,813,540	6,963,833 †	3,354,835 †	53,132,208

* All figures in Malaysian dollars (M$3 = US$1).
† Federal development estimates for 1966 were $651 million; for 1967, $690 million.

[13] The source of these data is Mavis Puthucheary, "The Operations Room in Malaysia as a Technique in Administrative Reform," mimeo., prepared for the EROPA Seminar on Administrative Reform and Innovation (Kuala Lumpur, June 1968).

Table 12. Grants from the social and welfare lottery, 1960–1967

Recipient	Number	Amount ($ Million)
Mosques	1,800	27.6
Suraus	1,669	5.7
Religious schools	742	7.8
Temples/churches	644	7.4
Welfare bodies	n.a.	9.8
Flood, fire, storm relief	29	2.8
Other social welfare amenities	210	2.5
Total		63.6

These minor projects were gifts from a benevolent government. They were considered to be "development cover crops" of little economic significance, but as evidence of governmental concern prior to doing larger and more substantial projects like major irrigation and land development schemes. While projects controlled by the district rural development committees thus covered only a small proportion of the government's rural development expenditures, they were the most highly publicized. The modest "cover-crop" concept was often lost in the government's enthusiastic claims, which tended to be identified primarily with the small projects managed through the district rural development committees. A justification for this was that the government responded to the people's felt needs for any reasonable amenities, and they were expected to respond with self-help to solve their own problems. Thus an important stated objective of rural development was to produce behavior change among rural Malays, to make them more self-reliant, progressive, efficient farmers and participative citizens of a democratic nation.

The rural development program, so extolled by foreign observers, has not lacked domestic critics. One school of critics led by Professor Unku Aziz charges that the program did not and could not get to the root problems of Malaysia's poverty, such as farm tenancy, fragmentation of holdings, landlessness, indebtedness, and middleman monopoly and collusive control of rural services including supply, credit, processing, transportation, and marketing. These undermine the farmer's incentive to modernize because they deny him a fair share of the fruits of more productive behavior. Farm income per capita has not increased since Independence, and the number of farmers who lose their land each year exceeds by far the number of those fortunate few who find places in FLDA schemes. Among the major beneficiaries of an activity designed to promote rural Malay welfare have been the Chinese contractors who build the minor facilities financed by this program.

In rural development the government must attempt to communicate with, provide resources and services to, and induce attitudinal and behavioral change among a large and scattered constituency. Characteristic of such situations is ineffective communication between the bureaucracy and their clientele and often the rejection of the former by the latter. In the Malaysian rural economy virtually all the classical dysfunctions in these relationships were present. The bureaucratic agents—the agricultural, cooperative, and veterinary assistants—were too few in number and too poorly trained, both in technical information and in communication skills, to have an appreciable effect on farmers' behavior. They were burdened with regulatory and routine office work and avoided frequent contact with farmers. Government was attempting to improve the technical training of its rural cadres and to increase their numbers, especially in agricultural extension, recognizing that improving administrative delivery systems was indispensable to any significant agricultural development. This was all the more important because government could not rely on the private sector, entirely foreign or Chinese, to serve as change agents by providing new technological inputs and new forms of credit or marketing, but it hesitated to displace them because it feared the political consequences and realized also that it had no available substitutes for the services currently being performed by the middlemen.

To complement administration, government was experimenting with participative institutions, organizing farmers for self-help, for more effective interaction with bureaucratic institutions, and ultimately to exert pressure on government. Here it encountered the problems facing peasants in coping with complex formal participative organizations and the inability of its bureaucratic cadres to activate them. There were no traditional organizations that could be adapted for these purposes. The unresolved competition between the Cooperatives Department with its single-purpose concept and the Department of Agriculture, newly committed to multipurpose farmers' associations on the Taiwan model further strained the government's limited resources. Despite a few provisional successes in demonstration farmers' associations, where the Department of Agriculture was able to commit heavy staff resources, farmers' associations were still shadows in most rural areas. The Department of Agriculture had optimistic expectations that a network of 385 farmers' associations could replace the middlemen in the West Malaysian agricultural economy within fifteen years, but these ideas were not supported by staff development plans that might provide sufficient technical services to the new organizations. Moreover, they underestimated the complexity of the middleman's functions which farmers' associations were expected to replace, nor was there assurance that Taiwan-style farmers' associations, as an institutional pattern, could take root in the Malaysian rural culture.[14]

Rural development was not one of the DAU's priorities even though the coordination of rural services was included in its charter. It had no external pressure or demand from any authoritative linkage to investigate this problem. There was no sign of change readiness to serve as an element of opportunity among the staff of the Ministry of National and Rural Development who, on the contrary, were known to claim a monopoly of interest in this program and to regard the system as sacro-

[14] For the Department of Agriculture's position on farmers' associations, see Mohammed bin Jamil, "The Role of Farmers' Associations in Marketing Agricultural Produce," mimeo., prepared for the National Agricultural Marketing Seminar, 16–18 November 1967. The author is the director of the Malaysian Department of Agriculture.

sanct, a test of loyalty to Tun Razak.[15] The score on priority, pressure, and opportunity were zero, but the DAU did have some capability—an earnest, young officer from a poor rural background who has just returned after a course in public administration in England and was spoiling to work on this problem. To him rural development was the main challenge in Malaysia, and he was not convinced that it was happening fast enough.

He spent three months in detailed study of the rural development committee in a single district near Kuala Lumpur where the young district officer, a classmate at the University of Malaya, shared his interest in rural development. It was the most thorough study ever made of the operations of a district development committee. He analyzed all the minutes of the committee for two years, attended several meetings, interviewed most of the representatives of the technical departments in the district and several of the *penghulus,* village headmen, local politicians, and many individual peasants. His report was in three parts.

The first part confirmed many of the criticisms of the way the system was operating. The committee's deliberations were

15 The Ministry of National and Rural Development created in 1959 was originally intended to coordinate and monitor all the government's development activities. In fact it never did so. It directly controls only about 12 percent of development funds, mainly for the FLDA and MARA which operate autonomously as statutory corporations. Its main efforts have been community development, adult education, minor works, and control of the state development officers. It does supervise the national operations room in Kuala Lumpur, with its elaborate maps and charts, but these are maintained primarily by the operating departments which claim and spend funds and control development projects and programs. The national operations room has no effective monitoring function, nor is it staffed for this purpose. It comes to life only once a month when Tun Razak holds his dramatic regular or special briefings with senior officers and department heads, or when foreign dignitaries are briefed about Malaysia's development institutions and programs. The national operations room has not been institutionalized as a program-monitoring or management-control device.

confined to small construction projects and amenities. It never once considered problems of production or welfare, the ongoing services of government and methods of improving their utility to the peasants, or the utilization of the government's physical investments once their construction was completed. These issues were outside its scope. Such activities as rice production and marketing, control of livestock diseases, fertilizer use, school attendance, or family planning were never included in the red books or on the large wall charts. "Development" was defined as spending the development budget on schedule. Sessions of the committee were dominated by the local politicians querying the district officer and the technicians on the progress of current projects or proposing new projects. The projects proposed always fell into the preprogrammed range—mosques, community halls, feeder roads, wells—which characterized the red book program from the very beginning. Aside from the elected representatives, local people never attended nor was there evidence that they were ever consulted. The report concluded that little effort was made to identify the real needs or even the felt needs of the peasants.

Most of the technicians in the district made no effort to coordinate their work on behalf of their common clients except on projects included in the red books. They tended to pursue routine work oblivious of one another and even of their clients. Except on projects included in the red books, they continued to communicate through formal time-consuming written messages. Their cumulative impact on rural life was negligible. The farmers had no effective way of communicating their needs to administrators, and nothing in the rural development system was changing this situation. The operations rooms system proved to be "only a sort of structural change superimposed on an old system of administration leaving the officials, their method of practices and their mentality very much as they have been before the Red Book." To most of the officials and politicians, the operations room had become an end in itself. Procedures were carefully followed as prescribed from above, but the goal of rural development had been displaced by the means.

He then documented the success story of a district officer, who entirely outside the framework of the operations room and the committee, achieved a spectacular breakthrough in rice production. By mobilizing all the resources available in the district, including the technical departments, religious authorities, and local officials, and by concentrating on a critical set of production problems, this energetic and imaginative man achieved far more tangible benefits for the local farmers and at virtually no additional cost to government than had the district development committee in a decade of minor construction projects and amenities. Specifically, crop yields per acre increased 30 percent over the previous year, fertilizer use increased tenfold, and 95 percent of the farmers planted simultaneously in keeping with water-control schedules.

The third part of the report recommended an expansion of the operations room system to feature the ongoing programs of government, especially those that directly affected production and the living conditions of rural people. Each department operating in the district would be required to develop an annual program of activities; these would be reviewed by the district officer to establish priorities and insure interdepartmental cooperation, e.g., between the departments of Agriculture, Drainage and Irrigation, and the Federal Agricultural Marketing Authority. Together these would form the district's annual plan of operations. Each state department head would visit the district to review the priority and feasibility of the program of his service. Upon approval, the action programs, like increased rice production, poultry marketing, and organization of farmers' associations, with quantified goals where possible, would be included in red books and on the wall charts and would be scheduled and monitored in the manner already established in the operations room system. Thus state and district development administrations would be linked in the planning, operational, and evaluation stages. This new departure would be tested in several districts in a single state to determine its feasibility and to develop and test specific procedures for implementing the new planning and monitoring system. This would build on the existing operations room system, but extend it to a broader range of problems.

The reaction of the staff of the Ministry of National and Rural Development was less than enthusiastic. One of the senior officers, at a meeting that required weeks to arrange, proclaimed that "the operations room system is perfect, it is some of the people—the officers, politicians, farmers—who are at fault." The system had become a fetish, and its administrators were not prepared to budge. It had been valuable in its early days in demonstrating to the peasants the government's concern for their welfare and in inducing officers on the ground to coordinate their activities more informally and to implement projects expeditiously. Over time, however, it had become ritualized, frozen in its original form and thus unable to adapt to new and emerging needs.

Only Tun Razak could unfreeze it, and though he was deeply concerned by the political and economic evidence of stagnation in agriculture and was seeking to overcome it by such new ideas as intensive agricultural development districts and a new research and development institute, such feedback as this DAU study did not easily find its way to him. Neither the director of the DAU nor the incumbent Chief Secretary who endorsed the report were part of Tun's inner circle of advisors on rural development. To get agriculture moving in Malaysia would require far more resources, organization, and social reform than this report recommended, but its administrative proposals represented a start in unblocking a system that no longer was delivering the goods. Yet the DAU was at an impasse. It had ventured uninvited into a complex and controversial program area, had antagonized an important linkage group, but lacked the means to mount an effective conflict strategy or even have its modest recommendations seriously considered at higher levels.

Industrial Development

Unlike rural development, which requires attitudinal and behavioral changes among a large and scattered clientele, industrial development through private entrepreneurship is an example of the class of development administration problems in which government attempts to capitalize on already existing attitudes and behavioral propensities among a relatively small clientele by providing additional resources or improved opportunities for their expression. It is concerned mainly with facilitating growth rather than structural or behavioral change. Prospective foreign investors and local Chinese entrepreneurs are already economic men. They require (1) ready access on favorable terms to resources—land, credit, and perhaps trained labor; (2) information on the availability and costs of the factors of production, on production methods, and on markets; and (3) incentives through tax and other policy instruments to induce them to make their behavior consistent with the government's definition of public policy objectives. In this form of development administration, the problem is to get the administration and some politicians to overcome their propensity to control and regulate and to emphasize instead the promotion and facilitation of desired client behavior. In Malaysia, which has no obvious comparative advantages in manufacturing, a bureaucracy conditioned to routine controls, and ethnic politics in which those benefiting from governmental encouragement and concessions are likely to be of a different race from those controlling government, the administration of industrial development is beset by special problems.[16]

The manufacturing sector of the Malaysian economy began from a very low base at the time of Independence. By 1965 it contributed about 11 percent to gross domestic product and 6 percent to total employment. The average size of firms was small, 82 percent of them employing fewer than ten full-time workers. The first Malaysian five-year plan called for a 10 percent annual increase in manufacturing output, accelerating the

[16] As Malays push into manufacturing through the route of public enterprise, an example of the first class of development administration problems will emerge, to achieve technical competence and behavioral changes in the bureaucracy of the MARA, the agency responsible for facilitating Malay participation in modern industry.

rate of growth in this sector from the average of 8 percent which it had experienced in the previous five years. Presumably most of this increase would come from import-substituting industries and from first-stage processing of raw materials. No priorities for industrial subsectors were stipulated, and indeed so little study or research had gone into this subject and the government had so little capability to do so that no meaningful choice of priorities was possible. Government policy was (1) to create and maintain a favorable climate for private-sector activity, foreign and domestic, through tax concessions, modest tariff protection, and free convertibility; (2) to provide infrastructure such as power, transport, and industrial estates; and (3) to assist with such services as productivity training, industrial research, and standards. Manufacturing would be left to private enterprise except where necessary to strengthen Malay participation and even then the preferred method would be to develop Malay capitalists, not public-sector industry. In 1968 previously established tax incentives (pioneer industries) were liberalized by adding export incentives and tax bonuses for industries that produced a priority product, used large amounts of domestic raw materials, or located in less-developed areas of the country. From 1956 to 1968, 132 "pioneer industries" had been established in Malaysia with paid-up capital exceeding $300 million, but it is not certain how many of them would have set up even in the absence of tax incentives.

The effect of the government's policy was to encourage import-substituting industries protected by gradually increasing tariff levels. Since 60 percent of Malaysian consumption of manufactures was imported, there was room for considerable import substitution, but the Malaysian market is relatively small and likely to remain small by international technological standards. The result could be the development of a small-scale, high-cost industrial structure on the Latin-American model, importing many components, repatriating substantial profits, yielding few export earnings for the economy, providing little employment, and incapable of further expansion. The reality of six makes of cars produced in three very small auto assembly plants all benefiting from tax concessions, import quotas, and high tariff protection, and employing fewer than two thousand workers was a harbinger if the policy of indiscriminate tax and tariff subsidized import-substituting industry continued. According to EPU analyses, the most promising industrial line for specialization appeared to be wood products, but this had not been investigated in detail.

Industrial policy had inevitable racial angles. Like manufacturers anywhere, Chinese entrepreneurs welcomed tax concessions and tariff protection, but were apprehensive of any larger governmental role in industry, fearing that it would be used to promote Malay interests by denying opportunities to non-Malays, by using public funds to subsidize inefficient Malay enterprises, or even worse, by using the power of government to compete with and ultimately destroy legitimate private business. Malay intellectuals and younger politicians were demanding greatly expanded roles for Malays in the modern economy, and this meant industry. If this must be done by the route of public enterprise and by guaranteed Malay participation in new or existing industries, so be it, for to them Malay progress was a much more important value than private enterprise.

The moderate response of the Alliance government was to attempt to encourage Malays without hurting Chinese. The MARA Institute of Technology was created to help young Malays enter the modern economy. After more than a decade of experience in financing and providing technical assistance to small Malay enterprises, MARA is now venturing into larger-scale undertakings. Government has organized a National Investment Company in which eleven prominent Malays have become shareholders and received originally 30 percent of the shares in each pioneer industry. Some of them became prominent members of the boards of large foreign-managed enterprises, but there is no evidence that they have important influence in the day-to-day management of these firms or that they are using the resources at their disposal to develop more broadly based Malay entrepreneurship or management or to spin off truly Malay enterprises.[17] The scheme is regarded with cynicism by non-Malays as the unjustified enrichment of a favored few. This arrangement will not long satisfy more militant Malays, yet to Chinese it is preferable to public-sector Malay enterprise.

Many observers and local participants concluded that if the government genuinely desired industrial development, the organizational arrangements were more likely to frustrate than to facilitate it. Few officers in the government of Malaysia or in any of its agencies had specific training or experience in industrial economics, finance, technologies, or management. Government decisions in this area were scattered over several agencies, none adequately staffed. In the Ministry of Commerce and Industry was an Industrial Development Division (IDD) whose staff reviewed, processed, and monitored requests for pioneer licenses. A Tariff Advisory Board reviewed requests for tariff protection which were actually more important to nearly all prospective investors than the temporary tax relief provided by pioneer licenses. A development bank, the Malaysian Industrial Development Finance, Limited (MIDFL), technically private, but with large government participation and support from the World Bank, provided secured loans to relatively safe enterprises (including Yawata Steel and Imperial Chemical Industries) and had begun to make a few feasibility studies and provide limited technical assistance. MARA was beginning to move into government operated or joint ventures with Malay participation and control. Land must be secured from individual state governments, some of which had established industrial estates, but each case had to be negotiated with state authorities and approved by its executive council. To process pioneer certificates there was an action committee which met once a week and in

[17] See Sumitro Djojohadikusumo. Subsequent to the May 1969 crisis the Government announced a new economic policy which, among other things, establishes a target of 30 percent Malay participation and control in the modern sectors of the economy by 1990, to be achieved by economic expansion and not at the expense of opportunities for non-Malays.

which nine agencies were represented. Its purpose was to speed up, through informal clearance, an earlier procedure that required clearance by slow-moving, formal correspondence. The procedures were as complex and as slow as the organization was fragmented. Applicants were buffeted from one office to another, and those with enough power or political influence attempted to circumvent this process by dealing directly with the Minister of Commerce and Industry or with the Minister of Finance. The impact of any prospective investment on existing industries was carefully scrutinized, so that existing industries would not be hurt by investors benefiting from tax concessions. The effect was to throw many obstacles in the way of a potential investor, to invite influence peddling, and to discourage many legitimate ventures. Each case was subject to detailed and open-ended negotiation on such issues as Malay participation and starting dates. The underlying assumption seemed to be that the government was making valuable concessions to the prospective entrepreneur, rather than an urgent need to promote industrial investment, diversification, and employment.

Responding to frequent complaints about the fragmentation of its industrial development activities and the absence of a strong forward thrust, the government in 1965 resorted to its standard expedient, the creation of a statutory corporation. But it did not free the new Federal Industrial Development Authority (FIDA) from the same bureaucratic processes which created its need. Its chairmanship was conferred on the Permanent Secretary of the Ministry of Commerce and Industry, the same officer who had been presiding since Independence over the existing loose cluster of industrial development activities. The chairman retained his position as Permanent Secretary. Two full years were consumed in the search for a director. The choice fell upon a German administrator with no previous experience in underdeveloped countries at a time when the capacity of any foreigner to exercise direct administrative authority in the Malaysian government was rapidly disappearing. The advent of the FIDA eliminated none of the existing federal agencies embroiled in industrial development nor the control of the states over land. The FIDA was equipped with no funds for credit and no access to funds. Beyond that its charter was ambiguous. Optimists expected that it would soon be *the* government's instrumentality for industrial development, absorbing and superseding the existing fragmented setup. Thus, as with the Economic Development Board in Singapore, a prospective investor would deal with one strong agency, equipped with a full range of services, access to resources, and ability to produce quick and binding decisions that would help him to make and carry out investment decisions. But to the strict constructionists, including the chairman, the FIDA would be primarily an organization for promotion, feasibility studies, and service to prospective investors, but all authoritative processing of actions and all governmental decision making would remain in the hands of the government agencies and civil servants who had always handled them.

The FIDA was activated soon after its director arrived, and it soon became clear that the strict constructionists were securely in control. The FIDA had no effect on existing organizations and procedures except to add another participant. Bitter conflicts soon developed between the new director and the chief of the IDD in the ministry, who refused to yield any of his existing functions, or even to permit the FIDA convenient access to his files. They set up competing and duplicating operations rooms. In these decisions the director of the IDD was supported by the Permanent Secretary, concurrently chairman of the FIDA. Organization and staff recruitment were painfully slow because the stock of qualified persons was so limited and regular civil service procedures were applied. Though it had a training division, there was no provision for staff training. The director had difficulty communicating with the small and modestly qualified staff that he was gradually given, and he was unable to fix priorities either for investigation or for action. Meanwhile he sensed that much was expected of the FIDA, that he had little progress to show and not much more in prospect, that he was exhausting himself in a fruitless battle with the IDD for control of the processing of pioneer certificates, and that his organization seemed like an old-time civil service establishment rather than a development agency. Plagued by these manifold frustrations, the director requested help from the DAU.

The DAU was not unaware of the FIDA's plight. The EPU was disappointed at its failure to move more vigorously into industrial planning and promotion on which it counted for a 10 percent annual industrial growth rate and some help with mounting unemployment. The EPU felt that administrative confusion was blocking many investment proposals. The Treasury was disturbed that the birth of the FIDA had not been followed by the demise of the IDD. The governor of the National Bank was alarmed that his original expectation that the FIDA might become the single, dynamic focal point for industrial development was vanishing. Industry was not one of the DAU's first-phase priorities. It had no officer who knew the field and little spare capacity to divert to the problem. There was some external pressure, but not so potent that it could not have been set aside, and there was little likelihood that the key power figure, the Permanent Secretary of Commerce and Industry, would favor any changes or desired the DAU's involvement. To test the water, the director of the DAU informed the director of the FIDA that the DAU could intervene only if invited by the Permanent Secretary. When the requisite letter surprisingly arrived, the DAU felt committed. It was an important policy area, and the administrative crisis was obvious. The study would acquaint DAU personnel with a range of problems that would certainly concern them more deeply in the future. Though the risk was considerable, perhaps the DAU could achieve some useful, if limited, results from this project.

The DAU officers who conducted this survey soon confirmed the widely held suspicions about the FIDA. Its staff, with few exceptions, was basically untrained in industrial analysis or in the techniques of industrial promotion and was receiving little substantive or administrative guidance from the director, who was concerned mostly with contacting potential overseas investors. Small though it was, the organization was fragmented into nine watertight divisions, there was little internal communication, and what interaction existed followed standard civil service practices of written file passing and minuting. In the absence of priorities, officers worked on *ad hoc* emergencies or on routine processing of pioneer certificates so far as competition with the more powerful IDD permitted. There was no evidence of an industrial development strategy or even of specific promotional efforts. What should have been a vigorous and enthusiastic young organization showed unmistakable signs of stagnation. There were no plans for staff development except for recruiting the absurdly large number of forty foreign advisors.

The DAU's findings confirmed the generally held view that the jurisdictional dispute between the IDD and FIDA was producing delay and confusion which discouraged potential investors. It thus proposed the abolition of the IDD and the absorption of its functions by the FIDA. It proposed methods for simplifying and expediting the interagency clearance of procedures for pioneer certificates so that total elapsed time between application and approval would not exceed four weeks. In a separate study requested by the Treasury, the DAU reaffirmed the importance of retaining the Tariff Advisory Board as an independent agency, but recommended that its technical staff be strengthened and that the government provide better guidance on policy and priorities to govern specific decisions on tariffs. It promised later studies into the relationship between the FIDA and MIDFL both of which seemed to be engaging in small and uncoordinated feasibility studies and in minor promotional activities.

Between MARA and FIDA there was no overt friction, but there were no agreed principles or procedures to demarcate MARA's activities on behalf of Malays from the FIDA's on behalf of the entire economy. Yet MARA was in a position to veto pioneer certificates for other investors even when it had no clear intention or capability to enter the field. Moreover, MARA had ambitious plans to participate in joint ventures with foreign firms and finance and even operate substantial industries, even though it had virtually no personnel trained or experienced in industrial economics, accounting, marketing, technology, or management. It had no plans to train personnel who might appraise such ventures or manage the industries it planned to operate. The prospect of failure was inherent in this situation, and with failure would come increasing Malay frustration and rage which would probably be directed against Chinese and foreign-owned enterprise. Meanwhile, MARA's inability to fix on priorities was compromising the national industrial development effort.

These investigations were drawing the DAU much more deeply into the area of industrial development programming and administration than its original priorities had contemplated and were giving its officers experience and insights into administrative problems in this important sector. The main issue of controversy was the FIDA's relations with the IDD. The DAU, supported by the EPU, Treasury, and National Bank, recommended that the IDD be abolished and its functions incorporated into the FIDA. The powerful Permanent Secretary of Commerce and Industry, while accepting the other DAU recommendations on reorganization, held firm for the continuation of a separate IDD in the ministry. His position was that the FIDA, a statutory corporation and therefore "nongovernmental," could not properly be assigned policy-making and enforcement powers. These must remain in the ministry.

An impasse having been reached, the DAU was forced to call on the Chief Secretary for assistance. After several meetings and backstage negotiations, an agreement was achieved: an IDD would remain in the ministry, but its director would concurrently be director of the FIDA. Thus the debilitating conflict between the two organizations would be liquidated, and the DAU would be asked to develop a compatible division of function and flow of transactions between the units that would insure more expeditious treatment of investment requests. The ablest and most experienced MHFS officer in the field of industry (a Chinese) was appointed to these combined posts, while the erstwhile German director of the FIDA was advanced to the role of senior advisor responsible primarily for contact work with foreign investors. The United Nations Industrial Development Organization agreed to provide six specialists to assist in developing the main divisions of the FIDA.

At the policy and priorities level, much remained to be done to rationalize Malaysia's industrial development effort and to develop greater governmental capacity for industrial promotion. The immediate organizational crisis had been resolved, thanks largely to the DAU. Shortly thereafter, the DAU was asked to examine in detail MARA's internal structure, including its capacities and performance in industrial development. The DAU's staff was thus accumulating experience in an important area of development administration. A repetition of the unhappy rural development experience was avoided because the DAU's leadership insured that it was legitimately invited into the situation and the DAU was associated with a coalition of agencies that was strong enough to force a satisfactory outcome on a powerful and reluctant linkage.

What Three Years Have Wrought: A Cautious Appraisal

Three years is obviously too short a span for the definitive appraisal of any activities designed to achieve structural and behavioral changes and growth in capacity and efficiency in a large and relatively stable system. Nevertheless trends may indicate the directions the experiments have taken and provide the practicing administrator with feedback data that enable him to learn and to adapt.

For the DAU this process was facilitated by the midplan review in the summer of 1968—two years after the organization was launched and shortly before the first senior advisor was due to leave. The midplan review was sponsored by the EPU to appraise the implementation of the Malaysian first five-year plan at its halfway point and suggest necessary reprogramming. Like other government agencies, the DAU was asked to prepare a submission. The product was a tightly packed, 49-page, mimeographed, double-spaced document about the same wordage as the Montgomery-Esman Report three years earlier. It restated the DAU's purposes and operating doctrine, took stock (not overmodestly) of its activities and achievements, projected an expanded program through the second Malaysian plan period (1975), and claimed increased resources and additional functions.

Confident that the government-wide systems changes which constituted its first priority would take root, the DAU was laying claim to resources that would in seven years triple its professional staff and move it decisively into two areas: the administration of substantive action programs, which was one of the core concerns of development administration, and sophisticated modern management methods associated with computerized information processing and management systems. The credit it took for its achievements produced raised eyebrows among some readers and even protests among Treasury officers who disputed the DAU's claims to have initiated the reforms in financial and supply administration which the Treasury was now espousing. But there was no expressed opposition to the main thrust of the paper, its doctrine of administrative reform, nor to the ambitious claims to additional staff and expanded functions. The first tangible evidence of the latter was the Treasury's agreement to add to DAU's establishment four of the five additional posts it requested for 1969. The new organization and the values it represented had come a long way in three years.

Comparing the midplan review paper with the earlier baseline document, the Montgomery-Esman Report, one finds evidence of progress in nearly every area identified for priority. Major exceptions were (1) local government and administration, where the DAU had been inhibited because of the long delay of the Royal Commission on Local Government in issuing its voluminous report; (2) government-staff relations, where the Montgomery-Esman recommendation to explore more effective alternatives to the Whitley Council system was foreclosed by the deliberations of the Royal Commission on Government Salaries and the subsequent threat of a civil service strike; (3) administrative planning in the ministries and departments. The DAU doctrine that operating agencies must continuously monitor their performance and plan for structural and operational improvements had made little headway. After securing NCDA approval, the DAU organized and conducted a full-time, year-long program under a highly qualified American advisor to train management analysts who would form the nuclei of management units in the major ministries and departments and thus equip them with the capacity to plan and carry out management improvement activities. However, recruitment lagged and graduates tended to be diverted to operating jobs. With few exceptions, senior officers, untrained in the use of management tools, expected the DAU or another higher authority to tell them what improvements to make, just as they expected the EPU to do their economic planning for them. The doctrinal theme that line administrators were responsible for planning and management improvement activities made little headway against the culturally sanctioned respect for hierarchy and preference for externalized discipline. This system-wide change to which the DAU attached high priority encountered more initial indifference than acceptance.[18]

Not all the major Montgomery-Esman recommendations were adopted. Some were accepted in principle but met resistance and were not yet implemented, like specialization in the MHFS; but there was very broad forward motion, and the Montgomery-Esman Report had only promised "to produce dramatic results within a space of five to ten years."

The euphoria surrounding the DAU's status and achieve-

[18] As the scope of this indifference and resistance became apparent, it was clear that the introduction of management analysis in operating agencies would have to depend on a longer-term strategy. The management analysis course which had been initiated by and in the DAU was transferred to the expanding Staff Training Center (soon to be redesignated as the National Institute for Development Administration) as a permanent component of its curriculum. A DAU officer who had returned from the United States with a Master's Degree in Public Administration and specialized training in management analysis was transferred to the STC to organize and direct the new course.

ments at the time of the midplan review was deflated within a few months. The FEO, rejuvenated by its new director and redesignated as the Public Services Department (PSD), suddenly claimed jurisdiction over the DAU and all its activities and proposed to absorb its functions and staff. Though the DAU was successful in fending off this attack by invoking the protection of the Chief Secretary, it was clear that its successes and its prospects made it an attractive target for acquisition by an expansionist conglomerate and that its own leadership had insufficient status and power to cope with this threat except by resorting to higher authority. It also led to a reassessment of priorities.

How should the DAU respond to the PSD's possessiveness of reforms in staff training and the Treasury's of financial administration—reforms which the DAU had initiated and from the implementation of which it was now being excluded? Should the DAU fight for a piece of the action or should it accept as bona fide the conversion of the Treasury and PSD, accommodate to their greater power in the Malaysian administrative system, and shift at an earlier date than originally contemplated to the administration of action programs and office automation systems? The decision was to retain its interest in personnel and financial administration, but to move more rapidly toward opportunities in other areas. Since the Treasury and PSD were swinging with major reforms and the substantive program areas were actually the heart of development administration, the DAU could, despite its reluctance at being pushed around, make a virtue of necessity.[19] As it moved to its new building in March 1969, two and one-half years after its establishment, the shift in its priorities away from government-wide systems and toward program sectors was under way.

The institution-building research program posited certain

[19] It was clear that the PSD was much more inclined to accept reforms like staff training that produced widespread benefits throughout the bureaucracy than reforms like specialization or five-year postings in the MHFS which required changes in familiar practices and were thus perceived as costs rather than benefits by the PSD staff.

tests of institutionality.[20] Though the achievement of institutionality is inconceivable in a three-year period, some trends could be explored in the case of the DAU, whose development was being guided by the institution-building orientation. In addition to technical capacity to deliver innovative services at an increasing level of competence, there are four main indicators of institutionality: (1) ability to survive; (2) normative influence on linked organizations (spread effect); (3) attainment of intrinsic value in its environment; and (4) capacity to continue to innovate (innovative thrust).

Survival is a necessary but not sufficient condition of institutionality. Those in control of financial resources acquiesced in the DAU's expansion plans; a new building in the Prime Minister's compound was erected for the DAU's occupancy; some of the ablest and most promising young officers in the MHFS were assigned to it; there were no significant overt attacks on its doctrine and program. The PSD's attempt to absorb the DAU misfired; its encroachments on DAU's jurisdiction were being resisted. The DAU had met the most primitive test of institutionality—it had survived, and its continued existence was not in jeopardy. Moreover, its capacity to deliver innovative services was being demonstrated in practice, especially as its staff training program began to pay off.

For an organization barely three years old, it was remarkably successful in transferring its norms to important linked organizations. This spread effect related both to norms and practices representing fundamental innovations and deviations from established practices, and to linked organizations that are central to the structure of power in Malaysian administration. Few knowledgeable observers of Malaysian administration would have predicted that the Treasury would accept, even in princi-

[20] See Esman and Blaise, pp. 4–7. They were slightly modified in Esman's article, "Institution Building as a Guide to Action," in D. Woods Thomas and Judith Fender, eds., *Proceedings of Conference on Institution Building and Technical Assistance* (Washington, D.C.: Agency for International Development and Committee on Institutional Cooperation, 1969).

ple, such a radical experiment as program budgeting and would actively work on adapting it to local conditions less than three years after the publication of the Montgomery-Esman Report. The DAU cannot claim sole credit for this achievement, but outside the context of the administrative reforms it represented and promoted, this would not have taken place for many years. That DAU officers wrote the principal speeches on administrative subjects for the Chief Secretary of government, who was initially skeptical of the need for administrative reform, was another indicator of its normative effect. That its sweeping proposals for civil service training were accepted by the new director of the FEO is a tribute to the change readiness of the latter, but it is inconceivable that a new division of training and career development would be operative were it not for the intellectual influence of the DAU. The developmentalist orientation to administration which the DAU represented was being promoted also in the new university teaching programs for future civil servants and for practitioners. This is not to suggest that the DAU was uniformly effective in norm transfer, contrary examples being the resistance and indifference of several ministries to management planning and analysis and specific rejection of its critique of the administration of rural development. In the main, however, the DAU in three years successfully pushed new ideas and practices deep into the administrative system at several influential points. Its normative spread, while not yet deep, was broad.

That a three-year-old organization or the developmental program it represented could gain acceptance for its intrinsic value would be too much to ask. The institution-building model posits two tests of intrinsic value—autonomy and influence. While it had considerable latitude in the formulation of its program of action, the DAU had not achieved the high degree of autonomy that characterizes an institutionalized organization. It was still struggling for the right to retain trained officers without loss of promotional opportunity in a manner that deviated from the traditional rules still governing the larger system. It was embroiled in disputes with the PSD over the control of developmental activities which it had initiated. Its success in acquiring resources was a reflection of the larger system's willingness to give it a fair chance to perform, rather than a demonstration of its ability to claim resources because the society prized it highly.

Its ability to exercise influence was also uncertain. The DAU was able to expand into new areas, such as project management and industrial development, but when it sought to do so at the expense of another organization, in rural development, its institutional quality did not carry it very far. It was not called upon for special service during and after the crisis of May 1969. The DAU leadership painfully realized that it could not influence some decisions that it considered part of its legitimate domain. It was not consulted in a major decision to establish a large new organization for agricultural research and development, even though its terms of reference required that it be brought in on major organizational changes. And its ability to continue to operate in major areas of systems reform which it had initiated was being challenged.

Demands for its services, however, were brisk. The Cabinet itself asked it to study the integration of ministries, staffing problems in the Malayan Railways, and administrative relations between the federal government and the states of East Malaysia. The Royal Commission on Teachers' Salaries asked its help in analyzing the management of the national education system and for the computerization of personnel and financial administration. The National Bank and the Ministry of Health requested organizational studies that had to be declined for lack of available trained staff. At the same time there was continuing and widely diffused skepticism about the DAU in its main clientele area, the civil service, compounded of fear that it might propound threatening changes, doubt that much could be done to change the traditional patterns of public administration, and cynicism that the DAU would ever be allowed to go into the "real problems," identified variously as corruption, racial discrimination, and political interference.

In institutional terms, it was thus a mixed picture. The DAU was not yet firmly established, nor had its innovations become normative in its environment, nor could it rely on its institutional qualities to get what it wanted. It was not clear how long it would continue to be innovative and in what areas and how much it would have to accommodate to pre-existing power and norms of behavior. On the other hand, the environment had not denied it resources, had not rejected it, indeed had begun to take on systemic innovations with which it was identified and was making increasing demands for its services. Its staff capabilities were being rapidly upgraded by overseas training, which enhanced its prestige. The three-year-old was not institutionalized, but the trend seemed favorable, more perhaps for the program of reform and development than for the sponsoring organization.

In retrospect, there were two critical defects in the original design of the DAU. The first was in downgrading the status of its leadership far below what was recommended in the Montgomery-Esman Report. Tactically the failure of the initial group of change agents to fight this battle was a serious oversight. Its modest position in the administrative hierarchy impaired its ability to cope effectively with linkage resistances. This was compounded by the selection of leaders who were cautious in their style and did not have ready access to the main center of power, the principal enabling linkage, Tun Razak. Though compensated in some measure by the access and influence of technical assistance advisors, by the quality of its performance, and by the energy and commitment of its young staff members, the status of its leadership was a chronic drag on the organization and its objectives.

The second main defect related to doctrine and strategy. The American-inspired, apolitical management notion that the power of persuasion and demonstration could induce senior officials to undertake reforms with a minimum of compulsion proved to be unsuitable in the Malaysian administrative environment. It assumed a consensus on goals and activist motivations that was not present among Malaysia's senior administrators. Unless a highly placed official (e.g., the Treasury's controller of supply) could be converted, it was extremely difficult to make senior officials take initiative in grappling with their own administrative problems. In a service placing so high a value on hierarchy and on externalized discipline, officers expect to be told what to do and await instructions. The proposition that these deep-seated behavior patterns can be modified by cooperative investigations, patient persuasion, and demonstration was never convincing to the DAU's staff. They believed that unless a powerful figure adopts reforms (e.g., the director of establishments with staff training), a reform organization needs more clout than persuasion to get its ideas accepted and implemented. It was not sufficient for the DAU to rely on the support of its enabling linkages, the Prime Minister's Department or Tun Razak, which were costly to mobilize, or to develop coalitions of other more powerful agencies as in the industrial promotion case. It needed enforcement powers of its own or control of an important resource in order to overcome the resistances or lethargy of some client agencies. The DAU's aforementioned failure to persuade permanent secretaries and their senior colleagues to establish management staff units assisted by its trained analysts is a case in point. Mere enforcement power in the absence of cooperation investigations and measures to increase the knowledge and capabilities of officers, to provide better operating systems, and to hasten generational succession would have been counterproductive, for imposed solutions can be distorted in implementation or frozen and ritualized like the operations rooms. But as one resource in a comprehensive program of administrative development and reform, given the context of Malaysian administration, the DAU's original design should have incorporated greater enforcement powers. Where technological and cultural approaches to change were insufficient, effective political methods should have been available.

Little has been said here about communal issues. The explicit doctrine of administrative reform and development in Malaysia had never directly touched this sensitive nerve, the assumption being that improved governmental performance, increased efficiency, and more rapid economic development would be sufficient products of better administration and would fully justify the effort. But unless they also strengthened the political system, the benefits of administrative innovation in any society would be highly problematical. In Malaysia the overwhelming political problem is communal conflict. How better administration may influence the management of this issue, which is central for the survival of the Malaysian polity, will be the subject of the next chapter.

8

Administration and the
Management of Communal Conflict

The post-election rioting of May 1969 witnessed the breakdown of the Alliance political system, which had managed communal conflict in Malaysia for fifteen years. It is uncertain whether a functional substitute for the Alliance can be improvised. Though manifest tensions have relaxed, both communities are up-tight. Some Chinese are alienated from the political system. For the majority who are not, confidence in the capacity of government to protect their interests has been shaken. While fears of Chinese encroachment on their political hegemony have diminished for the time being, Malays are increasingly dissatisfied with their own economic and educational backwardness. More ominously, the emerging politicians of both races are inclined to be more categorical, more impatient, and less accommodating on communal issues than were their fathers who founded the Alliance and are passing from the scene. The younger Malay politicians are not only unprepared to compromise on Malay political control, but they also demand more aggressive structural changes in the economy to uplift the Malays even at the expense of existing Chinese stakes. While they condemn the establishment members of both races, especially the MCA capitalists, younger Chinese politicians, insist on open competition for all economic and educational opportunities, thus rejecting Malay privilege, and demand full political equality, thus rejecting Malay hegemony. The communities are mobilized increasingly along communal lines and prepared to assert maximum claims on government. Even moderate leaders of each community feel compelled to reflect some of the demands of their extremists if they are to survive politically. The communities are competing for the same scarce values. They are less prepared to accept the authority of traditional leadership, but alternative leadership, procedures, and institutions have not yet appeared.

The good will needed to mitigate such tensions is further strained by economic adversity. Despite impressive aggregate economic growth, economic discontent is mounting as the benefits of growth do not appear to be shared equitably among classes and especially ethnic groups. Per-capita income among rural Malays has not increased significantly since Independence, despite rising expectations. Malay hegemony in government and Malay privileges have assisted a small group, but failed to distribute benefits widely. Urban working-class Chinese feel neglected, both by government and their own elites. Unemployment is growing alarmingly, particularly among urban dwellers in the 16–25-year age bracket. The education system, an important route for upward mobility, is beginning to turn out thousands of secondary school graduates equipped only for clerical occupations, of which the number is limited, but with high material and status expectations. Meanwhile, urbanization, education, and mass communication are generating high expectations which the growth of the economy cannot fulfill. The resulting frustrations are felt most acutely by the urbanizing young Malays and by young urban Chinese. Lines are likely to be drawn more rigidly as frustrations mount, as government lacks the economic resources to satisfy the increasingly insistent claims for opportunities and benefits, especially from Malays, and has little maneuverability to trade off and mediate one set of claims against the other.

Those developments tend to confirm the hypothesis that in a plural society modernization will intensify rather than mitigate communal conflict.[1] Far from eliminating particularistic group loyalties, modernization tends to accentuate them as

[1] See Robert Melson and Howard Wolpe, "Modernization and the Politics of Communalism," *American Political Science Review* 64 (December

group awareness mobilizes men along familiar solidarity lines. As ethnic groups modernize, they increasingly desire the same economic, political, and symbolic values, and as the supply fails to satisfy these increasing and competing expectations, tensions mount. The tensions are magnified by inability to agree on criteria for the just distribution of benefits and costs among competing ethnic groups. Neither overarching integrative "national" appeals nor crosscutting occupational and class interests are powerful enough in the short run to supplant or displace the more primordial communal identities that become the major lines of cleavage and thus structure political issues during the process of modernization—and well beyond.[2] Especially perverse is the tendency of electoral politics to aggravate tensions as populistic politicians reach for the jugular issues that can most efficiently mobilize support among mass constituencies —precisely what occurred during the 1969 election campaign in Malaysia. The greater the autonomy of elites, however, the more likely that the inevitable communal issues can be peacefully negotiated and managed.

Before 1969 the Alliance politicians maintained effective autonomy and legitimacy and were able to manage communal tensions with minimum disruption to the society. Patrician in their style, they developed no facilities or institutions for intercommunal dialogue except in the national Cabinet and the executive committee of the Alliance Party, which involved the same small group of men, and at some state capitals in Alliance Party executive meetings. Communal issues were considered taboo, too sensitive for public discussion. They were not aired in intercommunal forums, even in university circles. This absence

---

1970), pp. 1112–1130; R. A. Schermerhorn, *Comparative Ethnic Relations: A Framework for Theory and Research* (New York: Random House, 1970); and Arend Lijphart, *Accommodative Politics* (Berkeley: University of California Press, 1968).

[2] The persistence of communal identity can be seen, *inter alia*, in recent Belgian, Soviet, Canadian, and Irish politics; their tendency to surface after dormant periods can be seen in the recent resurgence of Scottish and Breton nationalism.

of dialogue was epitomized by a national conference in 1967 on agricultural marketing organized by the the Federal Agricultural Marketing Authority. Not a single Chinese businessman was invited to this officially sponsored conference even though Chinese millers and middlemen handle virtually all the agricultural marketing and are highly organized. The technique of the Alliance leadership was avoidance. The less communal issues were publicly bruited, the less trouble they would cause. The fewer people handling these problems, the more likely a fair, peaceful, and viable solution. The more specific the issue, the more likely a reasonable compromise. This was a prescription for system maintenance by a paternalistic leadership negotiating on behalf of compliant constituencies. It was not productive of new approaches to conflict management, nor did it present opportunities for the identification and exploration of fresh action programs. It was not likely to be acceptable indefinitely in a more mobilized and politicized environment where younger men were demanding more participation in political decisions.

Aside from the Department of National Unity, which is still searching for its role, and the National Consultative Council, which meets only sporadically, the senior politicians and administrators who have been responsible for guiding the polity since the May 1969 riots have demonstrated great concern on communal issues but produced few innovations. Yet they recognize that they cannot persist with the tactic of merely keeping the lid on a potentially explosive situation. The search for accommodative answers will require a willingness to consider unorthodox institutional changes and the structured involvement of groups outside the political and administrative elite.

The members of this moderate elite are the principal expositors and guardians of the concept of Malaysia. They understand the system-wide requirements and accommodative processes that are necessary to maintain Malaysia. They are the targets of diffuse hostility and of increasingly incompatible demands articulated and thrown up to them through communal political channels. They have very narrow room for maneuver between these conflicting demands and limited instruments, especially since the Alliance's political machinery is less effective, for mediating such conflict and for evolving accommodative solutions.

Allocation of Scarce Values

There are several alternative methods by which governments may allocate scarce values, whether they be access to public land or educational places, jobs or contracts, parliamentary seats or the official status of language. All of them are practiced in Malaysia and predictably who gets what and how has serious communal implications. The Constitution allocates certain major political values—the symbols of the polity and control over government—to Malays, but it also accords non-Malays valuable citizenship rights, the privilege of participating in political life (in a junior role), and the opportunity to finance political activity and thereby to influence government decisions. Within the main outlines of this political system and the constitutional allocations which have already been discussed at length, values are allocated by a variety of devices.

1. *Free competition,* where individuals or groups compete, formally at least, on equal terms according to specified and objective criteria in open markets, so long as they follow the rules of the game. Examples are the allocation of university places by relative performance on open, competitive examinations, access to mining rights on a first-come, first-served basis, or the right to do business in any line of activity according to performance in a competitive market, which is an objective test of economic efficiency.

2. *Special opportunities* departs from free individualistic competition by providing members of disadvantaged (or privileged) groups with special preparation at public expense or with subsidies to increase their capacity eventually to compete on even terms. Examples in Malaysia are the MARA Institute of Technology which provides, free of cost to Malays only, enriched and extended training in the skills needed to participate

in modern industry, commerce, and finance. Another is the subsidy to Malay fishermen for the purchase of modern equipment, plus technical advice on how to use it. This method of allocation causes little direct pain to those who are ineligible since it does not exclude them from opportunities for which the disadvantaged are being prepared.

3. *Relative preferences.* This principle of allocation identifies preferences available on a relative but not absolute basis to certain classes of individuals. It gives a compensating advantage to persons who are considered to be handicapped in open competition and therefore encourages the development of their capabilities. Examples in Malaysia are the 5 percent preference in prices offered to Malay contractors for small public works jobs. Proposals by the recent Bumiputra Economic Congress that Malay-owned timber mills and trucking concerns be charged lower taxes than others is an example of such preference. In the United States the 5-point preference for war veterans in civil service examinations is another example (a method of preference which some foreign observers have recommended as a substitute in Malaysia for the quotas discussed in the next section), while the job retention rights for veterans in reductions in force in the U.S. civil service is an example of absolute, rather than relative preference.

4. *Quotas and absolute preferences.* This method assures that a fixed or minimum number or percentage of units will be allocated to particular groups. In Malaysia the absolute guarantee of four Malays to one non-Malay in appointments to the MHFS and similar quotas on the issuance of taxi and truck licenses are examples. A recent proposal to apportion seats in the university's faculty of medicine on a racial basis according to population ratios would be an instance of substituting this method—thus guaranteeing the Malays half the positions in the prestigious and profitable medical profession—for the present system of free competition by examination which yields only 15 percent of the places to Malays. Resolutions at the recent Bumiputra Economic Congress that government deposit at least 50 percent of its funds in the Bank Bumiputra and that non-Malay firms

receive no more than 50 percent of import or export licenses on controlled commodities are examples of this principle.

5. *Administrative control.* This method of allocation apportions resources and opportunities at the discretion of public officials, effectively eliminating objective criteria altogether. Thus access to public land in Malaysia is now determined on this basis principally by Malay politicians with the result that agricultural land is now virtually unavailable to non-Malays. Pioneer industry licenses increasingly depend on acceptance of a negotiated but unfixed quota of Malays in the managerial levels of the firm. When the MARA decides to go into public enterprise ventures and closes the field to non-Malay concerns, this will be another instance of allocation of economic opportunity by administrative decision.

As a practical matter many government allocations combine two or more of these methods. Thus eligibility for admission as a settler to a federal land development scheme provides an absolute preference for Malays, reserves a quota for ex-servicemen, and distributes the others according to a point system that is said to operate reasonably equitably except where informal political pressures intervene. Places in the national university are allotted according to competitive performance in the nationwide higher school certificate examination, but scholarship holders, predominantly Malay, are admitted regardless of their relative standing so long as they meet the minimum qualifying requirements in the examination.

Diagram 2. Allocative spectrum in Malaysia

Free Competition	Special Opportunities	Relative Preferences	Quotas and Absolute Preferences	Administrative Control

Pro-Chinese

←——————————————————————————→

Pro-Malay

Pro-Economic Growth

←——————————————————————————→

Pro-Communal Equity

The hypothesis in Diagram 2 is that the closer one approaches the point of free competition on this scale, the greater the benefits and the satisfactions to Chinese; the closer one comes to allocation by administrative control the greater the benefits and the satisfactions to Malays. Satisfaction to Chinese is usually tantamount to perceived deprivation by Malays, while satisfaction to Malays is perceived by the affected Chinese as deprivation in the perverse zero-sum game thinking that characterizes this relatively affluent culture of poverty. Because of their vast educational superiority, their willingness to work hard, and their ability to use resources and opportunities efficiently, Chinese have no fear of free competition and indeed have great confidence in their ability to compete. To them, the less government interference the better.[3] Malays feel unable to compete as individuals at this stage of their development with the aggressively competitive Chinese, insisting that governmental intervention in the allocation of opportunities is essential to assure them the chance to develop the capacity to compete in the future. Otherwise they will become "like the Red Indians in America," a hopelessly subject backward race in their own country. The more militant Malays are not satisfied with the equal opportunity doctrine, claiming that this policy can never permit them to close the gap. They demand greater use of quotas, administrative controls, and government-sponsored enterprises to force Malay economic participation as a group, even if it means limiting the opportunities of Chinese and even displacing them from some fields like rural trade, marketing, and money lending. How similar to those black Americans who now reject as inadequate the doctrine of equal opportunity— the original objective of the civil rights agitation—and demand preferential measures in employment, housing, and education, which predictably draw the fire of white groups who consider

---

[3] Chinese compensate for some of the discriminatory effects of administrative allocations and quotas by bribery and other forms of financial payment. Such payments increase their costs of doing business and are resented by Chinese. Malay intellectuals bitterly condemn their rulers and rank and file for this easy conversion of opportunities for cash and for thus making a travesty of Malay privilege.

them as reverse discrimination and violative of the principles of free and open competition.

The classical prescription for breaking out of this impasse is through economic growth. In Malaysia this would promise so many increments of opportunity for jobs, business activity, and income that the Chinese could be satisfied, even though the Malays advance at a faster rate and begin to close the socio-economic gap, due in large measure to the investment of public funds in their development. But herein lies another cruel dilemma. The closer one moves to the free-competition end of the allocational scale, the faster the rate of aggregate economic growth and therefore of resources available to government for the Malays. But the same policy that maximizes this economic growth will enlarge the existing disparity among the races. The benefits of growth will accrue largely to the Chinese, whose money, entrepreneurship, management, and labor produce it, and the benefits will be in two forms: greater concentration of income and an even greater control of productive resources in the modern economy. Thus the faster the rate of over-all economic growth, the less the prospect of economic equity at least for several decades. And this prospect is unacceptable to Malays, particularly the younger ones. If they have to make a painful choice, they would opt for a slower rate of growth with greater Malay participation in and control of the modern economy and greater equity in the distribution of a smaller quantum of social and economic benefits. It is doubtful that the present political system could be maintained under either of these conditions, and its dissolution would be accompanied by massive distress and bloodshed.

In Diagram 3, below, this dilemma is graphically indicated. The horizontal axis (CE–CE') stands for communal equity, the vertical axis (EG–EG') for economic growth. Any acceptable solution that reconciles these two desirable values would have to fall in quadrant 1. The optimum would fall along line AB. Malay preference would fall in the ABD sector, which emphasizes equity over growth, while Chinese preference would fall in the ABC sector, stressing growth over equity. With no

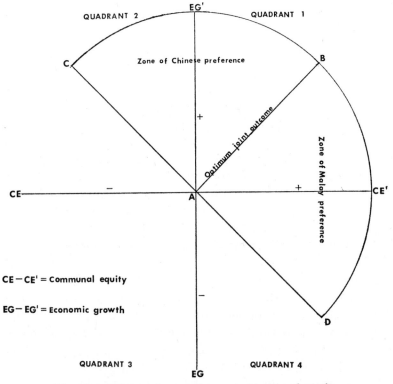

Diagram 3. Economic growth versus communal equity

institutional changes, the economy would probably move into quadrant 2 along line AC, economic growth accompanied by decreasing communal equity or greater economic power and welfare concentrated among the Chinese, not unlike the regional pattern in Pakistan during the later years of the Ayub Khan regime. If the extremist Malays were to have their way, the result would probably be in quadrant 4, perhaps along line AD, redistributing wealth, income, and control accompanied by negative economic growth, somewhat like Indonesia during the Sukarno period. This would produce a violent reaction among the Chinese. For Malaysia the main problem in public policy is clear: how to confine the outcomes to quadrant 1.

The time horizons of both groups are quite short, which is

another constraint on policy. Malays cannot be convinced that increasing inequity favoring the Chinese in the short run will eventually produce a greatly increased quantity of resources and opportunities that they will be able to capture through fiscal measures and thus achieve greater ultimate equity. Nor would they be satisfied to see both communities in the future advance at the same rate since this would result in a growing real gap between them. Advancing at rates that maintain but do not increase the real differences might be more acceptable if not so specified and if the rate of growth were enough to be widely felt and appreciated. This would put the solution in quadrant 1 below the line AB. The Chinese cannot conceive that any radical institutional reforms applied today to achieve equalization could possibly accrue to their benefit in the future.

Diagram 3 simplifies the alternatives since it does not specify the instruments that might be deployed to achieve the desired outcomes. The most obvious opportunity for trade-offs would exchange greater Malay participation in the modern economy for greater Chinese opportunities in government and in the symbols of the polity. Stated abstractly this would be unacceptable to Malays almost to a man. The idea of any diminution in the Malay style of the polity, one that would admit some Chinese elements into its symbols system, would be equally anathema. The Malays will have to be more secure in their confidence and sense of efficacy in the modern economy before they can accept any additional political participation by the Chinese, convinced as many already are that Chinese capitalists exercise great *de facto* political power.[4]

Moreover, the Chinese ask how in any practical or acceptable sense they can yield or share more economic power with Malays, even if they were willing. The poor Chinese is already fretting over the denial of agricultural land, the quota system on various licenses, and Malay preference for scholarships and government jobs. Aggrieved at discrimination, he feels he has nothing to share. Wealthy Chinese, while moving away gradually from

[4] A popular slogan: MCA-Malayan Chinese Association—Money Conquers All.

family to corporate-style enterprise, are hesitant to accept Malay partners; allegedly they will not work hard, they prefer immediate consumption to investing their profits in the growth of the business, and they are unable to resist the importunities of their relatives for jobs and other benefits. The result all too often is the Ali-Baba firm, with effective management and control in the hands of Chinese. Young Malays find it distasteful to work in a Chinese-owned firm, inevitably a Chinese social system, in which Malays feel awkward and uncomfortable with the direct pattern of human relations practiced by the Chinese even toward one another. To Chinese, acquiescence in government-sponsored enterprise in which their taxes are used to set up firms that compete with established Chinese businessmen or to close avenues of economic expansion to Chinese entrepreneurs would be looked upon as extremely unjust.

Wealthy Chinese do support large-scale training efforts to prepare Malays for roles in the modern economy. This they see as no immediate threat to themselves, and they agree that Malays must become more active in modern business—but, of course, they must get there on their own steam. Subsidies to small Malay enterprise, distribution of shares in pioneer industries to Malays (*bumiputra* capitalism), even pressure on foreign firms to admit Malays to managerial positions are accepted cynically as something for nothing to a few Malays and no great threat to Chinese. But they consider substantial publicly financed enterprise, whether in areas they have not yet entered or particularly in areas where they are active, and the closing off of resources or opportunities for their economic exploitation on a racial basis threats to their economic and political security. In their present mood, Chinese especially the Malaya-born and the middle class, would like to erase the stigma of second-class citizenship, but they see no practical way to share economic power with Malays.

Clearly the time is not yet ripe for the type of group accommodation visualized in the trade-off model just discussed. There is evidence of individual accommodation among a few urbanized professionals in joint medical practices, architectural firms,

257

and law partnerships, in the government agencies where members of both races accommodate in work situations, in universities and other teaching organizations, and to some extent in trade-unions. These instances of interpersonal accommodation among members of the three main ethnic groups, though not without strains, are highly civil and indicate a possible path of development in a society that will continue to be socially and politically plural, but where individuals and groups can co-exist and work together in harmony. Such accommodation is, however, not the norm, nor is it politically very significant. To the contrary, the prospects are for heightened intercommunal tensions over the allocation of scarce political and economic values for which both groups are increasingly competing, their expectations growing faster than the society's ability to gratify them. The task of artful conflict management, including the search for agreed criteria for the distribution of benefits and costs, will remain the primary agenda of Malaysia's public leadership.

Avoidance Model of Conflict Management

The strategy which the Malaysian governmental elites used before May 1969 to manage communal conflict can best be designated as an "avoidance model." Where possible, public discussion of conflict-laden communal issues was avoided. In doctrinal output the abstract themes of intercommunal harmony and understanding were emphasized, with appropriate warnings against "bad elements" which sow communal discord. The society was congratulated on the good will and the attitude of live and let live that had been achieved; trends toward the emergence of a Malaysian personality were identified—no more than a few weeks after the dust settled from a bloody communal riot. The underlying expectation was that over time the spirit of give and take would pervade the thinking and the behavior of responsible members of all communities, a wider set of common national loyalties would emerge, the communities would accommodate, and perhaps ultimately a new integrated culture would appear.

In the critical interim between then and now, the government's posture was essentially one of responding to events. As pressures from their constituencies pushed communally charged issues through party channels, the Alliance coalition tried to cool them, to break them down, and to improvise settlements that would suffice at least temporarily. When the Chinese demanded a Chinese-language university—a demand that the MCA leadership could not control—the result was a Chinese-language feeder college to be financed half by government, half by the Chinese community and to be named for the Malay Prime Minister, Tunku Abdul Rahman! The UMNO did not like this solution, but accepted it because it seemed to buy peace and promised to preserve the constituency of their Chinese partners in the Alliance. Shortly thereafter, the UMNO political channel produced a demand generated by Malay medium schoolteachers for a National University, fully accredited and teaching only in the Malay language. The government, in turn, accepted and implemented this demand. The Alliance was thus whipsawed between conflicting communal demands, but was usually able to control them. Its posture was (1) to accommodate these demands where possible, (2) to soft-pedal public discussion and controversy, (3) to compromise and settle such claims quietly in the small group of notables who compromised both the Cabinet and the Executive Committee of the Alliance Party, and (4) to use the power of government and of the Party machinery to repress, by force if necessary, unmanageable claims. Thus the machinery of both parties, especially of the UMNO, was used to repress the strident opposition that developed to the delicately balanced compromise on language policy worked out in the Cabinet in August 1967, and the police and army were called in to suppress the communal rioting in Penang later that year.

Little effort was made to anticipate communal problems before they became critical issues, no effort to study these problems in advance, no building of new institutions to work on them or to stimulate meaningful dialogue or exploration of accommodative or integrative patterns of action. The underlying fear was that any serious public discussion of such issues, even in controlled institutional settings, would be more likely to raise inflammatory passions than to produce solutions or even meaningful habits of discourse. I have noted how the government rejected a recommendation for a commission of inquiry to examine the causes of the communal riots in Penang in November 1967. They calculated that a more positive search for patterns of accommodation and a more diffused and public exploration of communal issues would yield more problems than the system could peacefully handle. It is fair to say that the Alliance leadership also preferred a quiet and controlled style of decision making.

Given the propensities for conflict in Malaysia, these conflict-avoidance methods worked reasonably well in the decade and a half preceding May 1969. The volume and intensity of demands were relatively modest, the polity had enough uncommitted resources to apply to the resolution of overt conflicts, and the charisma of the Prime Minister, who symbolized the policies of communal reconciliation and conflict avoidance, was available to cool the disputants.

The shock of May 1969 demonstrated conclusively that such practices would no longer suffice. Malaysia could not rely exclusively on the wisdom and the authority of its notables of both races to regulate communal conflict. Their authority was being successfully challenged by younger men from broader social strata in both communities. It became clear, moreover, that spokesmen and representatives of the groups directly affected would have to be drawn into the discussion and resolution of communal issues. In his preface to the NOC's *Report on the May 13 Tragedy,* Tun Razak acknowledged that "important matters must no longer be swept under the carpet . . . the objective of national unity must be confronted squarely . . . and a Consultive Council [convened] where issues affecting our national unity will be discussed fully and frankly."[5] To treat communal conflicts as taboo for public discussion, to react issue by issue at the point of crisis by improvised solutions arranged

[5] P. vi.

in camera by a handful of notables would no longer meet the need for more sustained intellectual inputs to guide public policy on these issues, nor provide opportunities for more educated and more politicized constituencies to participate in the search for viable patterns of accommodation.

The avoidance model was dead. But what would take its place?

Mutual Deterrence Model of Conflict Management

Malaysia's communal politics amount to mutual deterrence —a two-party game. Both Chinese and Malays are strong enough to inflict unacceptable damage on the other, and the majority on both sides recognize and appreciate this possibility. The pluralistic character of both major communities and the information gap between them create major elements of uncertainty about their mutual aspirations, expectations, and intentions. Also uncertain is the behavior of some elements in each community which do not feel bound by the decisions of the majority of their fellows and are prepared to resist official decisions or to provoke controversy and even violence.[6] As in any mutual deterrence situation, both competing parties also have incentives to cooperate in order to avoid mutual destruction and urgently need reliable signals, including the points at which their demands are negotiable.[7]

After the crisis of May 1969, the absence of a legitimate political spokesman for the Chinese and the erosion of the UMNO's authority among Malays impaired this model. Unless the political system can reflect the essentially bipolar character of Malaysian society, it will not be able to process the major communal issues which are the salient problems of Malaysian

[6] The Labor party militants and some secret society members among the Chinese, who are alienated from the political system and less well organized or disciplined groups of Malay nationalists who can be aroused to violence against alleged threats by Chinese to Malay hegemony.

[7] Thomas C. Schelling, *The Strategy of Conflict* (London: Oxford University Press, 1963).

society, nor provide legitimate and effective representation for the elements that comprise the major ethnic groups. No other pattern has emerged or is likely to emerge except a repressive and highly unstable one-race government. That is why a workable political process will require a functional substitute for the Alliance system and why the search for that substitute must be the first order of political business.

In Malaysia the two-party zero-sum game can be converted to a three-party increasing-sum game. The third party is not the other racial communities, for they are too weak politically to affect outcomes in West Malaysia.[8] The third party is the governmental elite, the senior political and administrative group, whose primary functions are systems guidance and conflict management. Their functions are to attenuate communal conflict by the following tactics:

1. Increasing the volume of benefits to be distributed so that conflicts can center on sharing the increments of a growing quantum of resources and opportunities is a major rationale for planned economic growth to which the government of Malaysia has been committed. To be effective, it must have two additional elements: a major concern with the distribution of the benefits of economic growth, both inter- and intracommunally, even if these retard or distort optimal growth paths, and noneconomic rewards which, in addition to intrinsic value, provide cultural, social, and political returns and can, in some situations, be traded off for economic satisfactions.

2. Cultivating mutual responsiveness so that each community may be sensitive to and consider as legitimate the needs perceived by the other. In Malaysia there is widespread agreement in principle to this objective, but little actual knowledge of the perceived interests and needs of the other community even in elite circles and little opportunity to participate in reliable information exchanges which would make such responsiveness possible.

---

[8] In East Malaysia, the Kadazans of Sabah and the Ibans of Sarawak as the largest communities are potentially major political forces, though at present politics in these states are dominated by better organized, urban-based Malays and Chinese.

3. Facilitating and enhancing structured opportunities for communication and bargaining at numerous points so that more reliable flows of information may facilitate mutual accommodation, issue by issue. This process will also encourage group learning and reperceptions of interests in the light of what might be intercommunally feasible. One function of the third party, government, is to see that such agreements, representing not static Constitutional principles but moving and shifting patterns of policy can be effectively reflected in governmental action programs.

4. Assisting the competing and cooperating communal groups to take advantage of opportunities to realize benefits conceded by or acceptable to the other party. If, for example, Malays would agree that Chinese taking scholastic examinations in the Malay language would not be subject to racial quotas, or if Chinese middlemen agreed that Malay farmers using new rice seed would be charged lower interest rates on crop loans, government could help individuals qualify for and realize these communally accommodative benefits.

5. Searching for measures that provide joint or shared rewards to both parties or "integrative solutions," which are not mere compromises but which provide substantial benefits to both parties, who in the process have redefined their interest in the solution. Methods which strengthen their common identity or attachment to common symbols of the polity can be encouraged and tested. Styles of thinking and of behaving along more integrative lines may develop, especially among educated youth, independently and even in contempt of ordinary communal bargaining and accommodation by their elders, if lines of communication can be kept fluid.

6. Maintaining the capacity to use force to preserve peace, discourage confrontational tactics, and enforce decisions arrived at by structured bargaining arrangements or by authoritative devices. This capacity is indispensable to the governance of a society as conflict-prone as Malaysia where accommodative measures as well as others imposed by public authority must be enforced against recalcitrant members of either group, and the overriding power of government must remain manifest and be

called into play when required for the measured application of coercion necessary to sanction decisions taken by legitimate processes. This is why the elites must maintain a measure of autonomy from their communally structured constituencies.

The function of the government elites, including both the senior politicians and the senior administrators, would not be merely to mediate between the communities. Often mediators are unable to implement the decisions and agreements they generate. In this case the mediators are also the system guiders and the rule enforcers, and thus combine authoritative with mediative roles. An administrative state permits this valuable combination of roles so long as the elites succeed in maintaining reasonable autonomy and legitimacy. Some members of the governmental elite do thus perceive their roles, except that they are not adequately equipped to carry out these functions and so exercise them only in the face of emergencies.

How would these processes work? A case is agricultural marketing, one of the most critical and chronic areas of communal conflict. At present the Chinese resist any disturbance of the institutional arrangements, including the role of middlemen. Militant Malays, on the other hand, wish to eliminate the Chinese middlemen altogether. These positions are incompatible and could lead to violent collision. The parties speak to their constituencies and at one another, but they do not communicate on this all-important issue, and there are no opportunities for structured dialogue. Assume that the government is able to provide new seed strains and other inputs which if properly used could return much higher yields to the farmers. Government could supplement this with one basic institutional change —to provide supervised crop loans to farmers who use the new seeds and other inputs. They could then, as a result of negotiations in one area of the country, persuade and demonstrate to the middlemen that with higher incomes, farmers would be able to purchase so much more for their personal consumption and for their farm requirements and would require so many more services (like machinery repairs) that the middlemen would be more prosperous as merchants, millers, and servicemen than they now are as money lenders. Would this not be the kind of increasing-sum game that would satisfy all parties, develop role complementarities, and reduce a major element of communal tension? Perhaps the measures agreed to would vary from one area to the other, and so might the styles of negotiation and bargaining, but the processes of mutual accommodation would be underway and the governmental elites, the third party to these dialogues, would be the problem definers, the initiators, the brokers, the facilitators, and the enforcers of the agreements that emerged and of the processes of communication that might prove to be more important in the end than any of the individual outcomes.

How feasible is this set of proposals? Can the quality of intercommunal relations be modified by the actions of a paternalistic government? In Malaysia government has been satisfied to maintain the peace rather than to search for new patterns of communal interaction. Yet the broader role suggested here seems to be feasible (1) because of the legitimacy and continuing recognition of the need for effective administrative institutions, the appurtenances and styles of the administrative state; (2) the broadly shared sense of need for political arrangements which will avoid violent communal conflict; and (3) the probability that senior administrators can be better equipped in the future to undertake such sensitive assignments and carry them out successfully. Politicians may play two roles in these arrangements—as spokesmen and advocates on behalf of competing communal interests and as members of the mediating groups. The performance of this mediating role requires coalition politics which attenuate communal demands in the search for solutions that will maintain the system. Administrators, their status protected from the immediate repercussions of communal conflict, will participate on behalf of the polity itself as members of the third party.

There is empirical evidence to support this role. One recent case was in Pahang, the largest East Coast state. There a group of senior politicians and administrators worked out an arrangement by which a Chinese firm would be awarded a long lease for a large tract of state land, in exchange for which 20 percent of the land would be allotted to Malay small holders for whom the firm would clear the land, plant the basic crop, and provide processing facilities. This is a possible pattern for breaking the stalemate on the allocation of agricultural land on the East Coast. Similarly with Federal Land Development Authority projects, the heavy government investment in land development for the benefit of Malay settlers has been sweetened for the Chinese by allotting them profitable contracts for clearing the land and planting the rubber or oil palm. At the district level and on a more modest scale, issues of potential communal conflict are managed by expedient compromises mediated by the district officer and the local politicians. I propose that this pattern be expanded so that it may become an explicit responsibility of senior administrators, for which they should be specifically trained, and that the process be carried out at numerous points and on groups of related issues where communal interests intersect, rather than, as during the Alliance regime, only in the national Cabinet and at the highest levels of the Alliance, and only when issues were about to assume crisis proportions. This is the way a two-party zero-sum game can be transformed into a three-party increasing-sum game.

A Further Step: The Guidance Model

Malaysia's leadership has decided, in principle, to move from the avoidance model to a guidance model, in which government anticipates communal issues, designs alternative patterns of action, improvises possible trade-offs, and develops accommodative habits of thinking and behavior. The shock of the May 1969 riots demonstrated that government cannot allow its most important problem, communal conflict, to develop autonomously. It must instead be prepared to invest more intellectual energy and political initiative in planning for communal accommodation and in implementing these plans than for the simpler problems of economic growth which may be thwarted unless the communal problems of control and distribution of benefits can be mastered.

Government is thus groping for a guidance strategy. An effective strategy would incorporate three ingredients. Two are long-standing elements of public policy in Malaysia, but the third represents a radical innovation. They are (1) insuring a climate of growth and opportunity; (2) maintaining a strong governmental presence; and (3) stimulating and structuring intergroup communication.

1. *Insuring a climate of growth and opportunity.* The very evident logic of this approach is to provide a growing quantum of resources and of personal options that will help to satisfy the growing economic demands of all groups and thus mitigate the tensions inherent in all social change. This economic reasoning deals with only part of the phenomenon of unsatisfied demands. It does not dispose of the problems of control, distribution of benefits, perceptions of equity, and relative well-being, or with noneconomic values. Nevertheless, the availability of increasing income and opportunities for education, jobs, and social mobility provide a cushion against group tensions. Additional tax revenues can be redistributed, more or less painlessly, in services to economically unsatisfied groups. Without this growth and the public awareness of it, zero-sum game thinking in its most brutal form takes hold of public decision making and nullifies efforts at group accommodation. On the other hand, visible evidence that things are going well economically can create an atmosphere of confidence that makes accommodation easier for all parties; even though they will dispute the fair distribution of benefits, the first group's benefits are not so readily perceived as being at the second's expense. There is more to go around for every group and when this is recognized, the belief in pervasive scarcity and the resulting social distrust tend to be lifted and men can begin to practice the art of give and take; they can afford to be more generous in adjusting the interests of others.

There are several methods available for promoting and sustaining a climate of growth and opportunity. The first—and this was a strong rationale for the administrative reform program which this book is about—is to assure more effective public services, particularly in those areas closely associated with growth and opportunity. If, reverting to an earlier example, the government can develop a delivery system for the new rice seed strains which, combined with complementary inputs, enables Malay peasants to quadruple their per-acre yields (a technologically feasible possibility), and if institutional changes can be negotiated which preserve for the peasant a large proportion of the value of his additional output, but still yield more income than previously to the Chinese middleman, this would be a major move toward communal accommodation in rural areas. It would approximate the optimum development path in Table 13, economic growth with increasing communal equity. Such outcomes will not come automatically, but only as the result of more effective governmental performance. Much of the government's capacity to deliver prosperity and a greater feeling of well-being, especially to Malays, depends on improved quality of public services, which, in turn, depends on the far-reaching administrative reforms now under way.

Second is the need to maintain continued scope for Chinese economic activity. This is particularly important because Malays will be unable to yield any measure of their political hegemony to Chinese until Malays are demonstrably better off economically and better equipped to compete than they now are.[9] An essential—but perhaps not sufficient—compensation for the Chinese is to maintain unimpaired outlets for their economic energies. This means not only that the existing Chinese stake in the economy should not be abridged by governmental action, but also that the inevitable and, in my judgment, desir-

[9] It must be emphasized that the one thing Malay masses will fight for is to protect their political hegemony. This was cleary demonstrated in May 1969 when their political control seemed momentarily threatened. A rumor in 1967 that with the retirement of the Prime Minister and the accession of Tun Razak, Tan Siew Sin, head of the MCA and Minister of Finance, would become deputy prime minister raised a howl of protest among Malays, including a provocative editorial in the newspaper of the UMNO youth. The unwillingness even of moderate Malays to concede a political role to Chinese other than as junior partners or oppositionists is one of the hard facts of Malaysian politics.

able ventures into medium and large scale public-sector industry to achieve Malay participation in modern enterprise should not injure existing Chinese firms. It also means that public lands should be opened for Chinese enterprise. Otherwise, the Chinese will feel boxed in economically, and the entire strategy may collapse. They will not only become increasingly alienated politically, but they will cease to invest in Malaysia, and the very growth and expansion on which this strategy depends will be choked.

A substantial portion of the tax yield on Chinese-induced economic growth—about 20 percent—can be invested in services to Malays which augment their competitive potential or in MARA industrial enterprises or public land development schemes which increase Malay participation in the modern economy. Some of this Chinese-induced growth could thus be converted to communal equity. This will not happen, however, unless the public services which translate these tax revenues into benefits for Malays are administered far more effectively than they have been in the past. This is one way that administrative development and reform fit into a guidance strategy. By providing employment for middle- and working-class Chinese, these continuing opportunities for Chinese enterprise will mitigate somewhat the resentments felt by rank-and-file Chinese against Malay privileges of which they feel they are the economic and symbolic victims. To prevent further estrangement of Chinese from the political system, it is important that Malay privileges, formal and informal, should not be extended beyond their present scope.

2. *Maintaining a strong governmental presence,* including the ability and the willingness to repress communal threats to the system depends both on ability to accommodate demands (treated as the first and third elements of this guidance model) and ability to manifest and use the necessary force. In Malaysia government has been respected, even among its enemies, for its ability and willingness to meet challenges to its authority with effective force, even though its methods are frequently harsh (including preventive detention) and its weight is felt more

heavily by non-Malays than by Malays. This respect was shaken among non-Malays by the use of public force during the May 1969 riots in a manner which they considered far from impartial.[10] It is vital that government correct both the image and the reality if future use of its powers of coercion are to regain respect and legitimacy among all communities.

In a situation as conflict-prone as Malaysia, the willingness of government to use force to maintain intercommunal peace and to curb excessive demands on public authority, especially those which are communally generated, is a *sine qua non*. Accommodative measures alone will not maintain public authority under conditions of intense strain. The abusive use of force can make accommodation more difficult and can actually weaken governmental authority, but its measured use to restrain and control intergroup conflict is essential, especially when the conflict challenges the authority of a government devoted to fostering intergroup accommodation.

This element of the strategy is conservative in its bias. It contemplates no radical changes in the structure of the regime, and it emphasizes measures by which the managers of the system can regulate conflict among its components. It is no substitute for the need for improved processes by which constituent groups can articulate their interests through participative processes and bargain among themselves and with government agencies in the manner contemplated in the next section. Despite what is claimed for the creative possibilities of conflict and confrontation,[11] intercommunal tensions in Malaysia need to be restrained rather than stimulated. It is far more likely that unrestrained communal conflict will be destructive of existing human values than that it can generate new approaches to accommodation. Therefore participative political processes must be accompanied by official coercion, used decisively for deterrent effect and, where necessary to impose the public order

[10] The police generally acquitted themselves well. The charges of partiality were leveled primarily against the military.

[11] Lewis Coser, *The Functions of Social Conflict* (Glencoe, Ill.: Free Press, 1956).

essential to mere coexistence, not to mention the search for improved patterns of accommodation.

3. *Stimulating and structuring intergroup communication.* The Malaysian environment has been singularly devoid of dialogue among communal groups. Such communication has occurred primarily at the senior levels of the Alliance Party and to a much lesser degree at the state levels. Elsewhere communal talk is either muted to avoid delicate confrontation or expressed through newspapers or public statements, where members of the communities talk at one another. Issues have been avoided or fixed positions proclaimed, but there has been no real communication and thus no dialogue. Moreover, there has been no serious exploration of accommodative action measures, except for those that are forced by imminent crises. The mutual deterrence situation has been a standoff between groups who recognize the dangers of overt conflict, but have no structure for engaging in dialogue or for probing and confronting the legitimate interests of the other. The achievement of accommodative habits of thinking, decisions, and behavior must engage more than a handful of senior politicians. It must involve a wider circle of politicians, those who also articulate group interests, of senior civil servants, and community leaders. There can be no guarantee that increased communication will yield increased affection or even understanding, but without dialogue there can never be even the negotiated search for accommodation, and the lines of conflict will become even more rigid. To stimulate dialogue is the business of political leadership, *but it must also be structured and guided by public authority to restrain the provocation inherent in meaningful dialogue under these conditions.* To release the honest expression of communal interests, to provide buffering, to restrain violence, to probe and identify workable compromises, to stage and watch over experiments are the creative roles which official leadership must assume in Malaysia.

The dialogue and the experiments can be most productive if they eschew abstraction and ideology and attempt to grapple pragmatically with real issues. Such real issues as land for the

Chinese, criteria governing access to educational opportunities, achieving greater efficiency and equity in agricultural marketing, and providing more business opportunities for Malays need to be faced by controlled and guided dialogue. Structuring communications processes that may lead to more accommodative solutions and, more importantly, to accommodative involvements and habits of thought must occur at many levels of group interaction, of which the following are examples.

First, local government institutions must be reactivated and strengthened. They are useful avenues for building accommodative relationships among groups. In Malaysia, however, they have been conceived less in this light than as technical instruments for performing minor local services. The governmental elites, political and administrative, have been impressed with the incompetence, frequent corruption, and undue play of political influence in town and local councils and with the control of the larger cities by opposition non-Malay parties. Thus they have systematically cut back on local self-government. The governments of most of the larger cities have been superseded and taken over by the states; local council elections have been indefinitely postponed. How much corruption, inefficiency, and machine politics can a society tolerate at the local level if these same institutions are contributing to intercommunal dialogue, problem solving, and accommodation? One method of stabilizing local government might be to combine elective councils with professional administrators trained not only to integrate local services with the activities of federal and state departments, but also to foster intergroup problem solving and experimental action. The present vacuum in local government deprives the society of a valuable resource for stimulating intercommunal dialogue and problem solving.

Opportunities should be found to foster communication among organized interests in the same sector, both at local and national levels. One example—perhaps the most explosive— would be the initiation of dialogue between organized middlemen and organized farmers. The Department of Agriculture is actively organizing multipurpose farmers' associations to speak for producers and to help them provide common services. They and the Federal Agricultural Marketing Authority threaten the power of and desire to displace the Chinese middlemen. Their immediate effect is to increase the bargaining power of Malay farmers vis-à-vis the already well-organized Chinese middlemen. To date, these government-sponsored activities on behalf of Malay farmers have increased suspicion and raised tensions. There is no effective dialogue at any level between the parties concerned, even though numerous issues could be bargained out in the interest of both, mediated by accommodation-minded politicians and administrators. There are ample opportunities for accommodation among middlemen and producers that will neither destroy the middlemen nor perpetuate the exploitation of Malay farmers. Some such agreements might be precipitated by or require implementation by additional and more effective public services. Group accommodation is never a static process, but requires continuous adjustment accompanied by pressure, hard bargaining, and occasional impasses, with public authority standing by to intervene. The point is that even in this most ticklish area of intergroup relations, there is room for constructive accommodation, but first the communication process must begin. There has been no communication except sporadically through communal political channels to the highest reaches of government at the moment that overt conflict threatens. The task of government is to structure and guide these opportunities for dialogue among the interested parties well in advance of the development of conflict situations.

Several steps can be taken to strengthen the governmental elites' capabilities to manage the processes of intercommunal dialogue and accommodation and to increase the intellectual inputs into governmental policy choices and action measures. The first has already occurred. A new Department of National Unity in the Prime Minister's Department has been set up to devote full time to the analysis of the communal implications of proposed government policy measures and action programs. When appropriately staffed, it will work with the Economic Planning Unit and the operating ministries and departments to initiate measures that may enhance communal accommodation. The proposed Tun Razak Institute might organize conferences for senior civil servants, politicians, and other community leaders on specific intercommunal issues. The university might establish an institute on intergroup relations for research and teaching in depth on the sources and the management of intercommunal conflict; it could, in the Malaysian laboratory situation, become an international center for the study of intergroup relations. Whatever the particular instrumentalities, the function of government is to set an authoritative tone which emphasizes the value of pragmatic accommodation and to equip the society with the structures, processes, and skills that facilitate and institutionalize dialogue and problem-solving behavior and restrain the excesses that such processes may provoke.

More controversially, government cannot ignore the role of the educational system in fostering accommodative habits. At present the school system is a greater source of latent conflict than of accommodation. While the initial strain would be hard to manage, the government should move toward integrating public education. To educate children in four different systems of primary schools based entirely on language teaches them nothing about accommodative behavior in their first six years of schooling, and their further education in two high school streams does little better, since most Malays take the Malay-language high school stream and most non-Malays enter the English stream. The nation-building benefits of a single educational stream, in which all children would participate equally in ethnically mixed schools, would outweigh the short-term losses in quality and the existing deficiencies of the Malay language for technical and scientific purposes. The single educational pattern toward which the system should move ought to be in the national (Malay) language, with English required to maintain the valuable openness of Malaysian society and other ethnic languages offered as optional subjects at all grades. Initially this change will be disruptive for teachers and students, as well as for families, but the prevailing structure of the educational system is not only inefficient but positively detrimental to communal accommodation. The inauguration of a single Malay-language teaching system would not be enough unless it were accompanied by measures which build accommodative interethnic habits directly into its teaching and social programs.[12]

Improved patterns of communal coexistence and accommodation cannot be achieved at the level of principle. The gap between *bumiputeraism* (the special position and privileges of the Malays) and "a Malaysian Malaysia" (open competitive access to all the values of society regardless of race) cannot easily be negotiated because in principle they are incompatible. The differences must be dealt with sector by sector, issue by issue, in an effort to evolve expedient compromises that enhance the possibility of peaceful coexistence. This will require structured communication, with government elites fostering and promoting accommodative behavior among the parties. To some issues there will be no ready solutions in the short run, and other agreements will become unstuck by experience. Thus the process will require continuous management by elites who enjoy some measure of autonomy from communal constituents.

The main argument of this chapter can be summarized in the following propositions: (1) intercommunal conflict is the most salient public policy issue in the Malaysian political system; (2) the present mutual deterrence pattern cannot be allowed merely to evolve without incurring unacceptable risks; (3) the policy of avoidance must therefore be supplanted by a positive guidance strategy structured by public authority; (4) the principle agents for conflict management must be the governmental elites, the senior politicians and administrators; (5) since one-race government would be highly unstable and noncommunal political organization is unfeasible, a functional

---

[12] The NOC government moved decisively in this direction by requiring the introduction of Malay as the sole medium of teaching in all government supported schools, beginning with the first grade in 1970 and adding a grade each year. Teachers are to be assisted in instructing in the Malay medium by special courses at Teachers Training Colleges. Shortages of teaching materials and texts in Malay are a continuing problem.

substitute for the Alliance system must be found which will provide legitimacy and effective representation and at the same time allow the elites sufficient autonomy to maintain the system-wide perspectives necessary to effective and credible conflict management; (6) though it has not been used and is not adequately equipped for this role, the civil service is a valuable, indeed an indispensable resource for the management of communal conflict.

Administrators as Conflict Managers

In an administrative state such as Malaysia, senior political administrators are involved in all allocative decisions controlled by government. They participate in the determination of (1) which values should be allocated by what mechanisms—whether new lands should be allocated among claimants by auction or lottery, whether the right to import rice should be determined by market mechanisms or by the Ministry of Commerce and Industry; (2) by what criteria each form of allocation should be governed—shall truck licenses be awarded on a first-come first-served basis or by racial quotas, should science teachers be assigned according to the availability of school laboratories or strictly according to high school population; (3) actual allocative actions, where criteria have been established and administrators function in their classical role as policy executors and where decisions have a large discretionary or judgmental element, as in the awarding of pioneer industry licenses or the siting of new schools. The closer one moves toward the discretionary end of the allocative scale, the more politicians become directly involved in individual decisions, but administrators exercise a major influence even in such cases because their expertise permits them to define the problem, organize the data, and often program the decision process. Inevitably they participate in decisions that are communally sensitive.

Several institutional attributes of Malaysia's civil service equip them to participate in the management of communal

276

conflict. They continue to command respect as legitimate representatives of public authority. While some Malay politicians and intellectuals attack them as insensitive to popular aspirations, complacent, arrogant, and conservative in their style; while many Chinese consider them inflexible, bungling, and remote from the real world; and while politics provides individuals and groups with alternative and often more effective channels for the articulation of demands, the civil service in Malaysia has suffered little from politicization and officers are secure in their status. The tradition of the administrative state remains and continues to confer high institutional respect on administrative incumbents, despite insufficiencies in the competence and the behavior of individual officers. This continuing respect is a resource which has not been deliberately committed to the search for communally accommodative problem solving.

The senior civil servants are the least parochial and the most cosmopolitan of all the elite groups in Malaysia. Their educational backgrounds have brought them in touch with members of other races as well as with modern ideas and life styles and have taught them the arts of accommodation. This has been reinforced by their work experience where they have associated, usually compatibly, with members of other races and have dealt with problems involving the interests of other communal groups. With few exceptions, they are above the cruder expressions of communal demands and hostility which often are evoked by grass-roots politicians and spokesmen for participative institutions. They are keenly aware of the potential destructiveness of communal conflict and its threat to the security of their own elite status. They have a clearer conception of the meaning of modern nationhood and the price this must exact in intergroup accommodation than those who have less stake in the survival and prosperity of Malaysia as a polity. In sum, these tend to be moderate men who are acquainted with the ways of civil compromise. This does not mean that they are indifferent to communal interests or have detached themselves from communal identities and sympathies. Many of the younger Malay officers are deeply committed to uplifting the Malays through stronger governmental initiative, which does not exclude greater pressure against existing Chinese economic power in such areas as agricultural marketing. It is nearly impossible in contemporary Malaysia to find anyone who can divest himself of communal sympathies, for this reflects the structure of the society. The senior civil servants, however, are communally the most moderate of all the elite groups in a society where nobody is above the struggle.

Malay predominance in the higher civil service might be expected to bias their mediating role in favor of Malay interests, or at least to be so perceived by non-Malays. In partial compensation, the Chinese are stronger in the professional services. Moreover, they are far better organized economically and better equipped for negotiation and bargaining than their Malay counterparts. When a functional substitute for the Alliance is formed, the Chinese will have the remedy of invoking political spokesmen when they feel the administrators are exerting influence to their disadvantage.[13]

[13] Some readers of this passage have disagreed with the proposition that Malaysian senior administrators could perform the mediative role because (1) they have shown little such capacity in the past (2) they are predominantly members of one ethnic group, the Malays, and therefore unable to be impartial or to evoke trust from the Chinese; (3) their performance during and after the May 13th outbreak confirms their inability to behave impartially in crisis situations. I agree with the first point as a description of the present situation, but believe that this deficiency can be overcome by training and generational succession as contemplated by the reform strategy outlined in this study. Point three is essentially unfair; the excesses were committed almost entirely by the military. There were few charges of obvious partiality by civil administrators, far fewer in fact than against senior politicians. While it is possible that administrators might favor the Malays, this could be compensated internally by training in their appropriate conflict-management roles and externally by the superior ability of the better organized Chinese groups to assert and argue their positions. This latter advantage would have to be accompanied by ready access on their part to politicians. This would depend, in turn, on reconstituting a functional substitute for the Alliance. It could not work with a one-race government.

The civil service controls the technical instruments which determine the effectiveness of governmental action. It is they who have continuing access to information derived from the government's feedback mechanisms and from sources external to government. They provide most of the intellectual inputs that define problems, shape policy choices, develop action programs, and deploy the resources of government in delivering public services. Choices of action programs and the effectiveness of governmental performance condition levels of public satisfaction and create opportunities for achieving accommodative thinking and behavior. That the same group of men who so critically determine how effectively government delivers the goods at the same time command respect as legitimate holders of power and are moderate in their orientation to communal issues identifies them as a valuable social resource for the management of communal conflict.

This definition of their role imposes a massive burden on the civil service—a burden that few of them now perceive as their proper function or are adequately equipped to carry. The prevailing role definition of the civil service, as described earlier, is essentially "administrative," faithfully executing the laws and the will of their legitimate superiors. They are more comfortable with the housekeeping routines of administrative management than with substantive policy or program issues. They have little feeling for a role as agents of social change or as mediators of group conflict. They do not perceive themselves as development administrators and few are psychologically or intellectually equipped for the role.

Nevertheless, I believe it is feasible to expand their functions far beyond their current dimensions. Many members of the MHFS are underemployed or working below their capabilities. Even though their growing sense of efficacy makes many of the younger and better-educated officers available for more demanding, active, and creative roles, the existing system does not evoke imagination or responsibility. For the most part, these officers are not adequately trained conceptually or technically for policy planning, program management, the guidance of social change, or the mediation of communally divisive issues. But the job is there to be done, and they are the group in Malaysia best equipped to do it. The training and career development program mapped by the DAU was intended to cultivate and to enhance these capabilities.

In social guidance activities, which are among the most demanding and sophisticated political arts, these officers would be associated with and supported by those politicians who, while responsive to the interests of communal groups, see their function as protectors of the political system and brokers among conflicting interests; they would conflict with other politicians who are instigators and champions of the maximum claims of communal constituencies. It would be essential to the survival of the system that the first group of politicians prevail over the second. Thus one of the functions of these administrators would be to support and strengthen moderate politicians who make moderate communal politics possible. To complicate their task, the very administrators who stimulate intergroup dialogue and search for accommodation must be prepared to resort to the measured use of coercion when government is confronted with challenges to its authority or with demands which cannot be satisfied through civic processes.

The management of economic development involves the distribution of benefits and costs among constituent group interests. In Malaysia there are significant intraethnic class and regional cleavages, but the most important ones identify themselves and are organized and mobilized along ethnic lines. Every significant decision involving economic growth or social welfare bears a load of communal consequences which no responsible public official dares neglect. The effects of social change are to escalate competitive demands and enhance political mobilization and thus to magnify the potential for communal conflict. So grave is this prospect that responsible men, particularly after May 1969, agree that communal relations cannot be allowed to run their course or to be resolved by the autonomous interplay of communally organized group interests. They must be overseen by men of good will, fostering the civilized resolution of communal issues and armed with powers sufficient to control conflict. This pattern was institutionalized by the Alliance coalition of constituent communally organized political bodies. The Alliance broke down because the leaders of its component organizations grew complacent in office and lost touch with their increasingly dissatisfied constituents who had stored up grievances against their own elites as well as against the other ethnic groups.

The management of communal conflict under conditions of social change and increased political awareness is a much more exacting task than in simpler times. Guiding the process of communal accommodation requires more than good will, more than coercion during crises, and more than the capacity of national political leadership in each constituent group to discipline or mollify the more militant demands of grassroots politicians. It requires sophisticated and disciplined intellectual inputs, the imagination to plan, the stamina to guide large-scale experiments, and the capacity to respond effectively to signals of trouble. These capabilities the politicians alone do not command; they require the support, participation, and guidance of administrators and technicians. Thus the objective of administrative development in Malaysia should be not merely to strengthen the technical and program-management capabilities of the civil service, important as they are, but also to build up their role as agents of social change and of communal accommodation.

The conceptual equipment and the operational skills required for these expanded roles will stretch the civil service beyond its present role definition and performance capacity. But the latent capacities exist, and a society which continues to reward them lavishly in income and prestige has a right to impose increased demands on its administrators. The politicians who impose these demands cannot do their job without improved administrative performance; the administrators, as they move beyond system maintenance activities, will find that they need the politicians for the communication and legitimization functions at which the latter excel. Social guidance and the engineering of communal accommodation in

Malaysia require both moderate politicians and moderate administrators, and each is utterly dependent on the other. The two-party mutual deterrence game is too unstable to endure without this third party. If they should fail, communal extremists will take over and, after the bloodbath, the military, utterly devoid of political or social-guidance skills, will be the receivers in bankruptcy.

The normative literature on administration continues to emphasize the instrumental function of civil servants to execute the will of their political superiors faithfully and efficiently. Any departure from this limited managerial role continues to evoke fears of bureaucratic usurpation, of self-serving, irresponsible, and exploitative power which must be controlled by nonbureaucratic institutions. A more relevant strain in empirical literature, however, points to the inevitable involvement by program administrators in policy choices and regards this as a normal function of men who control substantial skills, information, and strategic positions. The administrators in a modernizing polity such as Malaysia must be prepared for two additional roles: as agents of social change and as mediators of intergroup conflict. The composite comprises the policy, managerial, social change, and political roles which add up to development administration. Administrators are neither autonomous, nor are they merely controlled instruments of a political elite. They are neither guardians nor glorified clerks. They are participants in the power structure and in the social-guidance system. I see no possibility that any alternative power structure in Malaysia could yield an equal prospect of guiding this potentially explosive society along decent accommodative lines. The key to this strategy is to strengthen the Malaysian bureaucracy in all the dimensions that characterize modern development administration. This was the objective of the program of administration reform reported in this study.

To summarize the relationship between administrative reform and the political or conflict management role of administrators in Malaysia, there are two main links. First, the capacity of government to manage conflict depends in significant measure on its ability to design and deliver more imaginative and more relevant public services more efficiently. This set of objectives is served by improvements in the major management systems which enable government to make better use of its resources. Second, the role perceptions of senior civil servants, especially of the administrative elites (the MHFS), should be shifted away from passive housekeeping to a developmental self-image, and they should be equipped with the substantive knowledge and the operational capabilities that will assist them in performing this new role. These were explicit objectives of the reforms reported in this study. Capitalizing on the generational shift toward increasing personal and social efficacy among younger administrators, these strategies were calculated to enhance the capacity of Malaysian administrators to guide change processes, including the management of communal conflict.

That these strategies were instrumental to major publicly defined development objectives, such as economic growth and increased social well-being, reinforced their utility and increased their feasibility in the critical sphere of communal conflict management. At a time when the specification of the latter objective was considered inappropriate, especially for foreign advisors, this congruence of purposes provided the opportunity for the development of those administrative capabilities which may prove to be an invaluable resource for the management of communal conflict in Malaysia.

9

Administrative Development, Institution Building, and Guided Change

Any real-life study of administrative change must be embedded in a distinctive social context. Malaysia is both intrinsically interesting and suggestive of the problems of managing social change in an administrative state under conditions of intense and pervasive ethnic tension. The bipolar, mutual-deterrence standoff between Malays and Chinese preoccupies its participants and overlays every problem of public policy; other crosscutting forms of cleavage—class, occupation, region, and generation—tend to be swallowed up in the more salient ethnic conflict.[1]

Malaysia is an administrative state where government dominates nongovernmental institutions and administration overshadows participative organizations and processes. The transition from colonial to national control was not accompanied by political or social revolution. Administrative structures have not been politicized; they have retained their stability, discipline, and impressive capacity to contribute to system maintenance and thus to perform routine public services predictably and effectively. Yet despite strenuous efforts by national political leaders, the administration has not significantly

[1] Complex as Malay-Chinese relations are, this study has simplified the actual ethnic dimension of Malaysian politics. It has neglected the distinctive problems of the Tamil minority in West Malaysia and the even more intricate ethnic mosaic in Sabah and in Sarawak.

improved its capacity to integrate specialized programs, to adapt to new conditions, to innovate improved services, or to manage conflict. In ability to manage change processes, which is the core of development administration, it has ben deficient and unable to respond to demands for more dynamic performance.

Private enterprise, entirely foreign and Chinese, can handle much of the economic growth in the modern sector, but progress in the traditional and small-holder sector, mostly Malay, and the opening of opportunities for Malays in significant numbers to participate in modern industry and commerce requires active governmental and therefore administrative intervention. So do the development and operation of public works (highways) and social infrastructure (schools), not to mention the distribution of material and symbolic benefits and the management of communal conflict. Malaysia's civil service, well-educated, highly legitimate, and communally moderate, has been a much underutilized resource for economic and social development and for conflict management. The problem was how to enhance its capacity to perform the tasks of development administration in the distinctive Malaysian context.

Administration and Development: Alternative Strategies

There is universal recognition of the importance of improved public administration for economic and social development in low-income countries. The problem has been how to get it. On this subject there have been two major schools of thought. The first believes in working directly on administrative institutions and personnel through education and training, structural reforms, changes in procedures and systems, and modifications of incentives and rewards. This has been the main emphasis in technical assistance since World War II.[2] The second and less influential school of thought assigns priority to

[2] See Edward S. Weidner, *Technical Assistance in Public Administration Overseas: The Case for Development Administration* (Chicago: Public Administration Service, 1964).

modifying the social environment, arguing that administrative behavior reflects and is constrained by the value systems and the political structures of the society on which it depends.[3] Thus achieving cultural change or building nonbureaucratic structures to "control" administration or strengthening participative institutions are considered more significant than "tinkering" with administrative structures or processes. Not surprisingly, deliberately induced cultural transformations and the restructuring of political systems have proved low in feasibility both for internal and external change agents, but the less holistic approach of strengthening participative organizations and thereby improving the ability of constituents to interact with government agencies is drawing more attention and is likely to be an increasingly important theme in development administration.[4] In Malaysia externally induced cultural transformation

[3] William J. Siffin, *The Thai Bureaucracy: Institutional Change and Development* (Honolulu: East-West Center Press, 1966), and Fred W. Riggs, *Thailand: The Modernization of a Bureaucratic Polity* (Honolulu: East-West Center Press, 1966).

[4] Some proposals to induce administrative changes by transforming the external environment have been linked to revolutionary situations or to draconian campaigns like the Maoist cultural revolution which are beyond the scope of internal change agents or of external technical assistance in reasonably stable systems. Yet there is increasing recognition that the effectiveness of development administration, especially in that class of activities that involves induced behavioral change among diffuse low-income decision makers, can be fostered and may indeed depend on improving the capacity of clients to interact with government agencies and to take better advantage of public services. Intermediary organizations, operating at the interface between functionally specialized bureaucratic agencies and atomized clients can help to integrate specialized public services at the point of service delivery while assisting clients to define and articulate their needs and bring pressure on administrative agencies for more responsive and personalized performance. The main effects may be to close the informational and social distance gaps between officials and clients, improve the information flows to administrators, permit them to adapt their programs in response to this feedback, and increase the relevance of services to the public. Increased recognition of this relationship may lead to new attention among development administrators to the importance of identifying or actually organizing in-

or political change were out of the question; strengthening the administrative apparatus appeared to be feasible and to offer early and assured returns in governmental effectiveness; attention to participative institutions, while complementary, was secondary in time and importance and would not be feasible until the capacity of the administrative system to guide change processes was greatly strengthened.

In the reform and strengthening of administrative systems and structures, there are two basic lines of attack which are not incompatible but usually require a choice of priorities. The first is to concentrate on the central systems and structures which govern the entire complex of public administration activities and can thereby facilitate or inhibit performance over a wide range of public services. These central government-wide systems include the classical staff functions of budget and finance, supply, organization, procedures, methods, and especially personnel. The alternative is to concentrate on substantive action programs that provide direct outputs or services to society. This neglected perspective on public administration shifts the emphasis from the internal management of bureaucratic structures, decision processes, and operational methods to the delivery of services and their impacts on clients and constituents.

In the perspective of development administration, there are three major classes of output programs: (1) those which attempt to induce behavioral changes among large, diffuse, low-income clienteles, such as family planning or changes in agricultural practices; (2) those which provide additional opportunities and resources to smaller groups of clients who are already motivated toward developmental patterns of behavior, like industrial promotion; and (3) those which improve the effectiveness of developmental services provided directly by gov-

---

termediary structures through which they can work more effectively with their clients. This is one of the implicit assumptions of Title IX of the U.S. Foreign Assistance Act of 1966. For a discussion of this approach, see Martin Landau. "Linkage, Coding and Intermediacy: A Strategy for Institution Building," *Journal of Comparative Administration,* 2 (February 1971).

ernment agencies, like education and land development. All efforts at induced administrative change, whether they involve the central government-wide systems or any of the three classes of action programs, draw on three methods of inducing change: technological, cultural, and political. While effective programs of change involve combinations of all three methods, the class of change problem tends to determine the more effective emphasis, as indicated in Table 13.

Table 13. Relative effectiveness of change methods

	Change method		
Class of problem	Techno-logical	Cultural	Political
Central systems	I *	II	III
Class A	II	I	III
Class B	II	III	I
Class C	I	II	III

* I–II–III is a scale of effectiveness, with I the most effective.

Induced changes in the central systems and in services provided directly by government (Class C)—that is, activities which require changes in the behavior of bureaucrats—are most effectively based on new knowledge and practices (technological), supported by efforts to modify values and role definitions (cultural), and least of all by changes in incentives and rewards (political). Changes in behavior among large and diffuse clienteles (Class A)—for example, family planning—involve an important element of cultural change, reinforced by technological instruments and shifts in incentives and rewards when feasible. Class B problems—for example, industrial promotion—depend primarily on shifts in incentives and rewards, with some reinforcement in improved technologies, but little need for cultural changes. Since the changes attempted in the Malaysian situation were mainly directed at modifying the behavior and performance of bureaucrats, the predominant change tactics were technological. When emphasis shifts toward the administration of substantive action programs, which may involve behavioral and structural changes among client groups, there will necessarily be greater stress on cultural and political change tactics.

Under Malaysian conditions, ironically, a program of reform in development administration, which is strongly biased toward substantive outputs, nevertheless assigned first priority to modernizing the central government-wide systems because this was a prerequisite to more effective substantive programs. In general, a new reform agency is in a stronger position to be immediately effective when it can produce plausible technological models and when it can improvise simple changes in incentive-reward structures than when it has to rely either on technical experimentation or necessarily longer range and less predictable efforts at cultural change.

Administration and Conflict Management

The function of public administration in conflict management has been neglected in the literature on administration because conflict management is a political activity and legitimate administration has generally been regarded as confined to system maintenance or program implementation. How do societies cope with social conflict? In some systems with high levels of consensus on goals and means, much conflict is resolved through traditional organizations and procedures or through economic and political market mechanisms. Highly institutionalized political and participative structures, like parties and legislatures, successfully mediate many forms of conflict through bargaining and other nonauthoritative methods of social control. Where consensus is less complete, consensual methods must be supplemented by authoritative processes with resort to latent or even explicit coercion. These range from judicial processes to resolution by administrative decision or by the political discretion of governmental elites. Where consensus is weak and conflict potentials are high, the major burden of conflict mangement must be taken up by governmental elites. The most dangerous lines of cleavage in any society are communal (religious, racial, linguistic, ethnic) for they engage the most primordial loyalties in men. Where these are the salient cleavages, their management must preoccupy all sectors of the governmental elites.

In Malaysia, the classical example of a society that is conflict-prone along communal lines, the senior administrators constitute a stable, prestigious, and communally moderate element of the elite structure. They are untrained and unprepared in their role definition for conflict management and thus represent an underutilized resource for this function. Economic growth and more effective public services can contribute to the mitigation of communal conflict. One objective of the reform effort reported in this book was to improve the capacities of Malaysia's senior administrators to guide change process and thus contribute to the political or conflict management aspects of development administration.

Institution Building and Guided Change

Institution building is a strategy of planned and guided social change. It is particularly applicable to induced changes in relatively stable structures such as the Malaysian bureaucracy, especially when foreign technical assistance participates in the reform process. Central to institution-building theory is the formal organization which aggregates the technical skills required to perform innovative services and the commitments needed to promote, protect, and guide innovations in an indifferent and even hostile environment. A critical decision of change agents is the choice of leadership. Competent and committed leadership is essential both for building a viable organization and for managing its external relations or linkages. Leadership formulates and deploys a doctrine, a group of themes designed to achieve a shared sense of purpose and cohesion within an organization and to project a favorable image to the external environment. The program of the organization, its output, is an operational expression of its doctrine. Choices of activities are determined by the leaders' priorities as modified by their operational capabilities, environmental opportunities, and external pressures. Leadership must invest in the organization both materially and normatively, mobilizing and developing its resources in staff, funds, equipment, information, and authority. One purpose of program choices should be to enhance access to resources, which in turn reduces the cost to the organization of achieving change objectives. In so doing, leadership is continually confronted with the temptation to facilitate its access to resources by forms of accommodation to the *status quo* which have the effect of sacrificing or at least deferring its innovative purposes. Leadership must also focus on developing the internal structure of its organization so that it may have the technical ability, the communications capacities, and the authority system necessary to produce and deliver services and to interact effectively with its external environment.

In a complex society, organizations cannot operate in a vacuum. They must transact with other organizations and groups for resources, outlets for their services, and support. They must establish complementarities with other organizations, induce them to take up and incorporate their innovations into their own ongoing activities if the innovations are to become a part of the society, to be valued and thus institutionalized. Each linked organization and group has its own perceived interests which may be hospitable, indifferent, or hostile to the new organization and the innovations it sponsors. The identification and management of each significant linkage is a continuing problem for institutional leadership. It is both a learning and a political process. Because of uncertainties and unexpected events, plans that are set in motion for linkage management often go awry. Therefore, they must be continuously monitored and modified. With organizational learning, tactics and even important objectives may have to be adjusted.

Conflicts of interest may develop among organizations,

requiring institutional leaders to choose among accommodative and conflict tactics, to seek allies, to push ahead with innovative activities, or to trade off, sacrifice, or defer some innovations in order to salvage others. Moreover, change agents are not restricted to efforts to modify the behavior of existing organizations in their task environment. They may attempt to restructure the environment by sponsoring new networks of organizations, particularly among clients or constituent groups in order to increase their capacity to benefit from innovative services provided by the new institution and to develop new sources of support. Linkage management, with its learning and political features, permits innovators to make the most of their resources in the struggle both to survive and to innovate.

The end state toward which institution-building ventures are directed is a viable organization, technically competent to perform its innovative functions, securely established in its task environment, its innovations favorably valued and assimilated into the ongoing activities of linked organizations. Measurements of institutionality are the spread effect of innovations, the rate at which they are adopted by linked organizations, the respect they achieve as evidenced by the autonomy they are accorded and the influence they can exercise in their environment, and their capacity to continue to innovate. Institution building prescribes the process of building change-producing and change-protecting organizations. It is not concerned with normal organizational maintenance over time and adaptation to environmental changes, but only with the means by which organizations sustain their capacity to continue to innovate. Institutionality frequently biases organizations to conservative behavior as they gain a stake in the new *status quo* they have helped to create. When they lose their innovative thrust and become a barrier to subsequent changes, new change agents must emerge. Their tasks, in turn, are to revitalize existing structures or to build new ones to incorporate a new round of innovations.

The institution-building perspective proved to be a useful

strategy for guiding administrative reform in Malaysia. Intellectually, it was able to account for the problems that arose and for the successes and failures that were experienced in the early years of the Development Administration Unit. Operationally, it provided a model of the processes to be pursued, a check list of factors to be taken into account, a method of mapping the terrain, and a set of criteria for guiding decisions. The institution-building orientation is particularly useful for induced and guided change in relatively stable bureaucratic systems.

Elitist Change Processes

In the prevailing intellectual *Zeitgeist,* it is as heretical to advocate elitist processes of social change as to recognize any virtue in bureaucracy.[5] Yet my argument does both. Where rapid social change must be induced or where dangerous conflict must be controlled, where immobilism is to be avoided on the one hand or violence on the other, and where democratic practices have not been institutionalized, social guidance is required. In Malaysia, both problems converge and democratic traditions are weak; thus there is imperative need for social guidance by rulers who are in touch with and responsive to the demands of their constituents, yet enjoy sufficient autonomy to look at the polity in a system-wide perspective and negotiate and enforce viable intercommunal compromises. Guidance is by definition an elitist process. If the need is for induced change or conflict management or both, the question is seldom whether these processes should be managed, but by which elites. When elites lose control, immobilism or disorder are likely to follow. The danger in Malaysia was not elitism

[5] Elitism is the control of an organization or a political system by a minority which is not immediately accountable to its constituents. The social composition of the elite may vary from a traditional ruling group to revolutionary cadres. Their sources and degrees of legitimacy may vary greatly as may the combinations of persuasion, bargaining, manipulation, and coercion they employ to guide the system and maintain their rule.

but the prospect that the political elites were losing influence over their constituencies.[6]

Institution building is a guidance strategy and thus explicitly elitist, but it is neither an authoritarian nor a repressive process. While change agents and institutional leadership are endowed with some resources, these are not sufficient to impose changes on linked organizations in the political environment postulated by the institution-building model.[7] Institutional leadership must engage in transactions, exchanges, bargaining, accommodation, and similar political arts in order to extend their innovations. Their success is not predetermined, but results from skill in using their resources to induce changes among organizations and groups which also have interests to protect and resources for expressing them in an essentially political environment.

For developing countries with strong administrative and weak participative traditions, which simultaneously require structural changes and conflict management, changes are not likely to evolve naturally nor can major conflicts be managed in the absence of effective public authority. Thus guidance strategies are appropriate and indeed indispensable. Where senior administrators are part of the governmental elite, they represent a resource which should be committed to the pursuit of these objectives. The alternatives are to abandon developmental objectives or to find other elites, for in a country such as Malaysia these goals cannot be achieved by the diffusion of power or by populistic prescriptions. To abandon these developmental objectives would be unthinkable and no alternative elite appears as legitimate or as well equipped for the task, even if it were feasible to displace the present administrators and the politicians with whom they have been associated. Under these circumstances the rational procedure was to increase the capabilities of the underutilized adminis-

[6] The role of elites in successfully managing conflict in a religiously bipolar society (Holland) is analyzed by Arend Lijphart.

[7] The DAU's inability to impose changes, as I have noted, perplexed many of its staff members.

trative component of the governmental elite to participate in guidance activities. This took precedence over the subsequent but important process of strengthening and even building new participative institutions which can increase the influence of constituents on government and serve as intermediaries between specialized bureaucratic agencies and their atomized publics.

In states with high conflict propensity and weak democratic institutions, the inability or failure of one elite group to manage social change and to control conflict usually results in the collapse of a regime, followed by a period of turbulence and the ascendance of another elite. This process may produce beneficial political and social changes, but it can also be very costly in economic, welfare, and civic values, and the result is more likely to be rule by another elite group than a broadly based democratic process. Unless the existing elites are oppressive and incompetent and their successors are likely to be more humane and effective, the sensible strategy is to improve the capabilities of the existing elites to induce and guide developmental changes and to control destructive conflict. This was the situation in Malaysia where the displacement of the moderate Alliance–civil service elite would have led to severe communal turbulence with no possibility of an alternative democratic consensus and the ultimate prospect of a military regime. The reform strategy described and analyzed in this volume was based on these political premises. Both at the micro level—the single institution—and at the macro level—the political system—elite-based guided change strategies were indicated in Malaysia, not because they are intrinsically good but because they seemed the most feasible path to humane socio-economic development and conflict regulation in a change-resistant and conflict-prone society.

APPENDIX

"Training for Administrative Leadership: The Role of the Malaysian Home and Foreign Service"*

Introduction

There is a consensus of opinion that most Division I staff, especially in Superscale grades, in the Civil Service are involved in administration and management, regardless of whether they are in administrative or professional services. However, training in administration and management for this category of officers is grossly inadequate. Lack of appreciation for this form of training is largely due to the lack of understanding of the actual concept of administration. Administration is regarded as routine paper work such as signing vouchers, preparing memoranda on service, establishment and financial matters etc. and some of the higher clerical work. Administration is therefore something that can be picked up as one goes along and which requires no formal training.

The terms "administration" and "management" in this Chapter are used interchangeably to mean the activity connected with the mobilisation and direction of resources—human, financial and physical—for purposes of achieving the goals of the Government. Although used interchangeably, it is realised

* Extracts from Chapter IV of "Training for Development in West Malaysia," a Joint Report of the Development Administration Unit and the Staff Training Centre, Government of Malaysia (Kuala Lumpur, February 1968).

that there is a basic difference between the terms administration and management, namely that while management refers to the actual operations of mobilising and managing the resources, administration includes such activities as policy making and policy control. The difference between these two terms is therefore in terms of the level of the processes involved. Nevertheless, this distinction is not rigidly adhered to as there are certain areas of overlap between the two processes.

Though this report concerns training for administrative or management capability for the entire Division I staff of the Civil Service, it is felt that the administrative training of MHFS officers is more special in nature, in view of the special role and functions of the service and therefore requires separate treatment. Hence the question of administrative and management training for Division I staff is divided into two parts namely: (a) Training of MHFS for administrative leadership which is dealt with in this Chapter, and (b) Training of professional and non-professional officers as administrators, which is dealt with in the next Chapter.

The Role of MHFS and Need for Training

The MHFS or the Malaysian Home and Foreign Service, is a generalist administrative service, whose members serve at every level of the Government, whether federal, state or local levels, and are intimately involved in every aspect of the governmental activities and development efforts. Its scope and the functions are becoming wider with expansion of government activities. In addition, following the merger of External Affairs Service and the Malayan Civil Service, it has been entrusted with the new functions of foreign affairs.

The MHFS at present operates broadly in eight major areas of activities, namely: (a) Administrative management (finance and personnel management, procurement and supplies, and organisation and procedures). (b) Economic administration and economic planning. (c) Rural development (agriculture and community development). (d) Administration of social development (health, education, welfare and labour). (e) Land administration. (f) District administration and local government. (g) Foreign affairs, and (h) Internal security and defence. In addition, it is also concerned with many other miscellaneous matters such as parliamentary and constitutional affairs, intergovernmental relations, protocol and ceremonial work, immigration, national registration, etc.

The function of an MHFS officer is not routine paper work. He is now essentially a development administrator. The role of the MHFS is to keep government operations effective at all times by maintaining administrative expertise in these operations. Its role is to provide leadership in the areas of decision-making, policy formulation, programme planning and review, control and management of resources, programme coordination and implementation.

The effectiveness of government's developmental activities and the viability of government's policies therefore depend a great deal on the ability and the skill of the members of this service to perform its vital role. However, it is observed that there is a discrepancy between the role the MHFS should play and the role it is now performing. Generally, it has not been able to contribute much to departmental programmes by way of decision-making, planning and organisation and assisting departments to solve many of the administration and organisational problems of the department. The following situation is illustrative of the present role the MHFS officers are playing:

(1) Apart from the Treasury, FEO, EPU and a few Ministries, at the federal level and the land offices at the state level, MHFS officers, especially in the Timescale and lower Superscale grades appear to be either performing routine administrative and housekeeping work, such as service, establishment and financial work; or the "post office" role of passing papers; or such peripheral functions as servicing committees, application of rules and regulations and compiling estimates; or some miscellaneous work which cannot be specifically assigned to other officers of other services such as preparation of annual reports. They perform little or no substantive policy thinking

nor do they provide adequate support to the Permanent Secretaries or State Secretaries in matters of programme planning and policy analysis.

(2) A survey of the duties and responsibilities of the MHFS posts indicates that a relatively small number of MHFS officers are involved in a number of major programme and policy areas, particularly in social development, (education, health, welfare and labour), agriculture and rural development, and urban development. A large number is primarily engaged in administrative management activities, whether at Federal or State levels as shown in Table A. Even in these areas, especially budgeting and personnel management, officers are ill-equipped in terms of training and experience to make effective decisions and provide professional advice to departments. As a result, much of the thinking and problem-solving work are frequently done by officers in the Treasury, EPU and FEO. This, in turn, has created a number of administrative problems, two of which could be cited here. Firstly, officers in these central agencies are not intimately familiar with departmental problems and activities and as such are unable to make adequate and effective decisions to facilitate departmental operations. Secondly, decision-making becomes highly centralised, even over the most routine matters, resulting in unnecessary delays in the despatch of government business.

The above situation is mainly due to the fact that the Service has not reviewed its changing role in the light of changing situations resulting from Independence and planned development, and accordingly has not been able to increase its capacity to act. Testimony of departmental officers interviewed at federal and state levels reveals that the departments depend on or expect the MHFS to provide assistance by way of solving many of the administrative and organisational problems in implementing development programmes and in day-to-day departmental activities, by providing expert advice on solutions to administrative problems, or by dealing effectively with the FEO, the Treasury and the EPU on behalf of the departments. However, such assistance is generally not forthcoming, and if forth-

Economic administration and development (80)

Grade	Personnel administration	Administrative management (223) Budget and financial administration	Administrative management (223) Management and house-keeping	Foreign affairs (136)	Economic Planning	Commerce and industry	Monetary and fiscal policy	Public works, transport and housing	Other
Timescale	64	43	24	83	12	14	14	8	—
Superscale H/G	20	16	14	19	4	5	6	1	1
Superscale F/D	8	11	8	6	1	2	3	2	1
Superscale D and above	4	4	7	28	1	2	1	2	—
Total	96	74	53	136	18	23	24	13	2

Grade	Agricultural and rural development (23)	Social development (14) Health	Social development (14) Education	Social development (14) Labour	Social development (14) Welfare	Internal security and defence (35)	Land administration (60)	District administration (48)	Local government (10)	Other (38)	Total (667)
Timescale	7	0	2	2	1	17	45	39	8	17	400
Superscale H/G	6	—	1	1	—	9	6	8	—	4	121
Superscale F/D	6	1	—	—	1	3	6	1	—	6	66
Superscale D and above	4	1	1	2	1	6	3	—	2	11	80
Total	23	2	4	5	3	35	60	48	10	38	667

coming at all, falls short of departmental expectations. In short, it is the view of the departments that the MHFS is not able to respond speedily and effectively to departmental problems.

The inability of the MHFS to perform its role in providing administrative leadership is due largely to lack of training of its members. Training for MHFS as well as professional and non-professional services is pathetically inadequate. This is partly due to the fact that administration is still being looked upon as something involving detailed scrutiny over service, establishment and financial matters, and not as a process of management, policy development and programme operations and partly due to Malayanization. In the first place, administration is viewed as something static. Consequently the need for staff development in the MHFS in terms of formal as well as planned on-the-job training is not fully understood. It is still believed that the skill required to perform the type of administrative work as perceived could be easily obtained through experience. Secondly, Malayanization has put the entire civil service into a state of flux and the MHFS, in particular, has borne the greatest impact from the Malayanization programme. It is in this service that transfers were most frequent and the rate of turnover the greatest. The average tenure of office for an MHFS officer, with few exceptions, was less than two years, during the Malayanization period. Even after Malayanization has been completed, tenure of office of more than three years amongst the members of this service is rare.

Consequently, officers are not able to remain long enough to develop a thorough background knowledge and understanding of the intricacies of the administrative and departmental problems which they are required to solve.

Need for Training

That the MHFS is lagging behind in its capacity for action vis-à-vis the increasing complexity of administration is indeed a serious problem. If its skill and ability are not brought up to the mark through sustained and regular training, it may very soon become a superfluous service or a service of secondary importance whose members perform purely routine administrative work which departmental officers can undertake equally well, if not better.

It would be undesirable to allow the MHFS to be relegated to this position through lack of expertise and skill in view of the fact that under our administrative system, there are a number of vitally important roles which no other service could perform effectively. One of these is the political role.

Since society is becoming more and more politicised and people are becoming more aware of their political rights, programmes and policy issues can easily become politically sensitive. Thus policies and programmes should not only be economically feasible but should also be politically acceptable. While departments could produce their plans and programmes in the light of their own professional expertise, there is a need for such programmes to be studied, reviewed and assessed in the light of the overall political and social context of the country. Although departments should be alive to the political environment, it would not be practicable to expect them to respond fully to the political and social needs in formulating their programmes in the light of their own departmental interests and professional inclinations. This task has to be performed by the MHFS. The viability of the policies and programmes not only depends on thorough planning but also on the manner in which they are implemented. Here the MHFS has to perform the challenging task of defending the policies of the government, negotiating with interest groups, promoting developmental attitudes, convincing the public, and devising strategies to ensure acceptability and compliance with government policies etc.

Secondly, the MHFS is "neutral" enough to review competing departmental programmes objectively and to make hard choices regarding development priorities and resource allocations, and on the basis of objective and detached analysis of the programmes, to recommend to the Ministers on the choice of integrated and well-balanced policy alternatives.

Last but not least, because of the present career system in the Civil Service, the MHFS is the only service large enough to specialize in many vital areas of activities without affecting adversely the career opportunities of its members. Because of the increasing complexity of administration, specialisation is extremely necessary in such functional areas as budgeting, personnel administration, and management analysis, etc. and in such substantive policy and programme areas as fiscal policy, rural and industrial development, international relations, etc.

The performance of these vital functions means that the MHFS should be staffed by highly trained and highly qualified personnel possessing profound administrative skill more complex than those of the professional and technical officers and a great deal of mental adaptability. Thus, the ability that is required of the members of the MHFS should not be looked at only in terms of their ability to perform their daily duties but also in terms of the overall responsibility of the Service to ensure and expedite efficient performance of governmental activities and operations.

Consequently, post-entry training required of the MHFS officers is now a matter of urgency.

Recommendation

In view of the gap existing between the role the MHFS should play and the present capacity of the service to play this role due to its lack of expertise, the government should place intensive training programmes for MHFS officers at the highest priority in the training programmes in the Civil Service.

Training is an aid to development of skill and is in no way a substitute for learning through work experience. Hence, for training in the MHFS to be meaningful and beneficial in terms of both cost and purposes, it should be related to proper work assignment and career development. Training of the MHFS should be related to the present and future roles of the service and hence should be designed according to the present and future structure and functions of the service. In this respect development towards specialisation within the service should be given special attention. In line with the above principle, it is therefore recommended that the following pattern of training be adopted:

(1) Training for new recruits—induction and basic training.

(2) Training for full capability of performance, i.e. mid-level in-service training.

(3) Advanced-level in-service training—senior management training and advanced specialised training.

(4) Top management training.

Training Objectives: Targets of capability

The above training programmes are aimed at achieving in the MHFS, the following levels of competence:

Assistant Secretary level (Timescale): The officer would have a *good* knowledge and skill in broad areas of administrative management and development and the ability to apply a few administrative techniques to a moderate range of problems within his limited field of work. The proposed induction and basic training programmes plus adequate on-the-job training are expected to achieve this goal.

P.A.S. Level: The officer, on reaching this level, is expected to have a *deep* knowledge of a principal branch of a specialised area, either in administrative management area (personnel and finance) or policy and programme area (fiscal and monetary policy, agricultural, rural industrial or social development) resulting from additional year (or years) of in-service specialised training and supplemented by proper work assignment or posting. He should be able to apply this knowledge to a wide range of problems within the area of specialisation and to make decisions with sufficient understanding of the implications of these problems and solutions on other matters outside his speciality.

Under Secretary/Deputy Secretary Level: The officer, on reaching this level, would have an *authoritative* knowledge of the principal branch of a specialised area resulting from advanced specialised training and many years of specialised experience. He would be able to apply his knowledge to a complex set of problems and to make policy decisions with a deep understanding of the implications of these problems and solution on other matters outside his area of specialisation. In addition, if he is a deputy secretary, he should be able to assist the permanent secretary to discharge his functions as a top-manager.

Permanent Secretary Level: On reaching this level, an officer should have, in addition to the above knowledge, a strong managerial capability to direct and control large and complex organisation, resulting from advanced management training including refresher courses and many years of management experience. At this level, because of the very nature of the work involved, the officer requires skill and knowledge which cannot be restricted to any one specialised subject. Hence the advanced training programmes for top-level staff.

Recommendation

While training of the MHFS should be for both long and short term skills, it is felt that long term considerations should be emphasised. It is therefore recommended that special attention be given to intensive and long range training programmes for two critical groups of officers:

(a) Those who are now holding appointments in Superscale 'H' through 'F' (either substantively or in acting capacity), who would within the next 5 to 10 years (or even earlier), be holding top level management posts in Superscale 'D' and above. These officers would in the foreseeable future be responsible for exercising leadership roles during the 2nd and 3rd Malaysia Plan. They are now relatively young (mostly within age group of 30 to 40) and would remain in the service for another 15 to 25 years or longer. They are practically devoid of any formal training to prepare them for future roles and possess relatively short experience in relation to their present ranks, having had between 6 to 8 years' Division I service in respect of those holding Superscale 'H' appointments and 8 to 10 years' service in respect of those holding Superscale 'F' appointments. This group comprises 124 officers as shown in Table B. The breakdown figure for this group is as follows:

Superscale 'H'	26 to 30 years	4	
	31 to 35 years	50	
	36 to 40 "	28	
Superscale 'F'	31 to 35 "	9	
	36 to 40 "	17	
	41 to 45 "	16	
		124	Total

(b) Those presently in the timescale appointments, much younger than the above group (within the age group of 26 to 35) who would be holding senior-level management posts in Superscale 'H' through 'F' in 5 to 10 years' time (or even earlier). These officers constitute the bulk of the service (181 out of 564 officers, i.e. 32%). They are now relatively young in service, mostly having had between 3 to 5 years' experience, at the most, in the MHFS but who would provide potential and competitive material for senior management posts in the next 5 to 10 years' time. The breakdown figure for this group is as follows:

26 to 30 years	112
31 to 35 years	69
Total	181

In the light of the above factors, special emphasis should therefore be placed on the following training programmes for the MHFS: (1) Mid-level training for timescale officers. (2) Advanced training for Superscale 'H' to 'F' officers.

Training for New Recruits

INDUCTION TRAINING

The purpose of induction training is to provide new entrants with a good understanding of the nature and functions of the entire government and a working knowledge of their immediate duties and responsibilities. The induction training given to

Table B. Number of MHFS officers according to age distribution and grade as of 1.7.67

Grade	Age groups							Total number of officers	Total number of posts (stock)	Total number of vacancies
	23–25	26–30	31–35	36–40	41–45	46–50	51 Years and above			
Timescale	132	112	69	31	8	4	3	359	400*	41
Superscale H and G	–	4	50	28	21	12	2	117	121	4
Superscale F and E	–	–	9	17	16	15	4	61	66	5
Superscale D and C	–	–	1	5	13	19	9	47	57†	10
Superscale B and A and Staff Appointments	–	–	–	–	2	6	6	14	23‡	9
Total	132	116	129	81	60	56	24	598	667§	69

* Includes 10 supernumerary posts in Home Sector.
† Includes 2 posts in Foreign Sector filled by non-career officers.
‡ Includes 9 posts in Foreign Sector filled by non-career officers.
§ Exclude 10 Leave Reserve Posts and 25 Training Posts.

newly appointed officers in the MHFS is pathetically inadequate. Of the 167 officers appointed between 1.1.64 to 1.1.67 only 50 or less than 30% were given induction training at the Staff Training Centre. Taking into consideration that about 112 of these were direct entrants from the university (the other 55 were promoted from the MAS and State Civil Services), it is noted that more than 50% of the new entrants had been left to develop their own knowledge and understanding of their duties and responsibilities in particular and of our governmental system as a whole. Furthermore, even for those who were given induction courses, the training in some cases came rather too late. There are instances where officers were sent for the course after 2 years of appointment. It is noted that apart from the S.T.C. induction course, no orientation training is given at departmental or managerial level.

That induction training is important especially for the MHFS requires no further emphasis. Nevertheless, it may be pointed out that interviews with a number of induction trainees recently as well as serving officers have indicated that induction courses are extremely useful as they could greatly reduce the period of adjustment or "groping in the dark."

BASIC TRAINING

Basic training is referred to here as the attainment of work skill adequate for the performance of immediate duties. It is, however, not meant to be a once-and-for-all training as it should be followed by further in-service training in the course of an officer's career. Unlike the professionals, i.e., engineers, accountants and agricultural officers, who can immediately proceed to perform their professional work on appointment to the service, MHFS officers are virtually "non-operational" in the initial stages of their career. They cannot immediately apply the knowledge that they have acquired during their university education to actual work problems. Most, if not all, have to rely on their common sense to deal with many of the complexities of administration. Heads of department at times find it difficult to deal with the young MHFS officers in the ministries and central agencies in the light of their inability to really grasp or understand the fundamental issues and problems brought before them for solution. It is felt that it may take an MHFS officer at least the 3 years of his probation to be really at home with his role and function.

Basic training is also necessary for other services recruiting candidates with liberal educational background. This has been recognized by many departments recruiting such candidates for their Division I or II appointments, such as Postal (Assistant Controller of Posts), Telecommunications (Assistant Controller of Telecommunications, Traffic), Inland Revenue (Assessment Officer), Audit (Auditor) and Customs (Assistant Superintendent of Customs). Recruits in these services are given basic training departmentally either locally or overseas. Thus in the Postal Department, for example, new Division I appointees are sent for a 2-year intensive course at the British Post Office during their cadetship.

The MHFS is no different from these services and unless new appointees are given thorough basic training, their level of competence and performance would be considerably below that of their colleagues of the same status in the other services.

Basic training has been neglected in the MHFS. Of the 167 officers recruited between January 1964 to January 1967, only 6 officers have been sent for what could be regarded as basic training in the MHFS, in overseas institutions under the Colombo Plan or Federal Scholarships. All the 6 officers were actually confirmed officers who were promoted from Division II but were within the probationary period of 3 years. This lack exists because of the current emphasis on accumulation of skill and knowledge through work experience. This attitude has to be changed. While learning through experience is a good thing in itself, it is not and should not be meant to be the sole means of staff development. Furthermore it is time consuming. As administration in the context of development is becoming more and more complex, the present and subsequent 5-year plans cannot afford to wait for the MHFS officers to acquire the basic administrative skill and knowledge during implementation period. Indeed, the present neglect of basic training is a retrogressive step in view of the fact that in the former days MCS officers were sent for a one-year Devonshire course in the United Kingdom. This practice was discontinued shortly prior to Independence.

DIPLOMA COURSE IN PUBLIC ADMINISTRATION,
UNIVERSITY OF MALAYA

Reference is made to the proposed diploma course in Public Administration at the University of Malaya which the National Committee on Development Administration has agreed to utilise for purposes of training MHFS officers, especially those who are probationers. Under the scheme probationers would be sent for one academic year at the University to study theory and practice of public administration with emphasis on developmental aspects. The academic studies at the University would be followed by 4 months further practical course at the Staff Training Centre where trainees will be taught the detailed application of the various management tools in the areas of personnel and financial management, land administration, diplomatic procedures and practices, etc. The diploma course is meant to be undertaken during the third year of appointment. During the preceding 2 years, the probationers will be given on-the-job practical training by way of posting or attachment to a ministry or state secretariat for a period of one year and to a district or land office for another year or vice-versa.

RECOMMENDATION

It is recommended that the diploma course in public administration should in future be the basic training course for all probationers in the MHFS and should be the permanent feature in the training programme for these officers. The diploma course would be able to provide training for all future recruits, as it is expected that the rate of recruitment beyond 1969 would be in the region of 20 to 25. It is expected that a total of 30 participants would be admitted to each session of the diploma course.

Mid-Level Training

There are 153 officers in the timescale who have had between four to eight years' service on 1.1.67, those appointed between 1.1.59 to 31.12.63. Of this number, about 85 officers have been given short in-service courses of 2 to 3 weeks' duration at the Staff Training Centre in Petaling Jaya during the period 1964–67. In addition, 17 have been given in-service training in administrative management of more than 4 months' duration and 18 in-service specialised training, all at overseas institutions in Commonwealth countries, during that period. Therefore, in the past 3 years a total of 120 officers had been given mid-level training at the rate of 40 per year.

Although sufficient numbers have been sent for mid-level training, mostly at the Staff Training Centre, such training is not qualitatively adequate.

Mid-level training is defined here as training to give officers full capability of performance in their respective areas of responsibilities. Although in-service courses in administration and management at overseas institutions (mostly in the United Kingdom) are adequate in terms of duration as they last from 4 to 12 months, they are nevertheless, general in nature in regard to the course content and therefore could only provide the trainees with a general understanding of the principles and practices of administration, which is not sufficient for the MHFS. This is perhaps due to the fact that the overseas institutions are not in a position to assess the needs of the participating countries and also that such courses cannot be tailored towards the need of any particular country. In-service mid-level courses at the Staff Training Centre are more practically-oriented. However, in view of its very limited resources, the Staff Training Centre has not been able to provide training courses long enough in duration and concrete enough in substance to enable the trainees to study in some depth the various fields of administration and development. The courses conducted at the Centre are mostly of 2 weeks' duration with the exception of the Land Administration course which lasts for 4 weeks, and of other courses which run for less than 2 weeks. Furthermore, because of the scarcity of the teaching resources and the great reliance on outside speakers the course topics can only be briefly covered. Thus, for example, in Administration and Management Course 'B' (for confirmed officers between 3 to 5 years of experience) all the course topics with the exception of Project Management, are taught only in a two-hour lecture-cum-discussion session for each topic. The subject of Project Management is covered in one day.

The training courses, with perhaps the exception of Land Administration, cannot but merely scratch the surface of administrative problems and issues. Furthermore, administrative and management courses given to confirmed Division I officers could not be actually regarded as "mid-level" courses in terms of the definition given above, as they are essentially introductory or appreciation courses, designed to provide the Division I staff with elementary managerial knowledge as well as an introduction to the various administrative concepts.

Therefore, while these courses would be useful and sufficient to provide Division I departmental officers who are about to assume administrative duties with an appreciation of some of the common administrative and organisational problems, they are not adequate either in scope or in depth for the special needs of the MHFS. The MHFS officers, by virtue of their special functions need more skill and knowledge than could be provided by the present courses whether overseas or at the Staff Training Centre.

New Approach to Mid-Level Training

The tasks of government are becoming increasingly complex as the country progresses towards rapid development and economic diversification. As the MHFS is playing a key role in this process of growth—it is directly involved in the development of national policies, determining development priorities, controlling and allocating resources—it must perforce achieve a greater mastery in all aspects of the administrative processes and in every policy and programme area. The MHFS officers must, therefore, develop a clear understanding of the significant issues, problems and new developments essential to sound policy formulation, wise decision-making and effective programme direction. In recognition of the need for greater expertise in the MHFS and in view of the fact that it is practically impossible under the present complex situation to expect an officer of the MHFS to be equally competent in all fields of administration, the government has agreed to move towards specialisation in the service.

Recommendation

There should be a fresh approach towards the question of in-service training for the MHFS and that such training should be directed towards specialisation in the MHFS and towards building up full capability of performance of the officers in their respective areas of speciality.

Recommendation

It is recommended that the training be given in accordance with the possible areas of specialisation in the MHFS, namely:
Functional specialisation
  Administrative management
     (a) personnel management and manpower development
     (b) financial management (budgetary and procurement)
     (c) management analysis
Programme specialisation
   (i) International relations and foreign affairs
  (ii) Economic administration
     (a) economic planning
     (b) industrial development

    (c) international trade

    (d) fiscal and monetary policy

    (e) public works and transportation

  (iii) Rural and agricultural development—district and land administration

    (a) land administration and administration of natural resources

    (b) district development administration (implementation and coordination of rural development programmes, programme planning and operations)

  (iv) Social development

    (a) health

    (b) education

    (c) labour

    (d) welfare

  (v) Internal security and defence

  (vi) Urban affairs and local government

These would possibly be the six major areas of specialisation within the MHFS and the purpose of the training would be to create a new breed of officers in the MHFS, by developing in them a professional knowledge of their tasks, new attitudes and more solid foundation in those areas of specialisation. In-service training in the specialised areas would be in the following direction:

(a) *Administrative management specialists.* Personnel and financial administration are no longer a matter of applying or interpreting regulations. They are an important instrument of management. And as management becomes more and more a complex process, an MHFS officer is required to be an expert and innovative member of the management team. Similarly organisational and procedural problems are becoming more intricate as government expands its activities and departments continue to grow in size and to add new responsibilities. At the moment these problems are being solved on a trial-and-error and ad hoc basis, as officers have had no special knowledge or skill to identify these problems accurately and deal with them effectively. Officers in this group would, therefore, be trained to be functional specialists or management specialists in the following areas:

Personnel administration: systems and procedures such as selection, recruitment, promotion, discipline, employer-employee relations, manpower analysis, staff development, job evaluation, grading and classification of posts, salary administration.

Financial administration such as (1) Budgeting—budget procedures and budget analysis, programme and performance budgeting; (2) Procurement—procurement, contracting, stores administration.

Management analysis such as system and organisational analysis, management methods and techniques, such as work study and simplification, work scheduling and programming, performance standards, etc.

They would be posted to the Treasury, Federal Establishment Office, and the Development Administration Unit as well as to ministries and secretariats which require mastery of modern management methods. These officers would constitute the Government's management experts and "technical advisers" to departments and secretariats and would conduct competent analysis in personnel, financial and management matters for better decision-making and programme planning. This area is one of the most important specialisations in the MHFS.

(b) *International relations and foreign affairs specialists.* This specialised area would cover posts in the Ministry of Foreign Affairs and in the Overseas Missions as well as in some other ministries, which are concerned with our external relations and which require the skills and knowledge of modern diplomacy. Officers, to be fully qualified in the foreign affairs speciality, would require post-graduate and/or special training in international politics and economics, the processes of bilateral and multilateral diplomacy, in international law and in related fields. Within this foreign sector of the service a number of sub-specialities might be identified either on functional or geographic areas. However, it is felt that for the present moment a versatility in the foreign sector should be maintained because of its small size so that narrow specialisation is not feasible, at least in the foreseeable future. It would be sufficient for the foreign affairs officers to be "generalists" in the whole area of foreign affairs.

(c) *Economic administration specialists.* This area of specialisation would cover posts which require knowledge of modern economic concepts and economic analysis. Officers choosing to specialise in Economic Administration should be given postgraduate training in the various facets of economic policy and development economics. These officers would be posted primarily to the Treasury (Economic Division of the Treasury), the EPU, Commerce and Industry, Ministry of Public Works, Posts and Telecoms, and Ministry of Transport.

(d) *Rural and Agricultural Development—Land and District Administration.* This field would cover those tasks which focus on increasing the productivity and improving the general welfare of the rural people and developing their capability to participate actively in commerce and industry through rural development programmes. Officers in this specialisation would be found primarily in the Ministry of Agriculture, National and Rural Development, Lands and Mines and in the Secretariats. This area would comprise two sub-specialities, namely land administration and district administration. Land administration speciality would focus on the development and management of the country's natural resources, especially land, while district administration would be primarily concerned with management, direction and coordination of rural development programmes at field level. Although the specialities comprise distinct functions, they are nevertheless broadly inter-related areas. Officers in land administration specialty should no longer be trained purely to administer land in the static sense, namely alienation and acquiring land, solving land disputes, collecting land revenue etc. They should, with proper training, be able to promote development and economic growth through better management and utilization of land and its resources. Officers in the district administration group are expected, through academic training and experience to be masters in the entire process of rural development—in the control and management of development projects, in social change techniques, communications methods for purposes of motivating the rural people and changing their attitudes, and in production and marketing systems, etc.

(e) *Social Development.* Social development is potentially a major area of specialisation within the MHFS. At the moment, the MHFS is playing a very small role in the process of social development from the point of view of policy decisions and programme planning, as evidenced from the distribution of posts in the Ministries of Education, Health, Welfare and Labour. Yet the process of social development is not purely a function of medical, education or welfare officers alone. Social development is not just the question of instituting technical programmes such as eradicating malaria, family planning or eliminating illiteracy. It involves making fundamental changes in the values, attitudes, habits and practices of the people and instituting large changes in the character and features of our multiracial society, for purposes of achieving a viable and dynamic society and building up a strong social infrastructure for economic development. Social development is therefore an important function of the MHFS as it is predominant in any development programmes of the country whether in agricultural, rural and industrial programmes. Initially, MHFS officers in this specialty would be posted to the Ministries of Education, Health, Welfare and Labour. They should be posted or assigned to programme planning units in those ministries together with other departmental officers. They are expected, through specialised training and experience, to be competent policy analysts and to provide technical support to the Permanent Secretaries who are responsible for advising the Ministries on the choice of policy alternatives and ensuring success of the implementation of such policies. They should also be capable of assisting departmental officers in identifying major social problems and reviewing on-going projects for purposes of policy and programme formulation as well as testing the feasibility of programmes in terms of finance, manpower, organisation and political and social acceptance. Considering the fact that social development programmes, especially in the areas of education and health are consuming a large portion of our national budget, the number of MHFS officers in the four ministries concerned is extremely inadequate, i.e. 14. Most, if not all of these officers, below the Permanent Secretaries, are performing day-to-day administrative functions of personnel and finance. Although, in performing these functions they are involved in the problems of policy-making and programme planning, they cannot, in view of lack of training, provide the kind of policy analysis to their Permanent Secretaries to enable the latter to effectively exercise their leadership role in the area of policy. It is therefore recommended that not only should officers in this specialty be given intensive training in the substantive aspect of social and manpower development, but also the number of MHFS officers in these four ministries be at least doubled in the very near future.

(f) *Internal Security and Defence and General Administration.* Officers in this speciality are not expected to specialise purely in the two areas of internal security and defence, as there will be limited scope for advancement in this area. It is therefore proposed that officers should be trained and experienced in general administrative management, but should be assigned where possible to posts which would enable them to work in broadly related policy areas such as in defence and internal security, and would enable them to develop considerable expertise in the policy and operational problems of these important areas of government activity. However, a few potential officers should be selected and given advanced specialised training in the later stages of their career in defence policies and in military and police administration.

Recommendation

It is recommended that the in-service specialised courses should be established in two ways: (a) long courses of one year or more at post-graduate level; (b) shorter but intensive courses of 4 to 6 months.

It is felt that specialised training in some areas of policy and processes has to be considerably long to provide the officers with adequate knowledge and skill to be master professionals in their areas of specialty. This is especially true in the functional area of specialisation such as in finance, personnel management and management analysis, as well as in such programme activities as economic development, economic planning, and foreign affairs. Furthermore, such specialised courses would not be readily available locally for many years to come. However, not all could be sent for such specialised training. It is estimated that at the most a total of only 5% of the MHFS officers could be given such long intensive courses in any one year. In view of the fact that long intensive courses could only be given to a relatively smaller group of MHFS officers, short intensive specialised courses should be undertaken in respect of the other officers who need specialised training. Such short courses could initially be provided at overseas institutions but every attempt should be made to provide them locally as early as possible.

Recommendation: Overseas Training

It is not possible to initially develop local institutions to provide adequate training, especially in regard to the longer training programmes at post-graduate level covering a wide range of subjects. It is therefore recommended that overseas training facilities be utilized for both types of training in the initial stages of this training programme. In this respect, it is noted that overseas institutions notably in the U.S. and U.K. could offer great opportunities for specialised training in many areas of development administration suitable for the needs of the MHFS. However, for overseas training to be more meaningful and beneficial, attachment programmes should be followed where possible and well planned.

Recommendation: Local Training

On the basis of both practical needs and costs, it is not feasible to reply solely on overseas institutions to provide specialised training, especially short courses. While overseas training will continue to be an important feature in the programme of postgraduate specialised training for the MHFS, it is extremely desirable to provide shorter intensive courses at home as much as possible. In this respect, our present Staff Training Center has potentialities to be developed into a national institution of higher training in the area of development administration for middle and senior level staff in the civil service. The question of expanding and upgrading of this Centre is being studied in greater detail elsewhere in this report. It is expected that the Centre will be the nucleus of the proposed "National Institute of Development Administration," to be established by 1970. It is therefore recommended that starting from 1971 onwards short specialised training be provided primarily by the National Institute of Development Administration.

Recommendation

The question of specialised training in the MHFS would have to be studied in greater detail, by the Committee on Specialisation until such time as the Directorate of Training has been established, such as the types of training and nature of courses required for each area of specialisation, the number of officers to be trained in each area, the actual number to be sent per year, etc. It is therefore recommended that in view of the urgency of the need for specialised training and the need to train officers immediately, a Working Party of the Committee on Specialisation be set up as soon as possible to examine in greater detail the training requirements for each area of specialisation, to identify and evaluate the training facilities overseas which could meet the needs of each specialised area, to identify and select potential officers who merit training during the first phase of the training programme, to study the cost and other implications of the programme and to make recommendations to the National Committee on Development Administration.

Advanced Training

Advanced training for the MHFS is divided into three categories: (a) advanced management training; (b) advanced specialised training; (c) refresher training;

Advanced management training is aimed at providing officers in senior management level (in Superscale G/F/E and some in Superscale H) with an advanced knowledge in administrative concepts and techniques focussing on decision-making, policy formulation and co-ordination and on the processes and strategy of development as well as in various policy and programme issues and priorities. Officers trained in this direction are those with potentialities for advancement to top management positions and are expected eventually to proceed to such positions within a reasonable period of time. Unlike the advanced specialised training, advanced management training is relatively short, about 2–4 months' duration.

Advanced specialised training is training in greater depth in certain fields of study or specialised areas for the purposes of upgrading the knowledge and ability of the specialist to that of a master professional or "expert." Officers to be sent for this training are normally those who would have had intensive specialised formal training, preferably at post-graduate level. In the MHFS, officers with this training would constitute a corps of experts in the six major areas of specialty, namely: administrative management, economic policy, international affairs, rural and agricultural development, social development and internal security and defence. In addition to their normal functions they would act as "consultants" or resource persons to Ministries and departments in particular and to the Government as a whole.

At present, this type of capability is non-existent in the MHFS and the gap has to be filled by foreign experts. However, it is expected that as and when officers have been trained in this direction and have obtained sufficient experience, they should be able to replace those experts currently being employed on tenure basis such as in the Ministries EPU, DAU, and the Staff

Training Centre or on assignment basis to undertake certain projects such as budgeting and procurement, etc. It is extremely desirable that the Government should proceed to train MHFS officers for these roles as the employment of foreign experts should not be a permanent feature in this country especially when local talents could be developed to the same if not higher level in certain areas of administration. Furthermore, because of the constant turnover among the present experts due to the short-term nature of their employment, continuity in as well as effectiveness of the expertise are lacking. MHFS officers of this calibre could in future either hold top executive posts or advisory posts in the ministries and units in those ministries, i.e. EPU, DAU, etc. This form of training would be for a relatively long period and should therefore be given to younger potential officers in Superscale H through F, most of whom are in their thirties.

Refresher training is meant to keep senior officials in senior and top management levels abreast with the latest developments in their respective fields of operations and in related subjects and with the changing technologies in governmental operations such as the use of computers. This form of training would be given to those who have or have not gone for advanced management or specialised training.

At present, training of senior officers in any of these methods is practically non-existent. Of the 169 officers in this training zone, only about 4 have been sent therefore during the past 3 years from 1964 onwards. Of these two officers had been sent for advanced management training, one for refresher training and one for advanced specialised training. The latter was sent for post-graduate training in economics leading to a Ph.D. degree. A large number of these officers have already been promoted to higher appointments, i.e. to Superscale F in regard to Superscale H officers and to Superscale D and above in regard to Superscale F officers. Many of them are already of an advanced age so that longer courses would no longer be feasible for them as they would retire within the next 3–8 years.

Recommendation: Advanced Management Training

In order to ensure a higher level of quality and competence among these officers who will assume positions of responsibility and leadership in the foreseeable future, it is recommended that advanced management training be provided to as many of these officers as possible who should be selected on the basis of their potentialities and age.

Recommendation: Local Training Programme

It is observed that management training for this category of officers could best be provided locally on the following grounds: firstly, only a handful of officers, if any, who reach positions at Superscale F level and above could normally be spared from their duties for overseas training for a considerable period of time. Secondly, the training programmes conducted at overseas institutions for officers of similar status are with a few exceptions, generally arranged to meet the needs of the countries of origin. Hence they would not be suitable or useful for the MHFS officers apart from the mind-stretching exercise. It is therefore inevitable, in the long run, to establish Malaysia's own teaching programme for its senior management officers not only in the MHFS but also in other services as well as for those in statutory bodies. It is therefore recommended that a programme for advanced management training be established at the proposed National Institute of Development Administration starting from 1971.

Participation

It is most desirable for MHFS officers, especially at this stage, to undertake the course together with participants from outside the Service as well as outside the government, from the standpoint of both the character of the training programme as well as the returns to the participants. Hence, it is expected that a maximum of 15 to 20 MHFS officers and possibly twice the number of other participants would be sent for the course per year, at the rate of 2–3 sessions per year and at 15–20 participants per session.

Course Content

The main objective of the advanced management training is to assist these officers to develop sufficient skill to identify and analyse important issues, problems and new developments, as well as to provide a thorough understanding of current government policies, programmes and operations essential to sound decision-making and effective programme development. As such, the present conventional method of management training is no longer suitable. Officers of this level should not be confronted with a set course presented to the participants over and over again throughout the years but should be presented with a more dynamic programme focussing attention upon the major current problems and issues. The training courses should be flexible in nature which would vary in course content from year to year, or even within a particular year. However, since the participants have to have certain up-to-date knowledge in some aspects of management principles and techniques, the advanced management training could be divided into two parts—the first part containing fixed or regular topics such as project management and the second part containing variable topics.

Advanced Specialised Training

The total number of officers to be given advanced training in this direction would necessarily be small on the grounds of practicality and of interplay of many factors governing choice of officers for the advanced training—such as intellectual ability, aptitudes, motivations, academic and work performance, age, experience, etc. It would be difficult to assess the actual number of officers to be given advanced specialised training as this would depend on the needs for each area of specialisation in the MHFS. Assuming that each area would on average require a minimum of 4–6 of these specialists, the total number of such officers would comprise less than 5% of the entire MHFS establishment or about 30 officers.

Recommendations

It is recommended that the Government give special consideration to the advanced specialised training of about 30 or so officers with a view to creating a small corps of highly-trained specialists or "brains-trust" within the MHFS by the end of 1975. This would mean that the training of these officers will be spread over the 8-year period beginning from 1968.

Eligibility

The eligible officers would normally be those who would have had the initial specialised training at post-graduate level but this should not preclude others who would have been given the shorter specialised training if, by virtue of their ability and aptitude, they merit further formal training.

In view of the fact that there is now only a relatively small number of officers who have had formal specialised training (about 18–20), only about 2 or 3 officers should be selected each year for advanced training during the initial period, circa 1968–70. However the number should be increased to 4 or 5 from 1971 onwards and when more officers qualify for the advanced training.

Recommendation

In this connection, it may be noted that specialised and advanced training need not necessarily be broken into two parts and officers too could be sent for specialised training (e.g. at Masters Degree level) to be followed immediately by an advanced programme (e.g. at the Ph.D. level). It is considered that while it may be feasible at times to allow officers to proceed without break from their initial to the advanced stage in their specialised training, it may, under certain circumstances, be more useful for them to return to duty for a reasonable period of time before proceeding to the advanced stage. The period of interval should normally be between 2 to 5 years depending on the merits of the case and the prevailing circumstances. This arrangement would certainly be applicable to the younger officers in the Timescale. It is therefore recommended that there be a proper balance between the two methods of training and the choice of the methods should depend on a number of factors, including age, status, experience and potentiality of the officers and the exigencies of the service.

Recommendation: Selecting Authority

It is recommended that the procedure for identifying and selecting officers for the advanced specialised training be initially the same as that governing the specialised training programme, namely, selection and recommendation should be made by the Working Party of the Committee on Specialisation.

Selected Bibliography

I. Malaysian Pluralism

Allen, Richard. *Malaysia: Prospect and Retrospect.* London: Oxford University Press, 1968.

Arasaratnam, Sinnappah. *Indians in Malaysia and Singapore.* London: Oxford University Press, 1970.

Benda, Harry J., and John Bastin. *Modern History of Southeast Asia.* Englewood Cliffs, N.J.: Prentice-Hall, 1969.

Brackman, Arnold C. *Southeast Asia's Second Front: The Power Struggle in the Malay Archipelago.* New York: Praeger, 1966.

Djojohadikusumo, Sumitro. "Malaysia and Singapore," in Vol. I of *Trade and Aid in South-East Asia.* Melbourne: F. W. Cheshire, 1968.

Enloe, Cynthia H. "Multiethnic Politics: The Case of Malaysia." Ph.D. dissertation, University of California at Berkeley, 1967. Ann Arbor: University Microfilms, 1968.

Fallers, Lloyd A., ed. *Immigrants and Associations.* The Hague: Mouton, 1968.

Federation of Malaya. *Report of the Intergovernmental Committee, 1962.* Kuala Lumpur: Government Printer, 1962.

Federation of Malaysia. *Agreement Concluded between the Federation of Malaya, United Kingdom of Great Britain and Northern Ireland, North Borneo, Sarawak, and Singapore.* Kuala Lumpur: Government Printer, 1963.

——. *Toward National Harmony: A White Paper.* Kuala Lumpur: Government Printer, 1971.

——, National Operations Council. *The May 13 Tragedy: A Report.* Kuala Lumpur: Government Printer, 1969.

Fletcher, Nancy M. *The Separation of Singapore from Malaysia.* Data Paper 73. Ithaca, N.Y.: Cornell University Southeast Asia Program, 1969.

Gulick, J. M. *Malaysia*. New York: Praeger, 1969.

——. *Malaysia and Its Neighbors*. New York: Barnes and Noble, 1967.

Guyot, James F. "Creeping Urbanism and Political Development in Malaysia." Comparative Administration Group Occasional Paper (mimeo.). Bloomington: Indiana University Department of Government, 1968.

Hall, D. G. E. *A History of Southeast Asia*. Second edition. London: Macmillan, 1964.

Hanna, Willard A. *Eight Nation Makers*. New York: St. Martins Press, 1964.

——. *The Formation of Malaysia*. New York: American Universities Field Staff, 1964.

——. *The Separation of Singapore*. New York: American Universities Field Staff, 1966.

Hunter, Guy. *Southeast Asia: Race, Culture, and Nation*. New York: Oxford University Press, 1966.

Lee Kwan Yew. *The Battle for a Malaysian Malaysia*. Singapore: Ministry of Culture, 1965.

Levi, Werner. *The Challenge of World Politics in South and Southeast Asia*. Englewood Cliffs, N.J.: Prentice-Hall, 1968.

McGee, T. G. *The Southeast Asian City*. New York: Praeger, 1967.

Mahajani, Usha. *The Role of Indian Minorities in Burma and Malaya*. New York: Institute of Pacific Relations, 1960.

Mahatir bin Mohamed. *The Malay Dilemma*. Singapore: Asia Pacific Press, 1970.

Means, Gordon. *Malaysian Politics*. New York: New York University Press, 1970.

Milne, R. S. *Government and Politics in Malaysia*. Boston: Houghton Mifflin, 1967.

Popinoe, Oliver. "Malay Entrepreneurs: An Analysis of the Social Backgrounds, Careers, and Attitudes of the Leading Malay Businessmen in Western Malaysia." Unpublished Ph.D. dissertation, London School of Economics and Political Science, 1970.

Purcell, Victor. *The Chinese in Modern Malaya*. Singapore: Eastern Universities Press, 1960.

——. *The Chinese in Southeast Asia*. London: Oxford University Press, 1965.

Pye, Lucien. *Guerilla Communism in Malay: Its Social and Political Meaning*. Princeton, N.J.: Princeton University Press, 1956.

Rahman, Tunku Abdul. *May 13: Before and After.* Kuala Lumpur: Utusan Melayu Press, 1969.

Ratnam, K. J. *Communalism and the Political Process in Malaya.* Kuala Lumpur: University of Malaya Press, 1965.

—— and R. S. Milne. *The Malaysian Parliamentary Election of 1964.* Kuala Lumpur: University of Malaya Press, 1967.

Roff, W. R. *The Origins of Malay Nationalism.* Kuala Lumpur: University of Malaya Press, 1967.

Rogers, Marvin. "Political Involvement in a Rural Malay Community." Ph.D. dissertation, University of California at Berkeley, 1968. Ann Arbor: University Microfilms, 1969.

Silcock, T. H., and E. K. Fisk. *The Political Economy of Independent Malaya.* Canberra: Australian National University Press, 1963.

Slimming, John. *Malaysia: Death of a Democracy.* London: John Murray, 1969.

Stenson, M. R. *Industrial Conflict in Malaya: Prelude to the Communist Revolt of 1948.* London: Oxford University Press, 1970.

Tilman, Robert O., ed. *Man, State, and Society in Southeast Asia.* New York: Praeger, 1969.

Tregonning, K. C. *A History of Modern Sabah.* Singapore: University of Malaya Press, 1965.

Van der Kroef, Justus M. *Communism in Malaysia and Singapore.* The Hague: Martinus Nijhoff, 1967.

Wang Gung-wu, ed. *Malaysia: A Survey.* New York: Praeger, 1964.

Williams, Lea E. *The Future of Overseas Chinese in Southeast Asia.* New York: McGraw-Hill, 1966.

Wilson, P. J. *A Malay Village and Malaysia: Social Values and Rural Development.* New Haven: Human Relations Area Files, 1967.

II. Comparative and Development Administration

Braibanti, Ralph, ed. *Asian Bureaucratic Systems Emergent from the British Imperial Tradition.* Durham, N.C.: Duke University Press, 1966.

——, ed. *Political and Administrative Development.* Durham, N.C.: Duke University Press, 1969.

Eisenstadt, S. N. *The Political Systems of Empires.* Glencoe, Ill.: Free Press, 1963.

Gross, Bertram, ed. *Action under Planning.* New York: McGraw-Hill, 1967.

Heady, Ferrel. *Public Administration: A Comparative Perspective.* Englewood Cliffs, N.J.: Prentice-Hall, 1966.

——, and Sibyl L. Stokes, eds. *Papers in Comparative Public Administration.* Ann Arbor: Institute of Public Administration, University of Michigan, 1962.

Hsueh, S. S. *Public Administration in South and Southeast Asia.* Brussels: International Institute of Administrative Sciences, 1962.

Hunter, Guy. *The Administration of Agricultural Development.* Oxford: Oxford University Press, 1970.

LaPalombara, Joseph, ed. *Bureaucracy and Political Development.* Princeton, N.J.: Princeton University Press, 1963.

Lee, Hahn-Been, and Abelando G. Samonte, eds. *Administrative Reforms in Asia.* Manila: Eastern Regional Organization for Public Administration (EROPA), 1970.

Montgomery, John D., and William J. Siffin, eds. *Approaches to Development: Politics, Administration, and Change.* New York: McGraw-Hill, 1966.

Riggs, Fred. *Administration in Developing Countries.* Boston: Houghton Mifflin, 1964.

——. *The Ecology of Public Administration.* New Delhi: Asia Publishing House, 1961.

——, ed. *Frontiers of Development Administration.* Durham, N.C.: Duke University Press, 1971.

Siffin, William J., ed. *Toward the Comparative Study of Public Administration.* Bloomington: Indiana University Department of Government, 1957.

Swerdlow, Irving, ed. *Development Administration: Concepts and Problems.* Syracuse: Syracuse University Press, 1963.

Waldo, Dwight, ed. *Temporal Dimensions in Development Administration.* Durham, N.C.: Duke University Press, 1970.

Waterston, Albert. *Development Planning: Lessons of Experience.* Baltimore: Johns Hopkins Press, 1965.

Weidner, Edward W. "The Scope and Tasks of Development Administration: Recapitulations of Variations on a Theme," in *Meeting the Administrative Needs of Developing Countries.* Report of a project conducted by the American Society for Public Administration. Washington, D.C., July 1967.

——. *Technical Assistance in Public Administration Overseas: The Case for Development Administration.* Chicago: Public Administration Service, 1964.

——, ed. *Development Administration in Asia.* Durham, N.C.: Duke University Press, 1970.

III. Malaysian Administration

Abdul Kahar bin Bador. *Traditional and Modern Leadership in Malay Society.* Unpublished Ph.D. Thesis, London School of Economics and Political Science, Department of Anthropology, 1967.

Burridge, K. O. L. "Managerial Influences in a Johore Village." *Journal of the Malaysian Branch of the Royal Asiatic Society.* Vol. 30, Part I (1957), pp. 93–144.

Federation of Malaya. "Report of the Commission to Inquire into Matters affecting the Integrity of the Public Services." Kuala Lumpur: Government Printer, 1955.

——. *Report of the Intergovernmental Committee.* Kuala Lumpur: Government Printer, 1962.

Federation of Malaysia. *Budget Summary of Federal Government Expenditure, 1969.* Kuala Lumpur: Government Printer, 1969.

——. *First Malaysia Plan, 1966–1970.* Kuala Lumpur: Government Printer, 1965.

——. *Report of the Royal Commission on the Revision of Salaries and Conditions of Service in the Public Services* (mimeo.). 2 vols. Kuala Lumpur, 1967.

——, Development Administration Unit. *Land Administration: A Study on Some Critical Areas* (mimeo.). Kuala Lumpur, 1968.

——, Development Administration Unit and Staff Training Center (joint report). *Training for Development in West Malaysia* (mimeo.). Kuala Lumpur, February 1968.

——. Ministry of National and Rural Development. *Techniques Used for Developing Malaysia.* Kuala Lumpur: Government Printer, 1967.

——, Prime Minister's Department. *Organization of the Government of Malaysia.* Kuala Lumpur: Government Printer, 1967.

Hock, Tjoa Soe. *Institutional Background to Modern Economic and Social Development in Malaya.* Kuala Lumpur: Liu and Liu, 1963.

Jones, S. W. *Public Admnistration in Malaya.* London: Royal Institute of International Affairs, 1952.

Lim Tay Boh. "The Role of the Civil Service in the Economy of Independent Malaya." *Malaya Economic Review.* Vol. 4 (1959), pp. 1–9.

Montgomery, John, and Milton J. Esman. *Development Administration in Malaysia: Report to the Government of Malaysia.* Kuala Lumpur: Government Printer, 1966.

Ness, Gayl. *Bureaucracy and Rural Development in Malaysia.* Berkeley: University of California Press, 1967.

Paarlberg, Don, et. al. *Policies and Measures Leading toward Greater Diversification of the Agricultural Economy of the Federation of Malaya.* Kuala Lumpur: Government Printer, 1963.

Puthucheary, Mavis. "The Operations Room in Malaysia as a Technique in Administrative Reform" (mimeo.). Manila: Eastern Regional Organization for Public Administration, 1968.

Scott, James C. *Political Ideology in Malaysia: Reality and Beliefs of an Elite.* New Haven: Yale University Press, 1968.

Tilman, Robert O. *Bureaucratic Transition in Malaya.* Durham, N.C.: Duke University Press, 1964. This book contains a comprehensive bibliography of public documents relating to Malayan bureaucracy prior to 1963.

IV. Institution Building

Blase, Melvin G. *Institutions in Agricultural Development.* Ames: Iowa State University Press, 1971.

Building Institutions to Serve Agriculture. A summary report by the CIC-AID Rural Development Research Project, Committee on Institutional Cooperation. Lafayette, Ind.: Purdue University, 1968.

Butts, R. Freeman, John Hanson, John D. Montgomery, Jeri Nehnevajsa, and William Siffin. *Institution Building and Education: Papers and Comments.* Bloomington: Comparative Administration Group, Indiana University Department of Government, no date.

Eaton, Joseph, ed. *Institution Building: From Concept to Application.* Beverly Hills, Cal.: Sage Publications, 1972. This volume contains an exhaustive bibliography of institution-building literature, including the case studies sponsored by the Interuniversity Research Program in Institution Building which are not enumerated in this bibliography.

Esman, Milton J. "The Institution Building Concepts—An Interim

Appraisal" (mimeo.). University of Pittsburgh, Graduate School of Public and International Affairs, 1967.

——. "Institution Building in National Development" in Gove Hambidge, *Dynamics of Development*. New York: Praeger, 1964.

——, and Hans C. Blaise. "Institution Building—The Guiding Concepts" (mimeo.). Interuniversity Research Program in Institution Building, University of Pittsburgh, Graduate School of Public and International Affairs, 1966.

——, and Fred C. Bruhns. "Institution Building in National Development—An Approach to Induced Social Change in Transitional Societies" in Hollis W. Peter, ed., *Comparative Theories of Social Change*. Ann Arbor: Foundation for Research in Human Behavior, 1966.

Gant, George. "The Institution Building Project." *International Review of Administrative Sciences*. Vol. 32, No. 3 (1966).

Gautam, O. P., S. J. Patel, and T. S. Sutton. *A Method of Assessing Progress at Agricultural Universities in India*. New Delhi: Indian Council of Agricultural Research, 1970.

Goldschmidt, Arthur. "Technology in Emerging Countries." *Technology and Culture*. Vol. 8, No. 4 (1962).

Hill, Thomas M., W. Warren Haynes and Howard Baumgartel. "Management Education in India: A Study of International Collaboration in Institution Building." Cambridge: Alfred P. Sloan School of Management, MIT [1971].

Hirschman, Albert O. *Journey toward Progress: Studies of Economic Policy Making in Latin America*. New York: Twentieth Century Fund, 1963.

Huntington, Samuel. *Political Order in Changing Societies*. New Haven: Yale University Press, 1968.

Jones, Garth. *Planned Organizational Change*. New York: Praeger, 1969.

Loomis, Charles P. *Social Systems: Their Persistence and Change*. Princeton, N.J.: Van Nostrand, 1960.

Martindale, Dan Albert. *Institutions, Organizations, and Mass Society*. Boston: Houghton Mifflin, 1966.

Perlmutter, H. V. *Toward a Theory and Practice of Social Architecture*. Tavistock Pamphlet 12. London: Tavistock Publications, 1965.

Phillips, Hiram. *Guide for Development: Institution Building and Reform*. New York: Praeger, 1969.

Rigney, J. A., J. K. McDermott, and R. W. Roskelley. *Strategies in Technical Assistance.* North Carolina Agricultural Experiment Station, Technical Bulletin 189, 1968.

Rivkin, Arnold, ed. *Nations by Design: Institution Building in Africa.* Garden City, N.Y.: Doubleday, 1968.

Selznick, Philip. *Leadership in Administration.* Evanston, Ill.: Row Peterson, 1957.

Sherwood, Frank P. *Institutionalizing the Grass Roots in Brazil.* San Francisco: Chandler, 1967.

Thomas, D. Woods, William Miller, Harry Potter, and Adrian Aveni. *Institution Building: A Model for Applied Social Change.* Boston: Schenkman, 1972.

Thomas, D. Woods, and Judith Fender, eds. *Proceedings of Conference on Institution Building and Technical Assistance.* Washington, D.C.: Agency for International Development and Committee on Institutional Cooperation, 1969.

Thompson, James. *Organizations in Action.* New York: McGraw-Hill, 1967.

Index

337

*Administration and Development
in Malaysia*

Designed by R. E. Rosenbaum.
Composed by Vail-Ballou Press, Inc.,
in 11 point linotype Baskerville, 2 points leaded,
with display lines in Lydian.
Printed letterpress from type by Vail-Ballou Press,
on Warren's 1854 text, 60 pound basis,
with the Cornell University Press watermark.
Bound by Vail-Ballou Press
in Interlaken ALP book cloth
and stamped in All Purpose foil.

Library of Congress Cataloging in Publication Data
(For library cataloging purposes only)

Esman, Milton Jacob.
  Administration and development in Malaysia.

  Bibliography: p.
  1. Malaysia—Politics and government.   I.   Title.
JQ715.A5   1972   354.595'0007   71-173991
ISBN 0-8014-0685-4

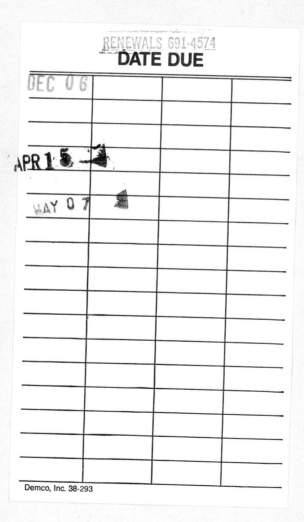